Cyrus Massoudi was born in London. After completing his studies at Edinburgh University, he moved to Iran where he spent three years on a journey of self-discovery, travelling and researching this book. He now lives in London with his wife and daughter, working as a writer, screenwriter and translator. *Land of the Turquoise Mountains* is his first book

'A fascinating insider–outsider view of a complex country we badly need to know more about. Writers like Cyrus Massoudi who illuminate our ignorance are vitally important.'

William Dalrymple

Land of the Turquoise Mountains

JOURNEYS ACROSS IRAN

CYRUS MASSOUDI

I.B. TAURIS

LONDON · NEW YORK

First published in 2014 by I.B.Tauris & Co Ltd
6 Salem Road, London W2 4BU
175 Fifth Avenue, New York NY 10010
www.ibtauris.com

Distributed in the United States and Canada
Exclusively by Palgrave Macmillan
175 Fifth Avenue, New York NY 10010

ISBN: 978 1 84885 637 0
eISBN: 978 0 85773 604 8

A full CIP record for this book is available from the British Library
A full CIP record is available from the Library of Congress

Library of Congress Catalog Card Number: available

Printed and bound by CPI Group (UK) Ltd, Croydon, CR0 4YY

For Edie Aryana

Contents

Preface   ix

Land of the Turquoise Mountains   1

Notes   237

Bibliography   241

Preface

So turns the world: her favours are soon passed,
All whom she nourishes must die at last.
One she will raise from earth to heights unknown,
One she will cast down from a royal throne;
But there's no cause to triumph or complain,
Such is the way she turns, and turns again:
Where are those heroes now, those champions, where?
Drive out such mortal thoughts that bring despair.

Ferdowsi, *Shahnameh*

Like many Iranians, my parents were displaced during the upheaval of the Islamic Revolution of 1979. They came to London, where I was born less than two years later. My schooling was as British as it gets, and though I spoke Persian at home, I grew up considering myself British but of Iranian origin. Iran was little more than an alien concept, a distant, mysterious land that belonged in my family's past.

Other than the language and the bizarre annual rituals of *Nowrouz* – the Iranian New Year that falls on the day of the vernal equinox – the only real connection I felt with Iran and its culture was through my grandmother. She would sit me on her lap and regale me with tales of mythical ancient kings and lion-hearted heroes doing battle with dragons and evil demons. Of all the characters in these stories it was Rostam and his mighty warhorse Rakhsh whose exploits would thrill me most. There was nothing this brave warrior would not do for king and country. He even took on the demon overlord, the monstrous White Deev, using the magical blood of his vanquished enemy to restore the sight of the king. My grandmother would embellish her stories with lines of poetry that she would try to teach me. Even though I was too young to fully grasp the meaning of these verses, I was moved by their beauty.

It was only when my grandmother gave me an illustrated children's copy of the *Shahnameh* that I realised where the tales had come from, that the verses she would recite were those of the great poet Ferdowsi. Entire afternoons would disappear as I obsessively thumbed the pages of this treasured book, transported to Iran – a magic land where anything seemed possible and where valiant heroes would sacrifice so much to protect it.

It was the *Shahnameh* that first made me curious about my heritage as a boy. Over the years that followed, this curiosity was fed and intensified by the steady stream of controversy, international incident and dramatic news reports that filtered out of Iran.

Throughout its history Iran has played a crucial role on the international scene. From the earliest encounters with Asian tribes in the north and the ancient Greek city-states in the west, on to its role in the evolution of the Silk Road, it has acted as the crossroads between East and West, a fertile breeding ground for the interchange of cultures and ideas, neither a part of the Arab Middle East nor of central Asia but a bridge linking the two. Since the early eighteenth century it has had first an expansionist Imperial and then Soviet Russia looming to its north, and in the nineteenth and twentieth centuries British India had bristled to its east. Currently, the Shatt al-Arab waterway and Hormoz Strait, both off the southern coastline of Iran, see nearly a quarter of the world's petrol supplies passing through them.

Outside Iran the country is viewed with suspicion, as a volatile and dangerous hotbed of Islamic extremism, its people oppressed by dated laws enforced by militias and morality police. Yet it is a country long-famed for its hospitality and one that is currently enjoying a burgeoning reputation for artistic and cinematic creativity. Beneath Iran's stringent Islamic exterior, behind the closed doors of many of the country's homes, there exists a reality very different from the image of the country presented abroad.

Iran is a chimera state: a confusing and confused hybrid of tradition and modernity, of reverence and rebellion; at once austere and extravagant, welcoming and forbidding. Every glimpse behind its sombre veil only serves to fuel the flames of curiosity, every snippet of a half-truth gleaned leads only to more questions – questions that I knew I would find answers to only in the country itself, the place of my origin.

During the three years I spent travelling around Iran, I became infatuated and infuriated by the country in equal measure. Somewhere along the way I came to see myself as an Iranian living in the West rather than a Westerner with Iranian roots. This change in the way I perceived myself prompted a question: what does it mean to be Iranian? This book is my attempt to find an answer.

Chapter One

Arriving in Tehran, the first-time visitor is instantly struck by new and unfamiliar images – lumpy black outlines shaped like Russian dolls waddling penguin-like along the streets, their sombre veils clamped in place tightly between their teeth, grizzled vendors peddling batteries, leather-faced men sitting in doorways drawing hard on cigarettes wedged deep between index finger and flat palm as though covering their mouths to yawn, fruit juice stalls with pomegranates piled high on their counters, money changers wafting bricks of currency at passersby and the odd goat being led ploddingly along under the weight of its laden saddlebags.

The clash between old and new, between tradition and modernity, is immediately noticeable. Crumbling brick bungalows are dwarfed by high-rise buildings, wooden carts selling the seasonal produce they've transported from the fecund foothills of the Alborz Mountains sit outside brightly lit shopping malls. Gleaming new Mercedes Benz cars speed contemptuously past ancient Paykans with their rusting exhaust pipes held in place by twine. Billboards advertising the latest smartphones and Patek Philippe watches compete for attention with banners proclaiming Islamic modesty and propriety. Posters of a severe-looking Khomeini contrast with murals depicting the compassionate gaze of the Imam Hossein, the seventh-century martyred grandson of the Prophet Mohammad, in whose name so many of the young men whose portraits also adorn many of the streets gave their lives as twentieth-century martyrs during the Iran–Iraq War of the 1980s. The most iconic of these murals found all over the city is the Stars and Stripes – except that the stars are human skulls and the red stripes, running vertically rather than horizontally, are the vapour trails of bombs falling onto a 'Death to America' slogan. A personal favourite is the image of a smiling young mother with a machine-gun in one hand and her tracksuit-clad toddler in the other chewing on a rocket as though it were a rattle. The slogan 'My children I do love, but martyrdom I love more' floats above their heads.

The walls of the sprawling compound of the former US Embassy are daubed with a series of anti-American jibes, the most striking of which is the now-familiar image of the Statue of Liberty with the face of a skull. The embassy itself has been turned into a base for the Revolutionary Guard. Another part of it is now a museum in which documents, hastily shredded by US personnel as the embassy came under attack on 4 November 1979, marking the start of the 444-day 'hostage crisis', have been painstakingly pieced together and proudly displayed to demonstrate the nefarious influence of America within Iran. These reconstructed A4 sheets sit alongside pictures of American 'crimes against the planet' and waxwork dummies of American diplomatic villains plotting around a table in the 'Den of Spies', as the compound has come to be known.

It is tempting to dismiss the posters, the murals, the imagery and the sloganeering as part of a pantomime of political rhetoric and propaganda, a projection of the regime's own self-perpetuating mythology. The more partisan information networks – taxi drivers, text messages and whispers in the bazaar – would indeed have you believe that these are merely manifestations of Islamic Republic obsessions and entirely state co-ordinated. But to consign all this, including the television images of flag-burning and fist-waving, as pure anti-Western propaganda would be as inaccurate as viewing all Iranians as malignant extremists hell-bent on the destruction of the West. The genuine divisions in society and the body politic were of course most eloquently clear in the aftermath of the 2009 elections, which brought out a wave of anti-regime anger culminating in the unexpected outcome of the 2013 presidential election. At the very least these events, personified in the election of the apparently reformist Hassan Rowhani, demonstrated that Iranian society and political attitudes are not monolithic.

Nowhere is the division of society more visible than amongst the women of Tehran. On one side is the hunched figure wrapped tightly in a black chador, a fold clenched between her teeth with only the area from brow to upper lip poking out from under the covering that preserves her modesty, waddling down the crowded alleyways of the bazaar, laden with groceries. On the other is the attractive *manteau*-clad young lady fully made-up, a colourful headscarf perched defiantly at the back of her head, peroxide-blonde streaks cascading from underneath it as her heels clip-clop down the leafy streets of northern Tehran from one fashionable café to another.

Tehran is of course not Iran – the sight of a *manteau* and colourful headscarf causes quite a stir in much of the countryside – but the capital city is a trend-setter and it is the place where Iranian youth is able to exercise its cultural and social influence most effectively. A much-cited fact about Iran is the staggeringly high percentage of the population under the age of thirty; over 60 per cent if official statistics are to be believed. In order to accommodate this burgeoning youthful population, universities are sprouting the length and breadth of the country. With Tehran housing the lion's share of the country's populace and only able to cater for a small portion of those seeking further education, the progressive ways of the capital are slowly spreading to more traditional parts through the student population. This permeation, bringing with it a more questioning set of attitudes, has only recently begun to reach the provinces.

But even in Tehran, the hub of a youthful and modern outlook, the all-enveloping chador still outnumbers the *manteau* in the majority of neighbourhoods, the exception being the affluent northern parts of the city. Nothing, though, is simple in Iran, and trying to make sense of the division between the progressive and the conservative is perhaps the most complex challenge. The modernity that has in many ways muscled itself into a very traditional country over the last hundred years, catalysed more recently by satellite dishes and the internet, has caused a deep-rooted schizophrenia in today's society; a society in which young people are as obsessed with Angelina Jolie as they are with the Imam Ali, as taken with Trance music and Tarantino as they are with mosques and martyrdom. Beneath the projected political machinations, beyond the hard-line foreign policy with its invective rhetoric and pantomime-villain façade, lies the real struggle: the internal conflict of a country desperately trying to come to terms with its own attempts at modernity.

★ ★ ★

A young man in khaki fatigues is being crushed under the tracks of an oncoming Iraqi tank whilst a rose weeps a tear of blood for the martyr. As I stared distractedly at this 6-metre-high mural that towered over the wide road leading into the centre of town, yet again reminded of the ever-present spectre of the Iran–Iraq War of 1980–8, I was snapped out of my reverie by Rahimi. An agency taxi driver in his early forties, he had long been the family's *homme à tout faire*, running errands for uncles and aunts to help make ends meet. Over the next three years Rahimi would become a staunch ally, ferrying me through the Tehran traffic and far beyond, all the while imparting his own brand of wisdom between bouts of laughter that rocked his middle-aged paunch and brags about the fourth satellite dish he had managed to cram onto his window-sill so that his wife could watch the latest Turkish soaps.

'You know I am a *mard-e jangi* too, Agha Cyrus,' he said, following my gaze. Literally translated this means 'man of war' and is how veterans of the Iran–Iraq War are often referred to. 'Two years I served at *jeb'he*, the front line.'

The war with Iraq was a gargantuan eight-year struggle between two oil-rich nations. On the surface, the war was a territory dispute that pitted Saddam Hussein against the equally notorious father of the Islamic Revolution, Ayatollah Ruhollah Khomeini. It resulted in one of the bloodiest, most destructive conflicts in recent Middle Eastern history. What triggered the war – whether a cocksure revolutionary Iran attempting to destabilise Iraq and protect its western flank, or an Iraq tempted to destabilise a rocky post-revolutionary Iran and protect itself from future Iranian meddling among Iraq's Shi'i population – is less important than how the war evolved.

On 22 September 1980, Saddam Hussein launched an offensive along some 480 kilometres of the disputed border into Iran's oil-rich south-western Khuzestan province. The poorly equipped and disorganised Iranian border units were easily overpowered as the Iraqi Army laid siege to various towns in the area. Iran, outgunned and technologically inferior, used the only weapon at its disposal to launch a counter-attack: sheer force of numbers. The Shi'i population of Iran was still riding the wave of religious fervour from the Islamic Revolution and the cogs of the propaganda machine began to whirr back into motion with great effect. Saddam, as the Sunni head of a secular party, was portrayed as intent on annihilating Iran's Shi'i population and his attack on Iranian soil as an act of war against the beliefs and principles of Shi'i Muslims. Men, women and children were called upon to emulate their revered historical Imams, Ali and Hossein,[1] and give their lives in the fight for justice. The ranks of the Revolutionary Guard and *Basij* voluntary militia swelled. Poorly trained and ill-equipped volunteers were sent to the southern border region by the thousands. Old men, young women and even children were sent in suicidal waves, drawing upon the martyrdom of Ali and Hossein for inspiration, to assault the entrenched Iraqi positions. The sheer number of the volunteers eventually succeeded in repelling the invading army but only after suffering huge losses.

By March 1982, the tide of the war had turned. The Iraqi forces had been pushed back over the border and it was the turn of Iran to go on the offensive. At this point the USA publicly announced its support for Iraq, with President Reagan declaring the USA would do everything in its power to prevent an Iranian victory. Iran's slogans and claims to export its revolutionary Islamic ideals, destabilising the region, were a serious cause for concern, particularly the prospect of the predominantly Shi'i oil-rich southern region of Iraq breaking away as a pro-Iranian autonomous Islamic state. In 1984 Iranian oil tankers began to be targeted by Iraq. The Iranian military were not long in retaliating. Soon even neutral ships were being targeted by both sides. America, worried by the threat to oil supplies and by the sky-rocketing prices of the precious commodity, increased its support for Iraq in the form of economic, intelligence and military aid. Despite this, the war rumbled on in a protracted stalemate at the cost of tens of thousands of lives. The better-equipped Iraqi Army was being held at bay by the better-motivated and more numerous Iranian ground forces. Seeing no end to the deadlock, the Iraqi Air Force began launching Scud missile attacks on Iranian cities. Iran reacted in kind but less effectively as a result of a weaker arsenal.

By July 1988, when no victory seemed in prospect for either side, Iran took the initiative to accept peace when Ayatollah Khomeini famously reversed all his previous rhetoric and declared he was prepared to drink from the 'poisoned chalice' of peace. The exact number of dead from both sides is difficult to gauge but most analysts put the figure somewhere between 500,000 and 1.5 million. It is now more or less universally accepted that the whole exercise was a grotesque and unnecessary folly in which two contradictory regimes slugged each other senseless until both collapsed exhausted.

★ ★ ★

Amidst all the slaughter, Rahimi was one of the lucky ones. As we drove through the traffic-laden streets of northern Tehran's Shemiran suburb, he told me tales of his time stationed in south-western Iran.

'Weren't you afraid?' I asked rather tentatively.

'Not at all,' Rahimi replied dismissively. 'You get used to bullets and shells pretty quickly. It's the other hardships that are most difficult. No food. No water. I was right on the front line, you know. The Iraqis were entrenched as far away from us as that building over there' – he pointed to an apartment block about 15 metres away from where he had parked the car – 'but it was those bloody scorpions that really got to us,' he said with a shudder. I looked at my companion with a mixture of surprise and bewilderment. The only warlike trait of this portly, mild-mannered, middle-aged man was a laugh that resembled muffled semi-automatic gunfire. I had so many questions but thought it best to wait for us to feel more comfortable in each other's company.

'I was in my car in Tehran once, though,' he continued unprompted, 'when a missile landed no more than 3 metres away. That terrified me. I didn't drive around town for weeks after that. It's a different mentality when you're at home, a civilian.'

As we drove on, the normally ebullient Rahimi fell silent. When we passed his local *Imamzadeh*, a small mosque-like shrine containing some relics of one of Imam Ali's descendants, Rahimi explained that some of the local casualties of war had been brought back from the front and buried here after the fighting had ended. The small courtyard was filled with row upon row of graves, a picture of the deceased embedded in each headstone – a special privilege granted to martyrs. The pictures showed fresh-faced boys on the cusp of adulthood, most younger than myself, many barely able to grow the *de rigueur* Islamic beard.

As we walked through the rows of young faces, Rahimi stopped before a photograph of a boy with an infectious smile: 'He was a school friend.' He walked on another few paces before pausing once more: 'He lived next door to me.' He went on to the row behind: 'He saved my life once,' his eyes shifted from the picture to the grave, 'I watched him die.' His voice was now very low. 'His brother,' he said pointing to a boy of no more than fifteen, 'is one of my greatest friends.' I silently breathed a sigh of relief.

'He now has one leg and one eye.'

Chapter Two

Just over a week after my arrival, the city underwent a sudden and dramatic transformation. Overnight, walls had been draped with banners of green and black and advertising boards plastered with pictures of a handsome, serene young man dressed in green. The usual lively clamour of the streets had been replaced by a funereal solemnity that seemed to give an added bite to the chill February air. It was Moharram, the first month of the Islamic calendar – a month dedicated to mourning the martyrdom of Imam Hossein, the grandson of the Prophet Mohammad and the third of the Shi'i Imams.

Hossein's death and that of his elder brother Hassan both stemmed from the long-running dispute over succession rights of the Umayyad Caliphate that Yazid had inherited from his father Muawiya and was desperate to legitimise. At the time of his death in 632 CE, the Prophet Mohammad had failed to name a successor. One school of thought among the Prophet's followers was that a determined leader should be chosen by consensus, the opposing view that leadership of the burgeoning Islamic community should stay within the Prophet's bloodline. Abu Bakr, representing the 'consensus' persuasion, emerged as the new leader of the community, creating a rift with the 'bloodline' faction who championed the claim of Ali to the caliphate. Abu Bakr had been closest to Mohammad and this, to many, furnished him with the necessary credentials. But Ali, the Prophet's son-in-law (through marriage to his only child, Fatemeh), cousin and first convert was deemed by many the worthier successor.

Resentment only grew when Abu Bakr named Ummar, an influential member of the eminent Meccan Quraysh clan, as his successor. This choice was considered by many to have been a political one based more on status and influence than on piety or true merit. A growing number of adherents of the fledgling faith backed Ali, a devout follower renowned for his sense of social justice. Ali was to be spurned a third time when Ummar was murdered by a Persian soldier in 644 CE and Uthman, another affluent member of the same elite Meccan tribe – the very tribe that, according to Islamic tradition, had shunned, derided and opposed Mohammad when he first brought them God's revelations – was named caliph. The belligerent Uthman gathered together an army and began quashing the brewing rebellions in some of Iran's northern and eastern provinces (many of which are now located in modern-day Azerbaijan, Armenia, Turkmenistan and Afghanistan) as well as attempting to cut off the tentative advances of the Byzantine emperor Constans II from the north.

The first of the Islamic conquests brought many converts and much wealth. A period of repression and corruption followed, culminating in Uthman being captured and hacked to pieces by his enemies in 656 CE. Finally the caliphate passed to Ali but his reign was fated to be short-lived. After just five turbulent years as caliph, Ali too was assassinated. His reign was blighted by constant political machinations and aggressions instigated by the Meccan and Damascene elite desperate to keep power amongst themselves.

Ali's eldest son Hassan succeeded to the caliphate, prompting Muawiya to raise an army and march against him. The two fought a battle but Hassan quickly realised his army was no match for that of the Syrians and agreed to cede the caliphate for the duration of Muawiya's life – but only on condition that it was returned to the family of the Prophet upon his death. A treaty that included a number of other stipulations was signed and roundly ignored the moment Muawiya was declared caliph. Hassan withdrew to Medina, where tradition has it that he was poisoned by his wife, who was under the nefarious influence of Muawiya. His death prompted yet more unrest and galvanised a group that came to be known as the *Shi'a-e Ali*, or Followers of Ali. Led by Hossein, Ali's second son, they rose up against the tyranny of the power-hungry, elitist Umayyads in the name of social justice.

In 680 CE a youthful Hossein (son of Ali, the assassinated kinsman and son-in-law of the Prophet Mohammad, and the Prophet's daughter Fatemeh) was making a pilgrimage to Mecca when he got word of assassins sent by the Damascene caliph Yazid. On hearing this, Hossein and his party, made up of his young family and a seventy-strong group of devout friends and followers, diverted their route towards Kufa. Before reaching the city on the banks of the Euphrates they were confronted by a detachment from Yazid's army and forced to camp on an arid plain, where they were besieged. The tragic events that followed have become etched into the Shi'i psyche, their potency only growing in resonance with the passing of time. So much so that every year an entire month of the Shi'i calendar is devoted to reliving and mourning these events. It was to witness their ritual re-enactment that I set off for the heart of Tehran.

★ ★ ★

In northern Tehran the streets were busy though the atmosphere was muted and heavy. Virtually every building was swathed in black and green material. Cars sped past, their rear windscreens screaming '*Ya Hossein*' in blood-red letters. Large tents and marquees had been erected beside buildings, their entrances curtained off with black fabric or plastic sheeting. These were *Hosseiniyehs*, areas where people could congregate and partake in the mourning rituals of the Moharram festival.

Further south, nearer the centre of the city, there was a palpable tension in the air, like the cloying intensity before a storm. People were milling purposelessly, waiting for something to happen. Young children handed out plastic cups of tea and *sherbet*, a traditional sugared fruit cordial.

'Drink. It is a *nazri*. It will bring you luck,' said Rahimi, draining one with a single gulp. People whose prayers have been answered by Imam Hossein give out *nazri*, a charity gift to the community as a gesture of thanks to the Imam. In a tradition that reflects the social justice and self-sacrifice so central to the Shi'i faith, rich cook for poor and poor for rich; how much is cooked is dependent on the size of the request made to the Muslim saint and one's means. Some hand out *sherbet* or tea, others cook for 1,000 people. *Nazri* food or drink is usually distributed via a local mosque or in the form of a banquet for the poor, but at Moharram time, with so many people around, it is common for these offerings to be handed out randomly in the street. As we drove further south into the heart of the city, we passed various streams of people congregating outside the metal doors of hidden homes, waiting patiently to pass through and collect the charitable Styrofoam boxes of lamb stew and rice.

Deeper into the city, in a run-down neighbourhood just south of the bazaar, a cluster of young men dressed in black were huddled around an older man whipping them into a frenzy with impassioned words and wild gesticulations. They leaped on the spot, the tails of their green head-bands bouncing against their shoulders, wailing the name of Hossein as clouds of condensation burst from their mouths into the cold air. Their faces were locked in a kind of intense trance as their palms thudded into their chests. This group of *sineh-zans* (literally the chest-beaters, beating themselves in grief at the memory of Imam Hossein's martyrdom) were *Basijis*. The *Basij* are the much-feared voluntary militia force who act as enforcers for the regime.

A little way down the narrow street, a goat was being hoisted into the air by its hind legs. A burly man held the writhing body still as another older man brandished a knife. With a single deft swipe the man's knife cut into the goat's throat. An arc of crimson tore through the air before spattering on the pavement near where I stood. Nearby, two goats happily grazed on a pile of litter blissfully unaware of their imminent fate. These animals were all to become part of the *nazri* meals that were to be handed out over the next couple of days. As I walked on, the older man began to skin the swinging carcass with expert strokes of his knife.

The streets became busier and harder to negotiate in the poorer southerly parts of the city. It was here that I came across a square teeming with people. In the centre was a large tent with smaller papier-mâché tents around it. These were supposed to depict the camp of Imam Hossein in 680 CE on a stretch of desert outside Karbala that was to become known as the Plain of Sorrow and Misfortune. Straw was strewn all over the ground. A wall of speakers bound together tottered precariously in the back of a battered pickup truck. An old man with eyes screwed shut belted out melancholy verses that floated through the crisp winter air. Suddenly a figure clad from head to toe in green appeared out of the tent, green feathers adorning his head. A collective sigh went up from the crowd, eyes welling with tears, transfixed by the man, who began striding purposefully around the tents. Just then another man dressed entirely in red and brandishing a sword appeared to jeers and whistles of derision.

The figures in green represented Imam Hossein and his party and those in red that of Shemr, commander of the evil Caliph Yazid's army, and his soldiers. On this stage the biggest tragedy in the Shi'i narrative was being acted out in front of an audience teeming with emotion. The *taziye*, or passion plays, are a long-standing part of the Ashura festival. In them the martyrdom of Imam Hossein is recreated in dramatic form. The *taziye* depicts how, for ten days, the Imam's camp suffered without food and water in the searing desert heat. The children suffered the most, their frail bodies ravaged by the effects of dehydration. As Hossein's camp grew weaker by the day, Shemr's army was strengthened by the arrival of reinforcements sent by Yazid, swelling their ranks by thousands. On the tenth day of the siege, the day that became known as Ashura, they finally attacked.

★ ★ ★

Hossein, green plumes reaching skywards, was chased around the stage by Shemr like a boxer looking to land the final blow. The *naq'al*, a narrator who intones the tale of Hossein's martyrdom in doleful verse tones, dutifully did his best to induce the tears of his audience. References to Hossein were sung like a sorrowful dirge, while Shemr's voice came out like a stentorian fog-horn. Perched on the bonnet of a nearby car, two men set the tempo of the piece on large hand-drums known as *daft*. Hossein stood before the women (played by men in black veils) and children of his family. The audience gasped in pity as he raised a baby swaddled in green to the skies. This baby was his six-month-old son Ali Asghar, so dehydrated he was on the verge of death. The Imam implored Shemr's troops to take pity and give him the water his family so desperately needed. The request was denied. Instead, one of Shemr's archers let fly an arrow, killing the baby held aloft in his father's arms.

The men in Hossein's party fought bravely, none more so than Abolfazl, but so outnumbered were they that soon all but Hossein had fallen to the sword. At this point Shemr scuttled off into the crowd only to reappear riding a white steed. The drums began to beat a faster rhythm; the wails of the *naq'al* grew louder and more frantic. The audience began to shift nervously, aware of what was coming. Shemr lifted his sword into the air and the horse lurched forward: the attack. A few more men in red appeared and rounded up Hossein's family. One member of the audience, a man well into his forties, began to get agitated and stepped forward as though wanting to help the captives but was soon shepherded back into the crowd by a member of Hossein's camp. As the performance reached its climax, there were many tear-streaked faces and harrowed looks in the audience. One mother covered her young daughter's eyes with her chador.

Hossein had been spared in the hope that he would accept Yazid as caliph but, when he refused to do so, he too was slain. Like his infant son, Hossein was mortally wounded by an arrow before being trampled under the hooves of Shemr's horsemen and decapitated. Seventy heads were severed and carried as proof of the gruesome massacre to the waiting Yazid in Damascus.

The stage was cleared as the audience sat in silence, absorbing the impact of the scene they had just witnessed. Despite the key role of audience participation in the proceedings, these passion plays are no pantomime. Many are moved to tears and the actors themselves often crumple in a heap after the performance in which they have given their all, impassioned by the tragic events recreated. 'The acting is powerful, though somewhat crude,' wrote Professor E.G. Browne, the revered British Orientalist, of the *taziye* he witnessed upon returning to Tehran in 1888 after seven months travelling the country, 'and it is impossible not to be influenced by the deep feeling evinced by both actors and audience.'[1] Sir Percy Sykes, the British soldier and scholar who travelled extensively in Persia, recounts an episode he witnessed just after the turn of the century in which he had 'seen the man who acted the part of Shimr at the Passion Play set on and beaten. Breaking away he rushed to the Governor-General for protection, screaming with fear and exclaiming, "I am not Shimr, but Your Excellency's cook!" Cases are known,' Sykes goes on to claim, 'in which players acting the part of Shimr have been killed.'[2]

Suddenly the *naq'al* picked up his lament once more, accompanied by the sombre beat of the drums. A procession shuffled into the square carrying a body shrouded in white on their shoulders. As they made their way around the audience I noticed that the outline of the body had no head. In its place a bloody papier-mâché stump could be seen poking out from the shroud as it came past. Shrieks of despair and cries of '*Ya Hossein*' filled the air as grown men and women began to wail and beat their breasts. Many of the younger children followed suit, caught up in the maelstrom of emotions. It was as though the crowd had just witnessed the brutal murder of a loved one, not a re-enactment of the death of a 1,400-year-old saint.

★ ★ ★

Far from eradicating the followers of Ali as Caliph Yazid had intended, the massacre at Karbala only served to galvanise the breakaway community. Intensified by the idea of sacrifice in the name of social justice – of the downtrodden taking a stand against their oppressors – the resonance of the martyrdom of Hossein and his followers was so great that it split the Islamic community in two and consolidated Shi'ism as the religion's second great branch.

Though the conflicts in which their martyrdom were rooted derived from political issues of succession, power and leadership, their names and their inheritance have become imbued with notions of a search for social justice and equity. As such, Ali and Hossein have become icons and role models for Shi'i Muslims, who make up between 10 and 15 per cent of the world's Islamic population and roughly 90 per cent of Iran's (with Sunnis making up roughly 8 per cent and the remaining 2 per cent being predominantly Zoroastrian, Bahai, Christian and Jewish). Iranians seek to emulate the 'purity' and 'wisdom' of their revered Imams, with the collective memory of their martyrdom having evolved into a key element of Iranian cultural identity. The beacon of Shi'ism has also functioned as a kind of medium with which Iranians can proclaim a national identity.

The submissive acts of piety carried out during Moharram became interwoven with the fabric of Iranian society after the establishment of Shi'ism as the national religion of Iran under the Safavids in the sixteenth century, but the origins of the mourning of Imam Hossein reach all the way back to 684 CE, four years after the fateful massacre itself. A group of Kufans who had embraced the Shi'i version of early Islam, racked with guilt at not having taken a stand alongside their Imam against Yazid's forces outside their hometown, congregated on the blood-soaked plain outside Karbala. Wanting to suffer as Hossein had done for their sakes, they rubbed the very dirt upon which the massacre took place onto their heads as they wailed and beat themselves in mournful anguish. Thus the ritual that has evolved into the Ashura festival was established. Through the repeated re-enactment of these rituals, the followers of Ali cultivated their newfound sect as a solid second branch of Islam that today includes such a large majority of Iran's population.

The potency of the emotion engendered by the martyrdom of Ali and Hossein and the notion of social justice on which the cornerstone of Shi'ism is built both played a pivotal role in the Islamic Revolution of 1979. On 2 December 1978, over 2 million Iranians poured onto the streets of Tehran. A week later, somewhere between 6 and 9 million people marched through the streets of towns and cities the length of the country. Throughout these demands for the abdication of Mohammad Reza Shah Pahlavi and the return of the exiled Ayatollah Khomeini, the Shi'i emphasis on sacrifice and a drive for social justice and equity were a powerful undertow in the flow of the Revolution. So it was no coincidence that these protests took place during the month of Moharram.

Throughout Tehran and other cities, towns and villages during these days of Moharram, one is greeted by the faces of these two pillars of the Shi'i faith, Ali and Hossein, more frequently than that of the Prophet Mohammad himself. During the holy month of Moharram, though, it is Hossein who takes centre stage and it is his idealised image which then appears in the rear windows of countless cars, alongside black banners and blood-red stickers.

★   ★   ★

A crowd had gathered outside a mosque I had wandered to. A burly young man adjusted a leather harness around his waist as people embraced him and landed encouraging pats on his sizeable shoulders. He was preparing to hoist the *alam*, a large metal frame embellished with flexible metal ornaments and long feathers of varying colours surrounding a painting of Hossein. This task is considered a great honour, exhibiting as it does two much-respected characteristics in Iranian culture: that of self-sacrifice on the one hand and that of the *pahlavan* – Herculean warriors epitomised by the legendary Rostam in Ferdowsi's *Shahnameh* – on the other. The *alam*, varying in weight and roughly 3 to 8 metres in length, heads processions that start out from each local mosque.

With a mighty cry the young man hoisted the hefty *alam* onto his shoulders as a procession formed behind him. Clad entirely in black, the men of the local community followed his tottering steps, keeping a funereal pace set by a handful of drummers in their midst. Some – the *sineh-zans* – beat their breasts with open palms. Most carried a *zanjir*, specially made wooden-handled chains which they brought rhythmically down onto either shoulder in time with the drums and the plodding steps of the procession. The women lined the streets and watched, perching on doorsteps, huddled under their chadors, or standing, tottering with emotion as the men of the community demonstrated their grief and passion for the martyred saint. The less pious men or those past their self-flagellation dates stood with the women, watching solemnly, clasping their right hand to their hearts, occasionally raising a handkerchief to dab welling eyes between heartfelt cries of '*Ya Hossein*'.

The tail of the procession was made up of young boys, some only three or four years old, armed with special mini *zanjirs* – smaller, toylike replicas in which the heavy metal chains have been replaced by light, plastic ones. Imitating their fathers in this symbolic act, they brought down the chains onto their frail little shoulders with bewildered looks. Bringing up the rear was a float carrying speakers through which a *naq'al* sang doleful verses extolling the selfless actions of the pious martyr and glorifying the events of his death.

The processions that set out from each local mosque congregated in the main road, forming a writhing, weeping, whipping sea of black in a kind of celebration of death. Everywhere were men and women with pained, doleful expressions and often streams of tears ran down cheeks as eyes and palms were raised heavenwards in anguish. The sobbing around me, especially by the elderly, was profuse and accompanied by the mournful mantra of '*Ya Hossein*'.

⋆ ⋆ ⋆

These days the public flagellation and breast-beating is more symbolic, more about keeping tradition and ritual alive than a true expression of atonement. It is as often theatrical as it is pious, so the sobs from the crowd function as a kind of applause, as if to acknowledge 'We came here to grieve, and the show has indeed reduced us to tears.'

Whether symbolic or an expression of true piety, no Moharram ritual is more theatrical than *ghameh zani*. A *ghameh* is a dagger-like sword, and *ghameh zani* literally means 'hitting with a *ghameh*'. This traditional act of devotion used to be performed publicly, alongside the breast-beating and self-flagellation, before being made illegal some forty years ago. In reality it is a ritualistic form of blood-letting in which the *ghameh* is beaten against the forehead, causing streams of blood to pour out onto the traditional white robes that signify the wearer's readiness to be martyred in the name of Islam. Though this still goes on publicly in the more provincial parts of the country, especially in the Azeri Turk-dominated northwest (the Azeris are renowned for their piety and strict observances of ritual), most devotees retire to the privacy of their own homes or to clandestine congregations to take part in these acts, which to an outsider can seem only like outright masochism. My best efforts to witness one of these gatherings were sternly rebuffed. These gatherings were private for a reason, I was told. My presence would be unwelcome and wholly inappropriate and my safety could not be guaranteed. But of course, it was whispered, there were still public displays of *ghameh zani* that could be tracked down in some Azeri-dominated settlements outside the capital. My curiosity piqued, I turned to the ever-resourceful Rahimi, who contacted an Azeri friend. Sure enough, he reported back with an address and a time for the following day, the tenth day of Moharram, the day of Hossein's martyrdom and the climax of the Ashura festival.

Shortly after dawn the next day, Rahimi and I drove north-west out of the capital, beneath the Alborz Mountains and their snow-dappled peaks shrouded in the morning haze. We were heading to a rough suburb of the town of Karaj, itself a satellite town of Tehran, called Ghaleh Hassan Khan. As we turned off the highway past a sprawling car-manufacturing plant, a series of sluggish processions were making their way into the village, which had been cordoned off by police officers. Coloured banners danced in the breeze at the head of snaking trails of black figures. Some of the women clutched picnic baskets and plastic bags full of food as they shuffled along towards the village.

Parking the car, we made our way through litter-strewn streets, past crumbling brick bungalows, and turned a corner to find ourselves faced with a swarming sea of black. The occasional white plume of an *alam* punctuated the otherwise Stygian monotony. We were suddenly in the midst of an orderly but large parade of self-flagellators, whose chains cut through the air, and swung over one shoulder before landing with a jangle and a patter on the men's backs. The dance was then resumed with another swing over the other shoulder, leaving grimy patches where the chains came to rest. The military precision of the chain-swinging was in sharp contrast to the amplified wailings of the *naq'als* and their various chants and cries to the martyred Imam.

At the heart of the village was a central square into which fed various narrow alleys carrying streams of chain-wielders, all clad in black. Individual processions were coming and going from all angles, some following one another, others fanning out to pass through the other. When two processions came head to head, the decorative metal frames of the *alams* at their heads would greet each other with a ritual bow. Occasionally these cumbersome metal frames would be spun around on the spot, whirling over the crowd, who ducked to avoid the heavy metal arms. At one point a *chadori* woman, distracted by the whingeing of her child, was caught unawares and took a nasty crack to the back of her veiled head before shrugging it off in the name of Hossein.

Palms raised to the skies were brought down rhythmically onto chests with a dull thud. Various techniques of flagellation were on display. Some preferred the single rhythmic whip, others had more elaborate movements to accompany an extra beat of the drum added between the metronomic swings. The chains would go up with the left hand, down onto the right shoulder, whip down to the side of the ribs while the right hand went up and landed on the right shoulder in fluid movements. Certain groups sauntered slowly, rhythmically, with a sort of side-step and swing of the arms.

The scenes were much the same as those I had witnessed the day before in Tehran, only on a larger scale; rather than crowds of hundreds, people were congregated in their thousands. The processions were more elaborate, too, with huge floats on which scenes of the Karbala massacre were being acted out, followed by stretchers with shrouded bodies. Hanging off the side of one such float was a time-ravaged old man weeping inconsolably and bringing his free hand down onto the dome of his bald head with repeated slaps of grief. Children chased each other through the procession, laughing with carefree innocence.

A huge portrait of Khomeini watched over the scene with an unflinching gaze. We pushed our way through the crowds, occasionally cut off by processions, in search of Rahimi's Azeri acquaintance. As we turned off the main thoroughfare, we saw a group of mourners gathered in a small square away from the main flow of the processions. Rahimi gave me a nudge and a nod and marched towards his friend, whom he had spotted at the heart of the throng.

As we approached, our Azeri contact turned towards us sobbing. Tears were streaming from his eyes, but the instant he recognised Rahimi, a friendly smile broke across his face. He dabbed his eyes with a sodden handkerchief and warmly introduced himself, all of a sudden quite light-hearted. I was left bemused by this emotional volte-face. Had this been simulated grief? The more I heard him speak, the better I got a sense of him, the more I realised that his grief was in fact very real, as was now his air of friendly banter. I would come across this ability of Iranians to switch with ease from one pack of emotions to another in a split second frequently in my travels.

★　★　★

In the square in front of us, three pyres had been built and decorated as tents representing the camp of Hossein and his followers. In one corner of the square was parked a rusty old Zamyad pickup truck with the ubiquitous sky-blue paint-job, speakers piled high in the back of it. Armed with his microphone and book of verse, the *naq'al* filled the air with his mournful recitations. Two groups of men – formed into snakes by placing one hand onto the next man's waist like a column of blind men – were being conducted in a mesmerising dance around the pyres by an elderly man waving a wooden sword. The dance looked more Native American than an Islamic mourning rite. One group of men wore black, the other covered their mourning clothes with white aprons – these the volunteers who were to shed their blood for Hossein. The dancing continued, becoming ever more intense, accompanied by the amplified verses sung by the *naq'al* booming from the speakers in the back of the truck. Every now and again the dancing, chanting and singing built to a climax, with both the men performing their rituals and the females in the audience weeping and wailing profusely. Tension gradually mounted in the frenzied atmosphere. After forty minutes the men in white aprons were shepherded down a little cul-de-sac, followed by the crowd.

I was swept along by the crowd when we came to an abrupt stop at a dead-end. Pinned against a wall, I was now just a metre or so away from the men in white aprons. Near me, a girl no more than ten or eleven years old was jumping up and down eagerly. 'This is my favourite part,' she announced to no one in particular. Suddenly to my right there was a young woman's scream. I turned to see the same elderly man who had just now been dancing and brandishing his wooden sword wrestling a little white bundle from the arms of the screaming woman. The bundle was a little boy, barely two years old, wrapped in the ominous white robe. A green hat was pulled from his head as he disappeared into the black throng looking terrified. The young mother's wails turned into a deep and desperate moan. Suddenly a blade glistened as it was raised above the writhing crowd before disappearing just as quickly back into the mêlée. Tears flowed all around. A man lay crumpled with emotion at my feet, weeping into the folded arms he had rested on his knees and repeating, '*Ya Hossein! Ya Hossein! Ya Hossein!*' Soon the baby was passed back to the chador-clad mother, beaming with pride as she pressed the bandaged, bloodied head of her child to her tear-streaked cheek. The young child had had the exhilarating experience of celebrating – yes, celebrating – the martyrdom of Imam Hossein.

Next up were the men. They knelt down one by one in front of the elderly man wielding the dagger. He brought the flat of the blade down onto the top of the first man's forehead with a firm tap. This was repeated a few times to draw the blood to the surface as the sensitive cranial skin swelled. After a few heavy taps, the man suddenly landed a single light blow with the sharp edge, as if flicking the dagger off the forehead. A trickle of blood meandered down the man's face before being wiped clean by a waiting attendant, who then squirted an antiseptic liquid onto the wound. The elderly man was then joined by another to help administer the devotional blows. The white-clad crowd jostled as they each pushed and shoved to have their scalps slit by the ever-active dagger. Some were so keen to commemorate Hossein's suffering and to show their piety that they demanded more: more blows, more blood, more feverish devotion. The elderly man raised the dagger in the air for another blow onto an already bloodied head, a glazed look in his eye, but just as he went to bring down the blade he was stopped by an outstretched hand. Two other men had been designated to temper the fervour and prevent things from going too far.

The blood from the heads of the volunteers, some as young as ten years old, was stemmed with strips of white cloth, while green and black scarves were tied around their heads. Now the crowd gradually reformed around the pyre. The intensely charged atmosphere of the fervid blood-letting was now dissipating as the dancing and chanting resumed. Dazed by what I had witnessed in the claustrophobic space of that small square, I giddily watched a large wooden pole, with an array of scarves dyed in traditional tribal colours tied to it like bunting, being hoisted in the air. An old man with stern, deep-blue eyes frantically waved the pole – a simple, tribal form of *alam* – through the air before bringing it crashing down onto a black shroud laid out on the floor. The men in the now blood-spattered white robes carefully wrapped the flagpole in the shroud, signifying the end of the ritual, and carried it away to the wailing of the women. The pyres were then set alight and as the smoke swirled around in the wind, scattering ashes over the thinning crowd, the *naq'al* sang his final dirge as the ceremony came to an end, the embers of the fire burning out in the wet, muddy ground.

Chapter Three

With the lifting of the black shroud of Moharram, Tehran once again underwent a dramatic change. The month of mourning had passed and with it the worst of winter. The spring equinox and all that it heralded was on the horizon. The snows that had dusted the northern edge of Tehran upon my arrival only a few weeks earlier were being pushed higher and higher up the foothills of the Alborz Mountains. Parks were once again full of life. Young and old were out walking, talking, drinking tea and working out on the bright-yellow exercise machines that had recently been installed in many public spaces. Youths clustered around fruit juice stalls exchanging quips that occasionally turned the cheeks of the young women the same colour as the pomegranate juices they sipped. The city and its inhabitants seemed relieved to have left the bleak times behind and reinvigorated by the prospect of the warmer months.

Traditionally, every Friday (the Islamic weekend) families, the length and breadth of the country, head out to their local *chelo kebab* restaurant to feast on succulent kebabs and steaming platefuls of rice. To celebrate this positive shift in atmosphere, I decided to do the same. Any narrative on Iran would be incomplete without a mention of *chelo kebab*, a dish as definitively Iranian as fish and chips is English or a hamburger is American. Sitting on an uncomfortable chair in a vast, low-ceilinged room decorated with garish floral tiles and colourful glass orbs that hung obtrusively overhead, I rubbed my hands together gleefully in anticipation of my first authentic *chelo kebab* meal.

First came an array of starters: garlic-flavoured yoghurt (*mast o moosir*), a plate of fresh herbs and radishes (*sabzi khordan*), *panir* and flatbread baked fresh in a *tanour* oven and *mirza ghasemi*, baked aubergines in a tomato and egg sauce laden with garlic. Under normal circumstances this would be considered a lavish spread in its own right but in a *kebabi* it merely serves as an entrée to the main event – foot-long kebabs of lamb or chicken accompanied by a huge plateful of highly buttered rice made even richer by the addition of a raw egg yolk. All of this is washed down with a jug of *dough*, a mint-flavoured yoghurt drink. Not a dish to be relished as a gourmet meal, a large part of the pleasure of *chelo kebab* is derived from the gluttonous way it is eaten: wolfed down by the overloaded spoonful. Although, even in the act of eating, you know serious indigestion is on the horizon, the thrill of the great gobble is indescribable.

A week earlier I had been intrigued by a bizarre haul of tatty objects shown to me by a friend raving about a flea market he had recently visited. 'If you want a real taste of Iran and what the country's all about,' he said excitedly, 'head to the *Jomeh Bazaar*.' Being close by and in desperate need of walking off my lunchtime overindulgence, I decided to wander down and explore this Iranian-style car boot sale. Every Friday (*Jomeh*), a dilapidated car-park in the centre of Tehran is transformed into a buzzing market-place as villagers and tribesmen from far and wide display their weaves and wares next to local traders.

A large concrete entrance led up into a grimy, carbon monoxide-saturated car-park overrun by a small army of peddlers. The swarm of bargain hunters and gawpers competed with the impatient horn-blasts and aggressive engine-revving of cars and motorcycles pushing their way to the upper levels of the building, which continued to serve as a car-park, their exhausts adding to the already squalid air. A couple of Cream and Rolling Stones records were perched in a cardboard box at one of the first stalls I came to. The stall owner saw my eye flicker with interest and swiftly reeled me in to peruse his bewildering spread. An old telephone disgorged wires out of a missing mouthpiece next to a camera that clearly had not been used for half a century. Calculators with cracked screens and missing buttons were lined up with regimental discipline on a moth-eaten throw. Seeing my interest in the more musical section of his stock, he proudly unveiled a gramophone that had been hidden from view. 'For the special customers,' he informed me with a quiet squeeze of my forearm. It was a wind-up with a needle, in pristine condition, which might well have found its way into the props department of a Hollywood studio.

Next to this stall, sitting proudly on a timeworn cushion, was a man with the distinct features and dress of a Turkoman. He looked as though he had just wandered in from the steppes of central Asia, the fortitude in his gaze seeming to speak of his descent from the armies of the Great Khan Timur, who invaded the country at the end of the fourteenth century. Laid out at his feet was a series of tribal-patterned carpets and floral headdresses. Beyond him, at the next stall, was an Afghan perched on his haunches beside a row of fabrics hanging from a misshapen pipe. A few pitches down was an elderly man placidly fingering his prayer beads. The pile of books in front of him contained a wide-ranging selection of German, Russian, French and English works, from regional histories and medical tomes to bird-watching and knitting manuals; there was even an eight-year-old IKEA catalogue in the mix. I unearthed a beautifully leather-bound two-volume Larousse French dictionary and agreed to pay the old man five pounds for it, prompting him to exchange his prayer beads for a pipe, which he loaded up for a celebratory smoke.

There was something here for everyone. Books, bags and belts were being hawked alongside chairs, tables, cutlery and crockery; carpets and clothes were displayed beside Indian fabrics and Uzbek silks. On top of that were the standard rings, bracelets, necklaces and knives of any self-respecting flea market and what can only be described as junk salvaged by dedicated foragers – all available for the best price negotiable following some energetic haggling, a fundamental part of most transactions in Iran.

The diversity of wares on sale was matched only by the spectrum of ethnic groups selling them. Arab, Armenian and Azeri had set up shop alongside Tajik and Turkoman. On top of that were the various tribes that comprise the rich and varied tapestry of Iran's ethnic makeup: Baluchi, Bakhtiari, Qashghai, Kurd and Lor. Their varying roots, like their wares, proudly on display in their distinctive features or by the colours and patterns of their clothes, all brought together under one roof by a common purpose – to persuade the wandering innocent to buy their tat; invariably, this wandering innocent obliged.

I was admiring the leather cover of my new dictionary on my way out of the market when I nearly walked straight into someone. My eyes were drawn to a pair of strange shoes with a pointed toe that curled upwards. Following them up, I saw a Mongolian herdsman staring back at me. His shoulders, arms and even his head were loaded with more than a dozen sheepskin throws, coats and bags. Here was a peddler far from home, eking out a living on the streets of Tehran by selling goods probably made by himself and his family. For a brief second I wondered why he had chosen to come all this way, but then I remembered that the link between our two countries goes back more than 800 years. Iranian history is littered with tribal disputes and incursions – some no more than petty blood feuds, others resulting in the foundation of new dynasties – but none can match the seismic impact of the Mongol invasions.

★ ★ ★

In 1218 a single, fateful decision set into motion a series of events that were to lead to the near-total annihilation of Iran. The imprisonment and subsequent execution of a group of merchants from the East by the governor of Otrar, a frontier town of eastern Khwarezm (modern-day Khorasan), provoked the ire of the wrong man. Temujin, better known by the title he adopted in 1206 – Genghis Khan – had previously sent an embassy to the ruler of Khwarezm with gifts and a message of goodwill, declaring that King Mohammad would be treated like his own son if he would agree to pay tribute. The king politely dismissed these men with an amicable reply. A second emissary was sent, a merchant caravan with instructions to develop trade links. It was these men who were executed by the governor of Otrar in King Mohammad's realm, and it was these deaths that provoked the most merciless and blood-soaked conquest of a much-ravaged land.

The Great Khan's armies tore through central Asia, laying waste to everything in their path. One by one the great cities of antiquity fell under the relentless onslaught of the nomadic hordes. Bokhara, Samarkand, Marv, Balkh, Herat and Neyshapur were all decimated. The cities that surrendered paid heavily in plunder; those that resisted were razed to the ground, their inhabitants slaughtered. Historians estimate that 1.3 million were butchered at Marv, 1.6 million at Herat and 1.7 million at Neyshapur, where the Mongols were said to have massacred every living thing, including the cats and dogs of the city, and piled up the skulls in gruesome pyramids of death. Neyshapur's famed university was reported to have burned for months. Bamian was wiped out of existence without even being plundered to avenge the death of Genghis's grandson, who fell during its siege.

Otrar itself fell after a six-month siege and the governor, the man responsible for bringing about this calamity, held out for another month in his palace before eventually being captured. He was brought before the Great Khan, who poured molten silver into his eyes and ears as retribution for the deaths of his envoys. Genghis Khan originally had no intention of invading Iran but the conquest of Khwarezm led him to believe that he was sent on a divinely inspired quest to conquer the world. The theme of Iranians being responsible, through short-sightedness and arrogance, for their own demise is one that recurs time and again throughout the country's history. At the time of his death in 1227, Genghis Khan ruled over an empire twice the size of the Roman Empire at its height; the largest contiguous empire in the history of the world to date.

The massacres and destruction had knock-on effects. The *qanats* – an ancient irrigation system of underground water channels making use of the water table and the land's natural gradient – were laid to waste and, with barely a soul left to repair them or to tend to the quickly desiccating fields, much of Iran reverted to the arid wasteland dotted with oasis towns it once was as famine engulfed the already beleaguered population.

In 1251 Hulagu, Genghis Khan's grandson, was sent by his brother Mongke on a mission to conquer the last bastions of the Muslim Empire and to establish a seat of power in Iran. This he did by conquering the seemingly indomitable Ismailis at Alamut, and by taking Baghdad and large parts of Syria. Only Egypt, under the Mameluks, managed to hold out against Hulagu. Back in Iran he founded the Ilkhanid[1] dynasty that ruled from 1256 to 1335. It was only forty years later, during the reign of Ghazan Khan (1295–1304), that the country began the rebuilding and recovery process in earnest. Ghazan converted to Islam before his accession to the throne in 1295. This signalled the beginning of the ascendancy of Islam under the Ilkhanids at the expense of the Buddhist and Christian beliefs that they had previously been promulgating. Of the many Buddhist temples built by the Mongols in Iran, not a single one survived to see the end of the fourteenth century.

Ghazan set about trying to rebuild Iran by introducing fiscal reforms (the most significant of which lowered and restructured exorbitant taxes) and revitalising agriculture by rebuilding the *qanat* underground water channels and introducing Asian crops and farming techniques. Like his predecessors he encouraged artisanship, scouring the empire for the most gifted artists, poets and astronomers to surround himself with. Trade flourished between East and West as the majority of the lands on the Silk Road were unified under a Mongol hegemony wholly intolerant of brigandage. Thanks to the close links with China, many new scientific and artistic concepts streamed into Iran, where they were fused with local knowledge, spawning a period of high creativity out of which came the Persian miniature.

★ ★ ★

A mild and sunny March morning made the stunning drive along the southern hem of the Alborz all the more enjoyable. I was on my way to visit Soltaniyeh, the most important building to have survived from the Mongol era. My spirits were particularly high as this was the first of my trips outside the capital and it was to explore one of the parts of Iranian history that holds the most fascination for me.

Some 300 kilometres west of Tehran lies the city of Zanjan, capital of the province of the same name. Being so far west, it is firmly in Azeri territory (which stretches from north-western Iran and beyond into the Republic of Azerbaijan), hence the predominance of the Turkic dialect spoken. Despite the fact that Soltaniyeh is a UNESCO World Heritage site, there is no direct exit to it from the motorway. Visitors are forced to drive an extra 35 kilometres to Zanjan and back by the old road. Pulling into Zanjan, I decided to wander around town and get a feel for it. Many Iranian settlements of similar size are, for the most part, indistinguishable from one another. The same tawny, one- or two-storey crumbling brick houses radiate outwards from a central bazaar – Zanjan was no different. The entrance to the town had been recently revamped, replacing the uninspiring old-road approach with a wide, tree-lined boulevard. Street names in Iran are limited to revolutionary terminology or names of martyrs, every village or town having an *Enghelab* (Revolution) and *Azadi* (Freedom) Street and an *Imam* Square. Most, though, are still known by their pre-revolutionary names (in other words, replace Revolution with Royal, Imam with Pahlavi, etc.), causing no end of confusion for the uninitiated like myself. An address referred to in speech by its former name is billed on street signs in its new appellation, causing frequent head-scratching and searching for streets no longer in existence. This confusing predicament is not aided by the Iranian propensity to respond to enquiries in the most unhelpfully laconic manner possible:

'Is this Pahlavi?'
'Yes.'
'So where's Vali Asr?'

'Here.'

'But we're on Pahlavi?'

'Yes.'

'So how do I get to Vali Asr?'

'You're on it,' *ad nauseam.*

★ ★ ★

What the bazaar in Zanjan lacks in size, it more than makes up for in personality. The high, vaulted brick roof lent an airy feel to the otherwise dingy, narrow alleyways overflowing with activity. Women in chadors scurried, weighed down by bags full of supplies, weaving their way through the obstacle course of piles of rugs, bags of spices and wrinkled old men nimbly pushing cartfuls of fabric around as seedy-looking young men with long, pointed shoes propped themselves up on piles of T-shirts, talking into their mobile phones. A small television was being ogled by an octogenarian beaming a toothless grin as he frantically fingered his prayer beads. I peered over his shoulder to see a skimpily clad Angelina Jolie firing an automatic weapon: a pirate copy of *Mr & Mrs Smith* playing in the bazaar of a town reputed for its conservatism.

As the city is famous for its knives, I felt obliged to purchase a Zanjani blade from one of the rows of cubicle-like shops, each displaying a dizzying array of weapons of all shapes and sizes hanging from or perching in every available nook and cranny, from swords and axes to ninja stars. After much deliberation and haggling I settled on a small flick-knife for a very reasonable price. As the shopkeeper handed it over, he informed me in a thick Azeri accent that I had chosen discerningly. *'Chineeye,'* he nodded in approval. I informed him that I wanted a locally crafted blade, not a Chinese import. He looked at me as though I were simple and, shaking his head in bafflement, placed a small, unostentatious pocket-knife on the table. He assured me that this blade would cut through metal and never break. Puzzled, I asked him why, extolling the local knife so, he considered it such folly that I opt for it over the Chinese one, which he admitted would soon break.

'The Chinese one has an adjustable spring mechanism and a fancy case.' I bought both.

Before leaving Zanjan I stopped at an old caravanserai that had been converted into a restaurant. Under the cool, vaulted brick ceiling I feasted on fine kebabs and fresh bread. A busload of young, boisterous basketball players poured into the restaurant shortly after me and scattered themselves over a few tables. Beside me a family sat cross-legged around a low table. The men sported the heavy stubble, dark shirts and tinted glasses that have come to be the badges of conservative supporters of the regime known as *hezbollahi* (*hezbollah* means party of God but in Iran the term is now loosely applied to anyone deemed pro-regime). The women wore black chadors pulled tight around their faces preventing even a single strand of hair from escaping. A young mother at the table cradled her new-born baby in her arms as it began to cry. She lifted a fold of the veil to her face and clamped it between her teeth as she extricated an alabaster breast heavy with milk. The basketball team was silenced, embarrassed yet transfixed by this brazen display.

★ ★ ★

Soltaniyeh is now a small, dusty, inconsequential desert village, but it was not always so. In 1304 the throne of the Ilkhanid dynasty, which reigned over the Persian lands of the Mongol Empire (what would now comprise Iran and parts of Iraq, Turkey, Azerbaijan, Armenia, Georgia, Turkmenistan, Afghanistan and Pakistan) from the mid-thirteenth to mid-fourteenth centuries, was passed from the heirless Mahmud Ghazan (1271–1304) to his brother Uljaytu (1280–1316), a title meaning fortunate in the Mongol language. 'The Sultan was born when his mother was crossing the desert which lies between Merv and Sarakhs. Her attendants, being obliged to halt, were afraid that the party would die of thirst, but upon the birth of the infant a heavy shower fell, and it was in commemoration of this that he received his title.'[2] Uljaytu decided to relocate the seat of the Ilkhanid throne from the more westerly city of Tabriz to a new capital, Soltaniyeh, which he dedicated to his father Arghun. The country's finest craftsmen and artisans having been forcibly gathered, a thriving city soon sprang up out of the barren desert dust, the centre-piece of which was the Mongol Khan's own mausoleum.

This was and still is an impressive brick building with a dome famed for its size. Edward Browne writes that 'nearly three hours before reaching … [Soltaniyeh] we could plainly see the great green dome of the mosque for which it is so celebrated'.[3] Even today, nearly 700 years after it was built, it claims to be the biggest free-standing and the oldest double-shelled brick dome in the world. At 50 metres in height and about half that in diameter, it is a symbol of the mastery of the bizarrely named 'squinch' – an architectural technique involving filling the upper corners of a room in order for it to be able to support a dome – that was pioneered by the Parthians, who ruled from the middle of the third century BCE until the establishment of the Sasanian Empire in 224 CE. This technique of mounting a round dome onto a square or rectangular structure was further developed and frequently employed by the Sasanians and has come to define Islamic architecture the world over in the ensuing centuries. Dr Arthur Upham Pope, the distinguished American archaeologist and expert on ancient architecture, describes the mausoleum as the 'ultimate triumph' of building with brick.

The size of the dome was immediately impressive from a distance, as E.G. Browne had remarked a hundred years ago. But upon drawing closer a visitor cannot fail to be captivated by the way its turquoise faience at once stands out against and merges with the impossibly vivid blue of the sky. A series of slender minarets rose delicately from the corners of the octagonal building on which the dome sat, as though holding the turquoise jewel in place. The inside of the mausoleum was disappointingly covered in scaffolding, a dog-eared computer print-out of a Khomeini portrait hanging from it for good measure. Teasing glimpses of the mosaic-work around the doorways could be made out through the metal web, but the view of the inside of the dome was almost wholly blocked by plastic sheeting.

A set of stairs led up to the second tier of the building, where an arch looked out onto the barren landscape; nothing but dust and scrub could be seen stretching off into a distant horizon punctuated by barely discernible angular peaks. It was difficult to believe that this had once been the western capital of the world's greatest empire. I came across a tight spiral staircase that wound up inside one of the minarets and bounded up it, imagining a fourteenth-century *muezzin* making his way up to summon the inhabitants of the thriving capital to their devotions. The top of the minaret had long since collapsed and, with a final twist up the stairs, I was blinking up at the untarnished azure of the desert sky. I turned around to find myself face to face with the mighty dome, I staring in wonder, the dome glowering back at me – yet another intruder among centuries of invaders, kings, warlords, mullahs, thieves, charlatans and even the occasional pious soul who had journeyed through here.

★ ★ ★

Uljaytu, having converted to Shi'i Islam after a dream he had whilst visiting the tomb of Ali at Najaf, harboured ambitions of bringing both Ali's and Hossein's bodies to be buried in the mausoleum he was building for himself. His intentions were understandably met with strong opposition from the inhabitants of Najaf and Karbala, who felt that they had sole claim to the tombs of Ali and Hossein. This opposition, coupled with suspicions of his own religious fluctuations – being baptised a Christian, converting briefly to Buddhism in his youth before becoming an adherent of the Sunni faith with his brother Ghazan and finally being inspired to turn to Shi'ism by a dream – meant that this ambition never materialised and it was only his own body that was interred under the lofty dome. Uljaytu's desire to create a burgeoning city worthy of the Ilkhanid throne and to leave a lasting legacy reflecting the absolute dominion of Mongol rule was not to be fulfilled. The city's reign as capital was as short-lived as his own. Just eighty years after his death, the once-thriving city was trampled back into the very dust from which it had been erected under the destructive hooves of the armies of the legendary Mongol warrior Timur, immortalised in English as Tamerlane (1336–1405). The mausoleum was the only thing spared.

In the late fourteenth century, Tamerlane and his army tore through Asia, conquering all in their path. So successful were his conquests that Sir Percy Sykes calls him 'the greatest Asiatic conqueror known in history',[4] a bold claim given the reputation of his compatriot and predecessor Genghis Khan and the great Achaemenian kings of the Persian Empire almost 2,000 years earlier, not to mention Alexander the Great, who, though not an Asian by birth, achieved his most dramatic conquests in these lands.

More than seven centuries on, this proud monument that Dr Arthur Upham Pope described as anticipating the Taj Mahal still stands firm, gazing out over the dusty plains of central Iran as, in the distance, the trucks, buses and cars on the Tehran to Tabriz road flash past showing little interest in one of the architectural wonders of the world.

Chapter Four

Nowrouz, the Iranian New Year, and its rituals can be traced back to the pre-Zoroastrian era, well before the sixth century BCE, being cult rites performed by migrant Aryan tribes that descended from the central Asian steppes and into Iran thousands of years before the birth of Jesus. Dr Ali A. Jafari, a somewhat controversial expert on Zoroastrianism, states that 'Tradition takes Nowrouz as far back as 15,000 years – before the last ice age.'[1] These rites were incorporated into Zoroastrianism, whose stint as the national religion – emerging in Achaemenian times from the mid-sixth century BCE and lasting until the fall of the Sasanians and the emergence of Islam in the mid-seventh century CE – cemented its place in Iranian society. So much so that since the Islamic Revolution of 1979, the Iranian government has attempted to abolish the 'heretical' *Nowrouz* celebrations on a number of occasions. But an overwhelming tide of public outrage put paid to these plans quickly enough. The significance and value attributed to the past is made apparent by the continuing import the *Nowrouz* rituals have in contemporary Iran. Iranians revel in the things that give them their identity – a messy mix of acceptance of Islam (yet their own Shi'i brand of it) with a deep adherence to pre-Islamic names, social rituals, a solar calendar and sense of Iranian-ness (yet rejecting any significant linkage to Zoroastrians).

Being the beginning of the seasonal year, the time for the natural cycle of rebirth and regeneration to start anew, the equinox marking the first day of spring in March is heralded as the commencement of the calendar year. Zoroaster, the prophet who brought the first and arguably most significant divine revelation sometime between 1800 and 1200 BCE,[2] was the first to proclaim a monotheistic doctrine. Zoroastrianism has often been misrepresented as a dualistic religion. Zardosht, as he is known in Iran, recognised Ahura Mazda as the one true God; eternal, all good, all knowing. It was from this one infinite being that Spenta Mainyu, the good spirit, emanated, and it was this spirit that went on to create the world. As Spenta Mainyu emanated, the universe harmonised (cosmically balanced as it is, with every force necessarily having its equal and opposite) by creating a counter-balance – Angra Mainyu, or Ahriman, the malevolent spirit. These opposing forces of good and evil are represented as much by light and darkness as by Truth (*Asha*) and the Lie (*Drauga*, the deceiver, *dorough* meaning 'lie' in modern Persian). (Incidentally this is the root of the Indo-European word 'drug', under whose influence one is misled from the path of truth.) Each essence has its cosmic realm, hence opposite the realm of light is the realm of darkness. It is from these opposing realms that the concept of heaven and hell entered Zoroastrian beliefs, later assimilated by the ensuing religions of the Book, namely Judaism, Christianity and Islam.

During the creation of man, Ahriman launched an attack on his opposing force and managed to corrupt the original seed of pure light, tingeing it with darkness. Thus the human race became the vessel for the cosmic struggle between good and evil, the soul its battleground. Three thousand years of peace and plenty were prophesied, with the forces of good suppressing those of darkness. 'The first period is a golden age of the rule of Ahura Mazda,' writes the late Professor Richard Frye, a highly respected professor of Iranian Studies at Harvard. 'Then come 3,000 years of warfare with Evil, a time of troubles. At the end of this period comes Zoroaster bringing a new force into the fray, which tips the scales to Ahura Mazda, and at the end of this age, 9,000 years from creation, comes the renovation of the world.'[3]

Scholars believe that many biblical concepts can be traced back to Zoroastrianism. Spenta Mainyu is equated with the Holy Spirit and Ahriman is thought to be the original Satan. Zoroaster explains the presence of evil in the world (an ongoing dilemma for religions of the Book, with Lucifer cast as a recalcitrant angel expelled from heaven) with his dualistic theory of struggling influences. Ahura Mazda, the creator, is a benign God who exists in his infinity in a quasi-Spinozan sense, leaving the spirits of Good (Spenta Mainyu) and Evil (Ahriman) to battle for the soul of man uninfluenced. 'Zoroaster thus,' writes the late Professor Mary Boyce, 'not only saw a noble purpose for humanity, but also offered men a reasoned explanation for what they have to endure in this life, seeing this as affliction brought on them by the Hostile Spirit, and not imputing to the will of an all-powerful Creator the sufferings of his creatures here below.'[4]

Guided by Zoroaster's teachings, mankind would eventually fulfil its divine potential, with the light of the human soul vanquishing the forces of darkness and annihilating Ahriman once and for all. With the Evil Spirit vanquished, Zoroaster foresaw an end to the material world, resulting in Good reigning supreme in a spiritual infinity of light. This apocalyptic ending, triggered by the miraculous birth of the *Saoshyant*, or World Saviour (from Zoroaster's own seed, preserved in a mythical lake), to human parents, is striking in its parallels to the biblical conception of the return of Christ and the Apocalypse.

★ ★ ★

The symbolism of *Nowrouz*, with the increase in daylight hours and the cycle of rebirth that the spring equinox heralds, becomes more pertinent still when considered with this battle between light and darkness in mind. Many of the ancient rituals linked with the New Year have, over the centuries, been adapted to become more compatible with Islamic beliefs in true, malleable, survivalist Iranian fashion. *Chahar Shanbe Souri* or 'Red Wednesday' is just one of these rituals. This night, revolving around the celebration of fire, kicks off the *Nowrouz* festivities on the eve of the last Wednesday of every year. Iranians take to the streets after dark to light fires – traditionally seven pyres are built one after another, reflecting the Zoroastrian conception of seven vaults of heaven and hell. Once lit, the fires are leapt over whilst the mantra '*zardiye man be to, sorkhiye to be man*', or 'my pallor to you, your redness to me', is chanted with each leap. One's ills of the previous year are cast into the flames to burn away whilst the glow and vitality of the fire is absorbed into the spirit. This ceremony originates from the Zoroastrian ritual of lighting bonfires on the roofs of dwellings before each New Year. These fires acted as beacons guiding the spirits of deceased ancestors who flew down from heaven to revisit their families, bringing providence with them and carrying away any ill fortune, thought to hang around one's head like a maleficent cloud.

On my street in Tehran, the residents had been stockpiling wooden crates and twigs for some days. As night descended on the final Tuesday of the year, they arranged them into seven small bundles and eagerly set them alight. The tranquillity of the mild March evening was shattered by ear-splitting explosions and bursts of light rolling one after another through the darkness. Smoke swirled up into the inky blackness of the night from countless fires burning brightly all over the country, whilst the streets below buzzed with the chaos of life. These days firecrackers have become an integral part of the *Nowrouz* celebrations and the youth that poured excitedly out into the dimly lit streets of the capital displayed their individual arsenals with great pride. The odd loud explosion had been piercing the hazy calm for a number of days leading up to this evening. Now 'Red Wednesday' was upon us, the bangs and bursts of light coming thick and fast. Teenagers huddled excitedly on street corners let off ear-splitting firecrackers to whoops of approval. Fireworks exploded overhead in coruscations of electric colours. There was a warm community feel to the proceedings, a sense of celebration, of freedom from the burdensome albatross of oppression. A young man strutted through the milling crowd like a cock in a hen coop, his hair gelled as high as it would stand before cascading down over his shoulders in an exaggerated mullet, a tight green T-shirt hanging off his wiry frame – this was a night on which any self-respecting peacock paraded his plumage.

'I've hung my speakers out of the window. There's going to be dancing,' he announced to the group of us that had perched on a street corner. Taking my hand lightly in his, he leaned into my ear. 'There's going to be girls,' he whispered with a wink of complicity. His friends and co-conspirators were unsuccessfully trying to synchronise the same CD being played on a car stereo at street level with that being played from the precariously suspended speakers above the empty courtyard. 'Please join us,' he added with a polite tilt of the head.

Sure enough, as the evening wore on and parents were battling to drag their overexcited children to bed, a couple of cars appeared packed with preened young ladies in tight *manteaux*. They were anxiously escorted into a courtyard where the young men and women of the area were congregating. The peacock suddenly appeared beside the speaker in the window and called for attention. He welcomed the new arrivals enthusiastically before upping the tempo of the music to cheers and whistles. The guys prodded one another excitedly on one side of the courtyard whilst, on the opposite side, the girls whispered and laughed amongst themselves, occasionally flashing an enticing smile. The scene triggered memories of awkward teenage discos, only these revellers were in their early twenties. One Don Juan took it upon himself to break the ice. Sauntering up to the girls, he soon had them giggling coyly into the side of their headscarves.

Reluctantly I scurried away and left them to it. I had another invitation I was keen to take up. A Zoroastrian friend held an annual gathering in the sizeable garden of his Tehran home – a chance to enjoy the festivities with adherents of this ancient faith. Unfortunately, not a single cab driver was willing to drive me across town and so my intentions were thwarted. The trip would have entailed sitting in three hours of traffic and the drivers were afraid of what might happen to their cars. 'Hordes of young men pour into the streets,' said one driver. 'They get over-excited. They launch Molotov cocktails and fireworks at cars. The poor guys, they've got nothing else to do. They just vent their frustrations pretending to celebrate.' That ever-present current of unrest, all too often expressed as a misplaced nervous energy, bubbles to the surface all too easily in Iran on any such occasion that creates large crowds.

★   ★   ★

The link between *Nowrouz* and the deceased has stood the test of time. The last Thursday or Friday of every year sees a mass exodus of Tehranis to the city's massive cemetery, *Behesht-e-Zahra*, just south of the capital, to make the customary visit to the graves of relatives and loved ones before the New Year. This modern interpretation of ancient customs was a different aspect of the *Nowrouz* ritual that I was keen to witness.

Once beyond the earthen-coloured brick dwellings of Tehran's suburbs, the road stretches off into a dusty horizon, leaving the chaotic city exploding outwards and upwards in the shimmering distance. It is on this arid plain that a verdant oasis has been created and immaculately maintained to accommodate the city's dead. Flags and Islamic banners dance in the breeze in front of large hoardings bearing images of Khomeini and various sayings – words of wisdom to his flock or revolutionary exhortations based on the bravery of the modern-day martyrs who made up a substantial percentage of the plots. Next to the cemetery, rising out of the desert haze, are the towering minarets and blue domes of the mausoleum of the late Ayatollah Khomeini himself. Here lies the man who made the Iranian Revolution.

The exterior of this monument is grand and imposing, if a shade Hollywoodesque. The interior, by contrast, is stark, simple and cold – more like a renovated aircraft hangar than a shrine to the father of contemporary Iran. The vast interior is dominated by a central chamber, at the heart of which lie the sarcophagi of Khomeini and of his son, Ahmad, shrouded in green fabric. Messages of prayer and reverence that have been slipped through the metal grille encasing the tomb pile up around its edge. Surrounding it are eight marble pillars and images of seventy-two tulips, each symbolising one of the martyrs that died alongside Hossein at Karbala. To accommodate the grandiose designs of the mausoleum dozens and dozens of graves and family plots, including that of my own family, were moved. The gaping expanse of empty plain that stretched off into the horizon behind begged the question as to why they had not just built the Khomeini shrine a few hundred metres to the right.

Hordes of families pour into the cemetery in the run-up to the New Year; the usually peaceful, tree-lined streets flood with streams of black. A near-constant flow of vehicles filled the car-park before disgorging entire families. I watched as an ancient motorcycle pulled in, its rusty suspension straining under the weight of four people. Father, mother and two little children were stacked and sandwiched onto the cracked plastic saddle. Stalls selling flowers and wreaths were mobbed by waddling black *chadori* matrons grabbing at the fast-disappearing bouquets. With the flowers in their grasp, the women attempted to regain their decorum and rearrange their chadors. Their Islamic modesty restored, they scurried off in search of their family plots. There was a vivacity that somehow did not seem incongruous in the cemetery. It was as though these visits, though solemn affairs, were in keeping with the sense of celebration that governs the rest of the *Nowrouz* period.

★   ★   ★

Woven into the symbolic rituals surrounding *Nowrouz* is the annual tradition of *khane tekani*. Literally meaning 'shaking the house', it is a spring clean which sees the otherwise drab exteriors of houses given life by the colours and intricate patterns of carpets being suspended for a good airing from roofs, windows and balconies throughout the land while every nook and cranny of the house is scrubbed. The ill fortune and evil spirits of the old year are washed away along with the dust and grime in preparation for the New Year. So too with clothing. *Nowrouz* is a time for new outfits; traditionally an entire family would acquire everything new, from head to toe. In short, this is the time of year when the slate is wiped clean, with a fresh start to the year symbolising the natural cycle so important in sustaining life.

Contemporary Iranians lay a table known as the *haft sin*, the Seven S's. These are seven symbolic items that begin with the letter 'S'; *serkeh* (vinegar), *seer* (garlic), *somagh* (a sour spice known in English as sumac), *seeb* (apples), *sabzi* (germinated seeds), *sekkeh* (coins) and *senjed* (a wild tree whose fruit resembles that of the mountain ash), although there are other variants. The origin of the idea can be traced back to Zoroastrian springtime offerings, and all are, in their different ways, symbolic of the desire for better health and prosperity in the coming year. The objects laid on the table beside the seven S's include the Holy Book (the *Gathas* for Zoroastrians, but most Iranian households will nowadays use the Qur'an), a goldfish (representing beauty in life), painted eggs for fertility and a mirror to indicate the importance of self-awareness. Ali Jafari, the Zoroastrian expert, said it well: 'The whole table, beautifully laid, symbolizes the Message and Messenger, light, reflection, warmth, life, love, joy, production, prosperity, and nature.'[5]

Chapter Five

One of the more recent trends to have associated itself with the *Nowrouz* period is that of tourism. The few with the means jet off to the States, Europe or Dubai; the majority, though, migrate either due north to *Shomal* (literally meaning north but in this case designating the Caspian shoreline, comprising Gilan and Mazandaran provinces) or fly south to Kish, a Persian Gulf island. Again, wanting to explore every facet of contemporary *Nowrouz* rituals, I decided to follow the crowd north to the seaside village of Nour where my maternal grandfather hailed from, being romantically impelled by hazy memories of a trip on my very first visit to Iran as a ten-year-old. I was soon able to hitch a ride to *Shomal* from the friend of a friend – an often invaluable means of travel in a country with limited public transport – and found myself in the passenger seat of a rusting Paykan car.

The journey east out of Tehran and through the Alborz is, if undertaken in the right season, one marked by changes in colour that tell its story more poetically than any pen. Following the treacherous path of ancient caravan routes, a winding road scythes through the immensity of the tawny mountainside like a human cry for attention. The only flash of colour to interrupt the drab rock came from the dark green and fleshy red of watermelons, piled skywards in the back of battered pickup trucks, and the bright pyramids of oranges being peddled by the villagers that lined the roadside. As the road wound higher and the air became crisper, the grey rock became veiled in the pure white of snow too high to be tarnished by the grime of our urban emanations, glistening in the bright sunlight against the otherworldly azure of the Iranian sky. The road meandered around the mountainside and down into the valley beyond, leaving the snow-laden slopes behind as low clouds heavy with moisture appeared, clinging to the brawny rock. The odd green shrub poked out of the desolation as though it could sense the moisture in the air. The dust of the valley floor far below gradually turned to mud, the mud into a stream and the stream eventually into a raging river. This river in turn generated vegetation; patchy at first, then slowly the banks became lined with lush grass and a canopy of green hid the barrenness of the mountainside above.

Forests, shades of green I had not seen since my arrival in Iran, carpeted the valley. Beyond this valley was yet another; greener, more lush. Further still foothills rolled their way towards the waiting sea, carrying trees right up to its inviting shores. By means of an hour-long meander through the mountains, we were transported from the arid emptiness to the south of the Alborz into a wholly different world – one exploding with verdant life, the air heavy with moisture. This is due to a microclimate created by the towering peaks trapping moisture blown in from the Caspian and creating a pocket of semi-tropical weather. Past the foothills and into the meagre flats that lie directly before the sea, swaying green fields of tea and shimmering bogs of paddy lined the road leading to the coast. Every so often we drove through a village, its shops laden with the inflatable toys and beach-balls that announced the imminent arrival of the sea next to large discs of deep-red pressed fruit (usually sour cherries) called *lavashak* flapping temptingly in the breeze.

Cowherds led their lumbering charges by the roadside, long sticks perched quaintly on their shoulders. The scene was unquestionably idyllic but there was something I could not quite place that was missing. It was only when I saw a farmer propped up against his plough chatting away on a mobile phone that I realised what it was. The bright colours of traditional dress that had made such an impression on me all those years ago were nowhere to be seen. Instead, the waistcoats and vivid red shirts had been replaced by jeans, baseball caps and replica football shirts. Reinforcing this impression of the relentless spread of globalism, only moments later I arrived at the first coastal town of the journey to discover the bawdy neon lights, rows of cars and towers of concrete that seem to be synonymous with seaside development the world over. The next town we came to was even more developed – more cars, more crowded and more concrete. I was absently gazing at the fluorescent plastic palm trees that lined the town's main boulevard when our car came to a stop. 'Welcome to Nour,' my driver-companion announced dryly.

The place was unrecognisable as the sleepy agricultural village of breeze-block bungalows surrounded by paddy fields that I remembered. It was now a burgeoning seaside town attracting thousands of Iranian tourists annually. Placards advertised motorboats and jet skis for hire. Shops selling useless trinkets jostled for space with bright, sleek fast-food joints with English menus. Every 15 metres or so a sign advertised holiday accommodation and the road was full of young men with gelled manes offering passers-by rooms for rent. Seeing I was young and single, one entrepreneurial chap sidled up to me and offered me a *veela* (villa) with an accompanying *Jeela* – a girl to 'make sure you have everything you need for your stay,' he added with a wink. I politely declined, informing him I already had somewhere to stay. 'Aha, *barikala*,' he said, congratulating me with a playful nudge in the ribs.

★ ★ ★

My grandmother owned a small holiday home in Nour and though she had passed away a few years previously, the house was still looked after by the ever-loyal Issa, a local goatherd she had taken in and employed as a gardener. Wanting a quiet, secluded corner in which to write, away from the incessant clamour of city life, I had sent word that I was coming to stay for a few weeks. Walking down the unrecognisable main strip of town, I was stopped dead by the sight of a rusting red gate sandwiched between the glamorous, sweeping entrances of two high-rise apartment complexes. I recognised it instantly as the gate of my grandmother's house. There was no sign of a doorbell so I shouted for Issa over the cracked wall. I heard some scurrying and whispered voices before the gate finally opened like a tentative yawn. Issa, his wife and two young children were standing in a row, as though to attention on the parade ground, to give me a royal welcome.

Thanks to Issa's diligence, the garden that my grandmother had been so fond of was immaculately kempt but, despite his best efforts, the house had fallen into a state of disrepair. The red band of paint that circled the tops of its white walls had been worn away by sand, wind and the corrosive humidity of the air. The high humidity levels around the Caspian coast had caused wood to warp and metal to rust. Inside, the cracked walls sagged in submission. The wooden boards of the ceiling had warped, crumbling away in places under the steady drip of leaks from the corrugated iron roof. The carpet was stained, threadbare and smelt strongly of mould. The furniture looked as knackered as the house, the kitchen worse off than the furniture. Wooden cupboards were bent out of shape as though refusing to shut in protest at our abandonment. The only parts of the house still with life in them were the bedrooms, or more specifically the beds, which came alive at night as the woodworm slowly but steadily crunched the bed-frames to dust.

Over the course of the next two and a half years I was to make regular trips to Nour. In fact, most of this book was first written there. Over cups of steaming sweet tea, Issa would tell me of his ancestral village in the mountains and the hardships they suffered every year with the onset of winter. He spoke of the spite with which many locals viewed the seasonal influx of city folk with their money and modern attitudes, and of the bizarre incongruities that spring up when two such differing lifestyles come together. When we were not setting the world to rights, Issa would stand by my workstation and gawk at my computer. He had developed an unhealthy fascination with my screen-saver: a space station orbiting the earth. At first, he stole surreptitious glances at it. Then, as he grew more comfortable in my company, he would stand transfixed for minutes at a time. It took many visits to Nour for him to finally ask what it was that he watched so contentedly.

Like everything else in the house, the telephone was in a state of disrepair and needed Issa's magic touch to work. When I first asked him about the phone line, he quickly disappeared and came back with a stepladder, which he positioned outside the window by the front door. Climbing it, he grabbed a handful of loose wires and began twisting them together in various combinations until I finally got a dial tone. He then hoisted these wires triumphantly above his head. He rebuffed my suggestion of taping them together. It would only work, of course, with him standing precariously on a rickety stepladder, his arms held skywards. When I tried to explain that I wanted to use the internet and that it would be for longer than a couple of minutes, he scoffed at the implication that he would not be willing or able to put up with it. And stay it out he did, seeming to hold up the heavens while the world was passing him by below.

* * *

With Issa's words about the tensions created by the arrival of the moneyed hordes from Tehran ringing in my ears, I wandered a few hundred metres down the road to a modern hotel that I had noticed on the drive in. The flashy cars in the car-park reflected the flashy clientele in the lobby. Girls sauntered, their dyed-blonde hair cascading impertinently from barely present headscarves, reminding me of a quip I had heard that 'there are more blondes in Tehran than in Stockholm these days'. Heels were perilously high, gaits exaggeratedly feline, the natural beauty of features masked under excessive make-up. It was not just the women who struck poses. Men with too much grease in hair styled too high flicked flashy watches a little too conspicuously. The latest mobile phones were glanced at and designer handbags switched from arm to arm, all with unnatural frequency. Not for the first time the image of the peacock, nature's greatest exhibitionist, sprang to mind. The waving plumes seemed to be wafting cologne and hormones across the large, open room. The electricity that seems to radiate dynamo-like in any place where substantial numbers of young men and women intermingle was almost palpable in its intensity.

These were the *aghazadehs* – the suffix *zadeh* means 'born of' so an *aghazadeh* is the sardonic term given to sons of clerics – the new elite who have usurped the playboy thrones of the *shahzdeh* princelings. Noses are unnaturally elfin, lips excessively plump; cosmetic surgery is not just acceptable but *de rigueur* – and that is just the men.

The disparity in wealth, the growing chasm that threatens to swallow the country whole, was more apparent in Nour than anywhere else I had thus far been. This provincial, farming-oriented town had, thanks to the *Nowrouz* holidays, attracted the cream of young, well-to-do Iranians, highlighting their excesses in the cold, rural light of day. The overtly garish stylings of the youth clashed more than ever with the sombre shrouds of the *chadoris*; the thirty-year-old rusting Paykans were made to look more decrepit than ever next to the sleek, seductive curves of brand-new Mercedes and BMWs.

A bright-eyed villager perched on the edge of his cartful of oranges, a scrap of cardboard resting on his mud-stained trousers announcing their price per kilo as he swung a sandalled foot to and fro, watching with a mixture of awe and incredulity as a group of girls, each with designer sunglasses larger than her face, clung to the Armani-clad arms of a buff man in his early twenties as he locked his BMW M5 with a loud squeak from 30 metres. The group brushed past the orange seller, oblivious to his existence, and walked into a gleaming chrome burger joint with an English sign. He spat, more with envy than venom, at the indentation left in the mud by a passing stiletto heel.

★ ★ ★

Every year on 13 *Farvardin* Iranians abandon their houses and head out into the great outdoors, where extended families eat, sleep, sing and dance the day away with the favourite Iranian pastime of the picnic. As with many cultures, the number thirteen is considered inauspicious, so this occasion, on the thirteenth day of the New Year, is an opportunity to bypass the perils and pitfalls of daily life. Folks while their time away in the safety of nature, far from the malevolent reach of evil spirits, in a tradition called *Sizdah be Dar*, or 'Thirteen Undone'. This ancient custom marks the close of the *Nowrouz* festivities and the end of the holidays. The government tolerates this pagan ritual by declaring it a celebration of nature rather than a pre-Islamic rite. Despite this, the influence of Zoroastrianism is conspicuous in the symbolism of the day's rituals.

The *sabzi* (germinated seeds) is taken from the traditional *haft sin* table and thrown into running water, usually a stream or river. Like the cleansing fire of Red Wednesday, the green shoots are said to ingest any lurking evil from the house that is then swept away by the fresh-flowing water. Nowadays interpretations of this custom are somewhat looser and more pragmatic. People without the time or inclination to get out of the city just toss their *sabzi* into the *joub* water channels that carry the Alborz melt-water through the city.

It is also customary to eat certain dishes on this day: *ash-e-reshte*, a thick vegetable soup (*reshte*, meaning root, is a spaghetti-like substance believed to bring 'roots' to new prosperity); *sabzi polo mahi*, rice cooked with herbs and white fish, the definitive *Nowrouz* dish; and *kahou sekan-jebin*, fresh lettuce dipped in a sherbet made from sugar and vinegar. If they do not go into the countryside, people with gardens often host parties at which these foods are served. It was at one of these parties that I found myself sitting on the lawn of a house in the northern Niavaran suburb of Tehran, chatting to an attractive young lady. As we were talking I watched curiously as she tied two pieces of grass together. 'Single girls do this in the hope that they're married by the end of the year,' she said with a smile.

★ ★ ★

Whilst it is true that much has changed in the enforcement of moral strictures since the early days of the Revolution – when make-up, public hand-holding and the sharing of a car with someone of the opposite sex who was not a family member were vehemently punished – it is also undeniable that many of the opportunities taken for granted by young people in the West simply do not exist in Iran.

Cars are one of the few enclaves of freedom available to the youth of Tehran. Away from the restrictive glare of parents and police, getting behind the wheel affords young people a bit of much-needed breathing space where they can talk freely with their friends and blast the pop music that is outlawed by the regime. So it makes perfect sense that courtship also becomes heavily reliant on a set of wheels. A couple of streets in northern Tehran are brought to a standstill every Thursday and Friday evening as the city's young go out on the prowl. Spruced-up young men pack into cars four or five at a time and drive up and down Jordan Street, keeping their eyes peeled for cars full of dolled-up girls. Afforded time and safety by the slow crawl of traffic generated by this activity, guys and girls wind down their windows and trade flirtatious quips. If a girl is suitably impressed by the elevation of a guy's quiff or the audacity of his chat-up line, she hastily hands over a pre-folded scrap of paper with her phone number on it, then turns away and does her best to act like a paragon of modesty. This is invariably hard to do as the roads are gridlocked and she is left face to face with the guy, who, if not the type to be stunned into embarrassed silence, only grows more brazen with her encouragement. Once their respective streams of traffic have carried them a suitable distance away from this awkward moment, they call each other and arrange a date. The more respectable of these dates are arranged for coffee shops but if the 'getting to know each other' step in the relationship is to be bypassed, it is back into the car and down a quiet alleyway or up a remote dirt track in the foothills.

The natural backlash against what, to a young mind, must seem a socially oppressive existence can cause youthful attitudes to be so determinedly hedonistic and defiant that they can seem downright foolish. I was given a taste of this firsthand one evening whilst being driven home by the son of a family friend who had taken it upon himself to be my guide to youth culture in Tehran. When his car was aggressively overtaken by a Nissan Patrol, he immediately gave out a yelp of excitement and put his foot down hard on the accelerator. Weaving in and out of the traffic at breakneck speed, he hammered the steering-wheel excitedly, deaf to my protestations. Terrified and bemused, I asked him what was going on. 'You'll see. You'll see,' he said, slapping me on the thigh. After a few hair-raising minutes in which we must have committed every traffic violation in existence but somehow managed to avoid serious injury, our car came to a stop at a red light. Alongside us was the Nissan we had been tailing. I thought we had been pursuing a long-lost friend or relative who also happened to be a rally driver. But when I glanced over I saw a girl not much out of her teens winking provocatively at us from behind the steering-wheel she could barely see over. 'This is how we do it here,' said my companion as my window dropped with a buzz.

'Your driving is almost as cute as you are,' he shouted at the girl as he leaned over me. A couple of minutes and an indecent number of lewd innuendos later, phone numbers were being exchanged over the irate klaxons of waiting cars as I squirmed uncomfortably in my seat.

'Let's hope *it* is as big as your engine,' said the girl as her Nissan sped off from the lights with a roar.

Chapter Six

The ebb and flow of life in Iran is dictated by its four very distinct seasons. Spring and autumn are ideal windows for travel, between the relentless heat of summer and the harsh inclemency of winter. Spring sees a magical transformation take place in many parts with the dry, dusty colours of tawny rock and desiccated fields of gold being replaced by the soft green of grass, the vibrant colours of wild flowers and the electric emerald of new crops. The Alborz Mountains and their surrounding foothills and plains explode with the soft whites and pinks of the blossoms of fruit-bearing trees and swaying red seas of wild poppies. My attentions, though, had turned from the verdant canopy of the north to the unflinching furnace that is southern Iran.

The south of Iran has been shaped by very different influences from those that have moulded the north, both internal and external, natural and man-made, creating a wholly different culture. Where the north was based around the caravans of the Silk Road, the south was shaped by ocean traders. Where the north was swayed by the ever-lurking presence of Turkic and Afghan tribes, the south saw migrants from the nearby Arabian world and the colonising vessels of the Portuguese, Dutch and British sail in and out of its history. Where heavy snows mark the long winters of the north, a never-ending summer scorches the south.

I was having dinner with some friends when talk turned to the Persian Gulf area and to the island of Qeshm. I mentioned having been intrigued by the history of European colonialism on the island and by its famous mangrove forest and lunar valleys. I thought nothing more of the conversation until my phone rang the following day.

'Are you Cyrus Massoudi?'

'Yes.'

'I understand you're interested in Qeshm?' The voice was gruff and unfamiliar, the tone neither friendly nor hostile. Was this the call I had been dreading ever since I landed in Tehran – the summons from the notorious security police?

'Why do you ask?' I countered, trying to sound calm. Any visitor to Iran will have heard tales of interrogations conducted in safe houses, usually seized from officials of the Shah's era. These were as much attempts to recruit informants or spread disquiet as the precursor to anything more sinister. 'And who is this?' I added tentatively.

'Never mind. Are you interested in Qeshm, yes or no?' I tried to recollect what I had said about Qeshm that might land me in trouble. I had spoken about European colonisers, about mangroves and sandstone formations. We had discussed a recent earthquake – but that was it, I was certain.

'Yes. In the history and geology …'

'Good.' The gruff voice cut me off before I had a chance to further plead my innocence. 'I have someone you should meet.'

And that was that. A few days later I was on a plane heading to Qeshm. The phone call turned out to be from the uncle of one of the previous evening's dinner guests – an uncle with an obviously dry telephone manner – and the 'someone' a man named Hossein who turned out to be one of the most unforgettable characters I was to come across in my time in Iran.

★ ★ ★

The history of Qeshm, much like many of the coastal regions of the Gulf and Indian Ocean, is dominated by the comings and goings of colonisers and sea traders. The Elamites are thought to have been the first to establish themselves on the island after the collapse of their empire based in western Iran around the tenth century BCE. There is evidence of maritime trade between the Elamites and Babylonians but this diminished following the reign of Nebuchadnezzar I (*c.* 1126–*c.* 1103 BCE), a decline that lasted right through the Achaemenian period as sea traders turned their attentions to the Red Sea routes. The trade routes of the Gulf were revived in the latter part of the fourth century BCE after the historic voyage of Nearchus. An admiral of Alexander the Great's, in 325 BCE he was ordered to navigate the Macedonian fleet westwards along the coast after Alexander's armies began to mutiny on the Indian campaign. Despite great hostility from the coastal tribes and a lack of food and drinking water, Nearchus managed to successfully navigate from India all the way along Iran's southern coast and dock the Macedonian fleet at Hormozia (modern-day Hormoz).

Persian and Arab historians only began chronicling maritime happenings in the Persian Gulf from the ninth century CE onwards. It is from accounts such as these that the voyages of Suleiman the Merchant, around 850 CE, grew in repute and went on to inspire what we now know as the tales of Sinbad the Sailor. Under the Daylamite Buyid dynasty (934–1055 CE), Qeshm enjoyed a period of prosperity and stability thanks to the burgeoning sea trade between northern Africa, the Gulf ports, India and China. With the collapse of the Buyid Empire, the island saw the arrival of Arab sheikhs from across the Gulf who conquered the neighbouring islands of Hormoz and Kish, establishing the Kingdom of Ormus. In the mid-thirteenth century, the island returned under Persian control and again prospered, this time as a key port in the slave trade.

The Portuguese arrived on the scene in 1507, during the early Safavid period, led by Afonso de Albuquerque. Deeming the islands of Hormoz and Qeshm strategically fundamental to controlling the Hormoz Strait – and therefore access to the Indian Ocean – they attempted to occupy them. Although initially repelled, by 1515 the Portuguese had assumed control of the islands, where they remained for the next hundred years until a new force sailed into the region's history. The British, in the guise of the East India Company, began to challenge Portuguese supremacy in the region in the early seventeenth century. In 1619 Rui Freire de Andrade was sent from Lisbon with orders to reinforce the Portuguese position in the Strait of Hormoz by subduing Persian resistance and seeing off the British threat. He succeeded briefly, building a fort on Qeshm Island and wresting control from the Persians, but was expelled in 1621 when an East India Company squadron, sent to collect a shipment of silk, allied themselves with the Persians in exchange for control of the castle of Hormoz and a number of other concessions. The battle for control of this key shipping channel was decided in February 1622 when, with the arrival of five British guns, the Portuguese fort was subjected to heavy bombardment. The garrison surrendered and Freire was captured and sent to prison in Surat on the west coast of India. William Baffin, the Arctic explorer in whose honour the eponymous bay and island on Canada's east coast were named, was a casualty of this battle.

In 1645 it was the turn of the Dutch to attack Qeshm. They failed to take the fort but did force a better trade agreement with the Safavid shah, Abbas II. In the early eighteenth century, expansion of the Omani kingdom led to a protracted war with Iran in which Qeshm was once again seized. The island was returned to Iran under the terms of a treaty signed between the two kingdoms, allowing the Omanis to build a naval repair yard on the island's southern shoreline.

For the next 200 years the fate of the island continued in this way, being defended by Persian forces against European colonisers and Arab expansionists. It was only in 1935, at the request of Reza Shah Pahlavi, that the last colonial foothold was relinquished in the Gulf islands with the abandonment of a British coaling depot on the small island of Hengam.

Qeshm remains geographically key to this day, located as it is to the north of the Hormoz Strait, a narrow waterway linking the Persian Gulf to the Arabian Sea. Roughly 20 per cent of the world's oil supply passes through the Strait, making it of vital importance not just to the region but to the global economy. When the 'nuclear crisis' refocused the world's attention on Iran, this body of water – bristling with civilian and military traffic, involving on the one hand the navies of the USA and its Western and Arabian allies and, on the other hand, the increasingly competent and capable Iranian Navy – took on even more political significance. Only a week before my trip, the Iranian Navy was conducting manoeuvres, testing their new underwater artillery by firing countless missiles in the vicinity of a small, uninhabited island called Larak, renowned for its beauty and wildlife. These manoeuvres were presumably for the benefit of the US Navy fleet anchored a short missile flight away with Iranian naval activity very much in their cross-hairs. I heard later of a fisherman finding an unexploded torpedo on the island that he salvaged thinking he might get a reward for returning it to the Navy. Back at his home, he was showing off this newfound treasure to his family – father, wife, brother and two toddlers – when the device was accidentally triggered, killing all instantly.

★ ★ ★

As I shuffled towards the cabin door and set foot on the steps of the plane I was hit by a wall of heat like the blast from an oven door being opened.

By the time I had got off the plane, collected my bags and negotiated the security checks, a sticky film of sweat had firmly glued my clothes to my body. The faint sea breeze did little to assuage the stifling heat. I quickly realised why I had been advised innumerable times to visit the south before May; 'otherwise you'll die' was the phrase commonly used – no exaggeration, I now realised. From early June to the end of August temperatures average over 50°C and, with an average humidity of over 80 per cent, even the slightest movement becomes an exertion. The 1,335 square kilometres of the island are mostly rocky, sandy and desolate, but there is a small mountain range whose volcanic origins have produced its dramatic rock formations. The island's economy was sustained predominantly by fishing until 1989 when it was declared a free trade port.

Iranians now flock to the island in droves to buy electrical goods at tax-free prices. I had heard of people spending small fortunes on a veritable Aladdin's cave that they went on to sell at huge profit in the Tehran bazaar. The government had recently limited the amount of goods one could take back to the mainland, where stringent customs officials wait to ruthlessly tax anything being imported. In typically Iranian fashion, entrepreneurs were rounding up strangers and paying for their trips to the island to make use of their goods allowance. Other more maverick bargain hunters had devised ingenious but often disastrous ways to smuggle their goods back to the mainland. One *chadori* woman tried to smuggle a refrigerator the few kilometres to the mainland on a dinghy. 'She didn't get very far before she had to be fished out by the coastguard,' I was told between snorts of laughter. Qeshm is also a hub for smugglers: alcohol comes in from India for consumption in Iran, where it is illegal, while the island is also a staging post for hashish and opium bound for Europe. DVDs also flood in from Thailand and the Southeast; 'Even sesky ones,' I was told by a beaming hawker pointing to his crotch.

Despite the island's many alluring qualities, it loses out in the tourism stakes to its much smaller, westerly neighbour. Kish became the pet project of the extravagant Mohammad Reza Shah, who wanted to create a luxurious pleasure island akin to pre-revolutionary Cuba. By the mid-1970s, hotels, nightclubs, beachside restaurants and bars had opened alongside Parisian haute-couture boutiques, exotic fabric shops and casinos. Even specially recruited French mademoiselles helped to create a flamboyant playground for the Iranian elite and high-rolling tourists from the Arabian Peninsula and Europe, all of this while Dubai was still little more than a sandy wilderness.

As with so many of the Shah's grandiose projects, it was stopped dead in its tracks by the events of 1979. The development of Kish was yet another example of excessive wealth and progressive Western morality being flaunted in a time of great poverty that the pious, traditionally minded population of Iran took such deep exception to. Seeing Madame Claude's brothel next to the neon signs of casinos represented the kind of misguided attempts to force a modernity that contributed to the undoing of the Shah's regime. In trying so desperately to attract the attention of the West, the Shah had managed to alienate his own people, oblivious to their traditional Muslim sensibilities. So, come 1979, the casinos and nightclubs were swiftly seized and destroyed or turned into headquarters for the Revolutionary Guard or other such militant wings of the new theocratic regime. The Islamic Revolution heralded the end of the burgeoning but tawdry Iranian tourist industry in the Persian Gulf that, in its heyday, could boast a direct Concorde flight from Paris and played host to such megastars as Frank Sinatra, replacing it with a policy as welcoming as an electrified razor-wire fence. Kish still attracts an estimated 1 million Iranian tourists a year, but the prospect of segregated, alcohol-free, heavily policed beaches does little to attract foreign tourists.

* * *

I hailed a cab and even before I had managed to tell him my destination, the driver had launched into an informative lecture on the mating habits of hawksbill turtles. He had recently witnessed that most curious of phenomena in which these turtles return to their place of birth in their thousands to lay their eggs and passionately recounted the spectacle. Tens of thousands of eggs had reportedly been collected on the beach of Shibderaz village over the previous few years and, the hawksbill being a critically endangered species, the local council have been working in conjunction with the UN Global Environment Facility to ensure an optimal survival rate for these giant turtles.

When, a few minutes later, we pulled up outside a row of houses elevated off the ground by stilts just over a metre high and my driver informed me we'd reached our destination, I was disappointed that the lecture had been cut short. As I was getting my wallet out to pay the fare, a placid voice from over my shoulder said something in the local Bandari dialect. My driver instantly smiled and refused any payment whatsoever, wishing me a pleasant stay as he drove off. I turned around to be greeted by the tranquil smile of Hossein. Seeing my bemused expression he said, 'Don't worry about it. He's a friend. Come in, coffee's brewing.' Everything about Hossein oozed languor and reassurance, from his salt-and-pepper mop and the soft cartoon-like features of his face to his easy demeanour and soothing voice. All of my concerns about spending a week with someone I had never met and knew nothing about were immediately dispelled. It was clear I was in safe hands. Not only did he seem to know every nook and cranny of the island, he also seemed to be friends with the majority of its inhabitants.

Hossein stands out as being different from everyone else I came across in my time in Iran. His generosity of spirit was free from the occasionally cloying and cumbersome affectations of the country's hospitality culture. Receiving a guest was not a duty but a pleasure to him, a chance to share the natural wonders of his beloved island. Where many Iranians have a tendency towards exaggeration and histrionics, he went about his business with understated assurance. While many Iranians profess a great love for the outdoors this is often limited to picnicking with packaged foods and flasks of tea on the hard shoulder of a busy road. Hossein was a true outdoorsman, most at home in the shady cranny of a deserted beach for days on end with no provisions but his trusty pocket-knife and a makeshift fishing-rod. In short, he was that most un-Iranian of things: a doer not a talker.

Over breakfast, Hossein suggested a plan for my brief stay on the island and once we had drawn up a suitable itinerary, we headed to the new bazaar in search of supplies. A bright white mall of gargantuan proportions based on the designs of similar Iranian-owned commercial hubs in Dubai, it sold everything from televisions to tents. A row of clothing shops offered a broad choice of the local apparel, from brightly coloured, Indian-looking translucent patterned voile chadors for women to the flowing, white ankle-length Arab robes known locally as *jimeh* for men. I was surprised to turn a corner and find a row of gleaming new Triumph motorcycles packed into a cupboard-sized showroom. Outside was a large hirsute man with an admirable handlebar moustache, jet-black hair greased back tightly to his scalp and pulled into a ponytail, wearing faded, ripped jeans and a bulky pair of boots you would not want to be kicked by; he was a veritable Iranian Hell's Angel.

From the escalators and fancy lights of the new mall, I followed Hossein's flaccid yet purposeful gait to the old bazaar. A succession of battered wooden stalls lining a couple of dirt streets was manned by leathery faces wafting fans to keep invading hordes of flies from overrunning the piles of fruit and vegetables on offer. Colourful mounds of local women scurried about buying groceries. Many of them wore *burkhes*, ornate masks covering the nose and eyebrows with gold sequins that shimmered in the strong sunlight. These, unlike the burkha and niqab ever more prominently adopted by Muslim women in the West, were not worn primarily for modesty or a sense of identity but as protection from the sun. As I took in the scene, Hossein glided between the stalls, exchanging handshakes and friendly greetings for groceries.

Our next port of call was a beachside bungalow constructed of breeze blocks so hurriedly piled on top of one another that it seemed as though two of the walls had been forgotten in the haste. Inside was a group of local fishermen we had come to buy fresh supplies from, *araghchins* wrapped around their heads. The *araghchin*, literally 'sweat collector', is a Middle Eastern sweat band. It is similar to the Arab *chafieh*, which is usually worn with the free-flowing white *jimeh* robe, almost as frequent in these parts as the Afghan-style *shalwar kameez*. We purchased a crab and three fish so fresh they were still gasping for air. One of the fishermen, with a bare chest and flowing white beard, proceeded to descale and gut the fish with a speed and dexterity that belied his advanced years.

The appearance and dress of these fishermen spoke of the history of strong Arab influence in the region. While the majority of Arab settlers in Iran followed in the wake of the defeat of the Sasanian Empire by the Muslim armies in the seventh century, the south had long seen an Arab influence, with many nomadic tribes wandering back and forth across the border with southern Iraq and trade relations stretching back many centuries prior to the Islamic conquests. The recent Gulf Wars have seen a major influx of Iraqi Arabs flooding through the south-western border into Khuzestan province. Despite this, less than 2 per cent of Iran's population are Arab and, though some pockets have preserved their ethnic identity and language, most are now fully assimilated into Iranian culture. Bearing in mind the history between the two countries and their being such a small minority, it is easy to understand why many of the Arabs now living in Iran, especially those that are Sunni, choose to keep a low profile.

Having stocked up on provisions and packed them in coolboxes full of ice, we jumped into Hossein's car and set out on a tour of the island. As we drove through the impossible heat I noticed high walls of rubble skirting the roads. 'They've been here since the war,' Hossein told me. 'They piled up tons of dirt along the coastline so that American warships in the Gulf couldn't see activity on the roads. It costs too much to do anything about, so it just sits here ruining the view.' Without warning,

Hossein suddenly turned onto a dirt track leading to a cream-coloured cliff-face glistening in the sun. 'It's too hot. Let's go see the grottoes.'

Various gaping black openings peppered the pallid cliff-face. These warren-like caves were reached via steps carved into the rock from a single opening at ground level. This series of connected passageways and natural windows was hewn in such a way as to act as an incredibly efficient air-conditioning system. The exact history and purpose of these caves is unknown, though they are believed to be from colonial Portuguese times. One theory is that they were used as a prison. Given the sizeable drop from the openings to the ground and the single, easily guarded exit this is certainly a plausible assumption.

From one of these windows a vast plain of sand and rock sprawled far into the horizon, littered by the odd shrub somehow capable of sustaining itself in these harsh conditions. In the distance small carpets of green could be seen, gardens irrigated by underground freshwater channels. Troops of camels indifferent to the midday sun plodded their way between dancing spirals as a twisting breeze whipped up the hot dust. Cliffs and rocky outcrops with angular breaks sat on the horizon, evidence of the continual flux of the earth's vast plates adrift on a subterranean ocean of fire. I sat and took in the bizarre landscape from the confines of my cool, rocky perch. Beautiful in its barrenness, the plain had an air of prehistory about it, untouched by the artifices of human endeavour.

That evening Hossein took me to a restaurant owned by a friend of his. As we drove up to the restaurant, I noticed the ruined walls of the fort built by Rui Freire de Andrade in 1621 to defend Portuguese interests from the advances of the British and the Dutch, the merlons of a buttress reaching up to the sky like plump fingers. Hossein's friend took us onto the roof of the building, where we lay with the stars above us and the sea at our feet. As our host fed us a rich dessert made from puréed rice sweetened and flavoured with cinnamon and rosewater, he disappeared downstairs only to return with a sitar. Sitting cross-legged on the edge of the roof, he cleared his throat and launched into an eerie Bandari ballad that instantly brought a smile to Hossein's face.

Exhausted by the long, hot day's driving, we thanked our host for dinner and crawled off the roof of the restaurant. Before heading home Hossein insisted we stop off at the beachfront to enjoy the evening breeze. As I lay on the sand, staring up at the stars, I was revelling in the tranquillity afforded by a night sky devoid of artificial light when a jeep suddenly reversed onto the beach and pointed a trailer out to sea.

'Smugglers,' Hossein said knowingly. Sure enough, a minute after the jeep had pulled up a small speedboat appeared out of the gloom and beached itself right in front of the waiting trailer. Within no more than a minute the boat had been hoisted onto the trailer and fastened before both disappeared into the darkness just as suddenly as they had appeared. It was only once back in Tehran that I heard rumours that Hossein himself had been a conduit for many of the staple goods in short supply during the lean years of the war, darting over to Dubai and Oman on a cigar boat.

★ ★ ★

Hossein had arranged for us to be picked up early the following morning. Our driver was a cheery African Iranian whose frequent belly laughs were highly infectious. Although historically Iranians have been more famed for emancipation than enslavement – Cyrus the Great freed the Jews from captivity in Babylon and every single worker to have built Persepolis, the famous Achaemenian capital, was purportedly paid for their labour – Iran's southern coastline is home to pockets of African communities brought over from the continent's east coast by Arab slave traders in the early Qajar period. Although Mohammad Shah Qajar issued a decree prohibiting the slave trade in 1848, it was not until 1929 that slavery itself was formally outlawed.

We were on our way to meet a fisherman friend of Hossein's at a jetty outside town with the intention of heading across to Hengam, a smaller island off the southern coast of Qeshm populated only seasonally by a small number of fishermen and their families. Hossein seemed agitated – or as agitated as his placid demeanour would allow. He was concerned the sea would be too choppy to make the twenty-minute crossing and, knowing how eager I was to spend a night or two on Hengam, was worried about leaving me disappointed.

As we drove through the sandy plains of the island, the wind that was threatening our excursion suddenly picked up, stirring the dust and sand into a hazy, shifting cloud. This soon thickened into a solid wall through which not even the road could be seen. The excitement of being caught in my first sandstorm was swiftly replaced by fear as a car coming the other way suddenly screamed past us out of nowhere, clipping the wing-mirror as it went. The fact that our driver could not see the end of his bonnet did little to curb his joviality – or his speed. Another car shot past us; this time a head-on collision was averted only by a sudden swerve of the steering-wheel. 'Heh! Heh! Close one,' was the reassuring response from the driver's seat. Just as my nails were disappearing into the tatty upholstery of the pickup, the wind dropped a little, and the sand with it. Through the clearing haze I caught sight of a troop of camels lethargically plodding along, indifferent to the abrasive barrage.

'Well, we're definitely not going to Hengam today,' Hossein said as we pulled up to the jetty, feeling the full force of the sea wind and seeing it whip the deep-blue surface with rolling streaks of white. The smiling fisherman came over and confirmed what we already knew. We would have to try again the following day. Rather than head back to town to spend the night indoors, Hossein suggested we drive to the northern shoreline of the island to explore the Hara jungle: 20,000 hectares of labyrinthine waterways and mud islands covered in nothing but mangrove trees, mudskippers and exotically plumed birds.

★ ★ ★

Our pickup pulled into the dusty drive of a ramshackle building with a large, rusting sign declaring the area a UNESCO Biosphere Reserve. This swamp only appears as the tide goes out, uncovering a hidden mass of mud islands bursting with the green foliage and exposed, straight roots of a mangrove forest. Hara, the Persian name for this salt-water tree, was coined by Abu Ali Sina, better known by his Latin name: Avicenna. This eleventh-century physician, astronomer and philosopher was so far ahead of his time that his famous works, *The Book of Healing* and *The Canon of Medicine*, were both key medical texts used throughout Europe and the Middle East until as late as the eighteenth century. The Hara jungle area claims to be the largest mangrove forest in the Persian Gulf and Sea of Oman. Over 200 different species of native or migratory birds are attracted to the forest and make it the island's most popular tourist attraction.

We were there not for the birds but to enjoy the simple thrill of spending a night under the stars in a wild and untouched environment. At the head of a vast series of muddy banks and saltwater channels that spread far into the horizon was an empty building being constructed to welcome tourists. Nearby, a cluster of locals smoking cigarettes perched on a series of wooden boats grounded onto the muddy bank. Hossein began to converse with them in the local Arabic-infused dialect, just one of the many spoken in Iran, reflecting the patchwork of ancient tribal lands which makes up the country.

Our request to be abandoned in the middle of the muddy wilderness was greeted by the sort of bemused looks that said, 'Why on earth would you want to do that?' As seems to be the case the world over, once our explanations were accompanied by an acceptable inducement, the incomprehension soon gave way to enthusiasm. Our equipment was loaded onto a boat and we were soon motoring through the waterways, satisfied that our adventure had been salvaged. After twenty minutes meandering through narrow channels and around muddy dog-legs, we came to one of the larger mud islands and the boatman grounded us onto the bank with a roar of the outboard motor.

Hopping down, we were immediately swallowed up to our knees by a pungent grey sludge. Slipping and sliding with every step, we proceeded to unload the boat. The boatman was paid half the agreed fee and left promising a prompt arrival the following morning to take us back to the mainland. As he disappeared back into the labyrinthine network of channels I took in the glorious isolation of the location. Other than a few long-billed wading birds and some mudskippers we were absolutely alone and with no realistic way of getting back to civilisation.

Beside us was a little wooden structure on stilts, a primitive one-man shelter. It was built by a local man some fifty years ago. He fled to this spot after an argument with his wife, built the shelter from bits of driftwood and proceeded to live here for the next forty years. 'Since he died,' the boatman had cackled before he left us, 'you gentlemen are the only other people to have wanted to spend a night here.'

★   ★   ★

I was watching a mudskipper haul itself out of the water and skip through the mud when Hossein suggested we go for a wander. We were soon trudging through mud and shallow rivulets of saltwater, heading back in the direction the boat had brought us from. With each step the soles of our feet would disappear into the mud, occasionally rasping on roots not sharp enough to pierce the skin but jagged enough to make it uncomfortable going. We came across hundreds of small, flat fish laid out to dry in the sun by a local fisherman. Once desiccated, Hossein told me, they would be taken to his village and ground into a powder frequently used in the local cuisine.

After twenty exhausting minutes, we reached a point where the river opened up and with sunset fast approaching we decided to go for a swim before it was too late. I had not even found a safe place to put down my camera before Hossein had stripped off and jumped headfirst into the murky water. Plodding to the water's edge, I was about to dive in after him when I saw a strange look on his usually imperturbable face. 'Everything okay?' I asked.

'Yeah, fine. Jump in. The water's great.' There was something suspicious about his reply, but determined not to lose face, I took a deep breath and dived in too. Taking a couple of strokes towards Hossein, I immediately felt a number of small, slithering things bumping against my body. Looking around, I saw we were surrounded by a swarm of jellyfish. Panic, rooted in traumatic childhood seaside memories, seized me.

'It's alright, they don't sting,' said Hossein treading water in front of me. We swam to the other bank, clambered through the mud and sat for a few moments looking at the river we were going to have to swim back across. Tens of thousands of little translucent balls floated close to the surface of the water the entire length of the river. Despite knowing they were innocuous, it took a fair bit of nerve to jump back in the water. Hossein chuckled quietly as my bravado was belied by the speed with which I swam back across the channel.

★　★　★

Later that evening, Hossein garnished a fish with a squeeze of lemon and some salt, wrapped it in foil and tossed it onto the coals of our campfire as the sun disappeared behind the muddy banks of the swamp. A near-full moon shone so brightly as to render our torches redundant. As its lambent rays caught the water's surface, I noticed the tide coming in unusually quickly. Looking from the full moon to our tents and then to the raised shelter, I sidled over to Hossein. 'Are we going to be alright here?'

'We should be. There's always the shelter.' His playful smile did little to allay my concerns, which were rising as fast as the water around us.

Later that night I was awoken by a loud rustling coming from the shelter. Groping my way out of my tent, I saw Hossein brandishing a large branch. A pack of huge rats was attacking the food supplies we had hung from a branch in the shelter. They had already laid waste to one bag, the remnants scattered across the shelter and the mud below, and were working on dislodging the second from its perch. As Hossein swatted at the rats, I found some sticks and tried to hook the bag away from their gnawing jaws. After a hard-fought battle, we managed to rescue enough food for breakfast, which Hossein put in his tent. As I was clambering back into my own berth, I saw him dart out and grab the branch. 'Just in case,' he said as he disappeared into his tent.

A quick inspection of the homestead the following morning revealed that the water had closed in to within 10 metres of our camp on three sides. As I inspected the damage done by the rats, the sound of a boat engine tore through the silence of the morning. Thinking this was our lift, we started hurriedly dismantling our tents. As the boat came around the corner, we saw that it was not our escort back but a boatload of *chadori* birdwatchers. Lowering their binoculars, they looked incredulously at the two dishevelled, semi-naked, mud-caked figures scratching their heads on a mud island in the middle of nowhere.

★   ★   ★

Arriving at our rendezvous with the fisherman in good time, we were relieved to find a calm sea and a waiting boat. Within no time we were bouncing over the waves of the Persian Gulf and pulling into a sandy cove on the westernmost point of the island of Hengam. Jumping into the water, we waded onto a beach about 150 metres in length and no more than 10 metres wide. Surrounded by a 15-metre-high cliff of crumbling sandstone, the beach was deserted but for the odd hermit crab scuttling across the wet sand. At the far end of the cove, sandstone mushrooms that had once formed the cliff-face sprouted out from the sea, their bases being slowly eroded by the ebb and flow of the tide. As we looked out to sea, the surf lapping softly at our ankles, Hossein and I both looked relieved to have traded the muddy mangroves and their giant rats for this tranquil cove and its crabs.

The midday heat was too unbearable to even consider putting up tents so, in the shade provided by a small cave, we started a small coal fire and left a fish to sizzle away in tinfoil as we went for a swim. With masks and snorkels Hossein had brought, we explored the coral reefs teeming with fish, the clear waters and bright sunlight bringing their vibrant colours to life. The flowering coral exploded with unearthly shapes and shades as shoals of fish all colours of the rainbow swept around in synchronised swirls of feeding. I was being enveloped by a particularly large shoal that danced around me as I moved my limbs when I noticed Hossein gesturing at me. I swam over to see him chasing a turtle, swimming alongside it as it glided gracefully through the water.

It being spring and with the corals blooming, it was mating season for many marine animals and we were treated to a spectacular display of courting by three squid. Two smaller, darker females hovered in formation flanking the larger, grey male who was so docile that we were able to dive down, look into its yellow eyes and stroke it unperturbed. The females would break formation slightly before re-forming with martial precision the moment we had retreated a safe distance. Hossein told me that when they mate, the skirt around the body of the male squid lights up with fluorescent coruscations of blue. I floated above them for a long while, wanting to witness this curious phenomenon firsthand, but I was left as unfulfilled as the waiting females.

As the sun began to set and we sat around the campfire that evening, Hossein and I swapped stories of adolescent adventures, chatting as we prepared our camp-fire meal. I was absorbing another of Hossein's increasingly bizarre tales as the night began to envelop us when I noticed a startling sight. The waves breaking gently at our feet were glowing. I looked at the lapping waters more closely and could see little fluorescent specks being tossed around in the surf. 'Luminous plankton,' said Hossein eagerly. We sat there mesmerised by the glowing waves breaking on the shore. Clusters of plankton swarmed in fluorescent clouds as though the ocean had become an enormous living mirror reflecting the heavens on its rippling surface.

We eventually tore ourselves away from the natural spectacle and turned back to preparing our last meal on the island. I was stoking the fire as Hossein was preparing the snapper he'd caught earlier that day when the ground beneath us began to shake with a low rumble. Realising what was going on, I leaped to my feet in panic. Hossein had barely even twitched. Southern Iran is located at the point of convergence of the African, Arabian and Indian tectonic plates and frequently experiences earthquakes. The island of Qeshm is also located between two of Iran's largest natural gas fields. In 2005, just over a year earlier, an earthquake measuring 6.0 devastated the island, levelling four villages and with a significant death toll. Over 400 aftershocks followed the main quake.

I looked up to the large sandstone overhang above our heads. Only an hour ago Hossein had been telling me how he always used to camp on the opposite side of the bay where the beach was wider. One day after a small earthquake, he had returned to find big boulders strewn across the sand right where his favoured campsite had been. Seeing a large fissure in the overhanging sandstone cliff directly above us, I frantically started pulling up the pegs of my tent.

'Where are you going to go?' Hossein said with a smile. When I looked around, I realised that I really didn't have anywhere else to go. The beach was so narrow that most of it had already disappeared under the rising tide. The previous night, impelled by the full moon, the tide had risen so high that it had come right up to the edge of my tent. I was convinced that the earthquake would cause the water to rise even higher. 'Don't worry, we'll be fine. The cliff-face is surprisingly comfortable.'

Hossein's blasé attitude was doing nothing to assuage my panicked state. As I stood there, my tent in my arms, some loose gravel blew down into my face from the cliff top. Seeing how worked up I was, Hossein helped me move my tent a couple of metres to the left and distracted me by instructing me to prepare the food. I had soon calmed down just enough to sit and eat dinner, albeit with one eye firmly on the soft sand-stone rock-face. The very same rock-face that had seemed so welcoming and had given the bay a sense of secluded serenity and protection now hung menacingly overhead, transformed into a looming threat.

I lay awake the whole night, straining my senses for any indication that the cliff-face might give way, but other than the sea gently lapping through the side of my tent again, the evening passed without any more drama. Dazed and slightly delirious, the events of the previous forty-eight hours played back in my mind: the jellyfish, the rats, the turtle, the mating squid, the plankton and the earthquake all swam around in my head like a lucid dream.

Chapter Seven

The ceremony known as *golab giri* is well known and much loved in Iran. It is the traditional process by which rosewater essence is distilled from a flower known as the *Mohammadi* rose, harvested over a three- to four-week period around May. I was keen to witness this ceremony, which I had heard about since my childhood but never seen. Iran's best rosewater comes from around the city of Kashan, 250 kilometres south-east of Tehran and on the edge of the Great Salt Desert of central Iran. Killing two birds with one stone, I decided to book myself on a two-day coach tour. Taking coach tours is not usually my idea of travel, but the tour has become a staple of middle-class Iranian activity and so I convinced myself that a little 'toor' would give me an entertaining insight into this particular corner of Iranian life. I was not to be disappointed.

The sight of an orderly queue of scowling elderly women did not augur a promising start. Amidst a sea of greying hair poking out from under sombre *hejabs*, I climbed onto the bus and was ushered to my seat. Just as I was weighing up whether to make a dash for it, an attractive young lady in a white *manteau* climbed onto the bus. She was joined by a young man whose hair was so smoothed down it looked as though he had been doing head-stands in an oil slick. This gentleman, the lady proudly announced, unprompted, to everyone on the bus as she audaciously whipped off her headscarf, was her fiancé. There were claps of approval and good wishes offered all round as the formerly dour matrons blossomed into smiles, accompanied by the obligatory chorus of comments like: 'Aren't they an adorable couple'; 'Their children will be handsome little things, won't they?'; and 'How beautiful she is. Her nose has been very well done.'

Having seated everyone, our host for the tour squealed the PA into action and proceeded with the customary welcome speech, at the end of which he added, 'Despite my appearance I'm a *kafar* [unbeliever], so relax.' He had a protruding, vulpine face and sported a greying beard (usually the badge of a *hezbollahi*) that did him no favours in a country where appearances count for a lot. His eyes, though, were warm, his voice friendly with a touch of playful impudence and his silver hair, on closer inspection, carefully groomed. As the 'toor' host gave his welcoming remarks, it became clear that we were occupying a microcosmic bubble which was leagues away from the image that official Iran liked to project of itself. Here was a young single woman travelling with her boyfriend/fiancé, both all fancied up, she whipping off her headscarf at the first opportunity, a middle-aged Lothario unashamedly joking that he was a *kafar* – and all this among a group of strangers who, despite never having seen one another before, somehow immediately understood that they were all of a type.

The 'toor' host announced that we would be going around the bus introducing ourselves and stating our professions. Having been repeatedly advised to avoid announcing any literary aspirations to strangers, I began to fret despite the seemingly sympathetic atmosphere. The thirty or so ladies ahead of me were getting into their stride and passing round pictures of their sons and daughters, many of whom seemed to have successful careers as doctors and engineers in Europe and the USA, affording me some time to come up with a suitable cover story. Finally it was my turn. When I stood up and announced that I lived in London and had come over to explore the country, I could feel the collective sigh of relief. From the front I heard one of the ladies call, '*Batcheh joun* [Dear boy], why don't you get rid of that awful beard? You terrified me when I saw you clamber onto the bus.'

The introductions served their ice-breaking purpose and soon our tour guide was drumming the jovial beat of an Iranian folk song on the microphone with his fingers. It did not take long for one of the more elderly ladies on the tour to leap to her feet and accompany him with her gravelly tones whilst pirouetting in the aisle, waving the hem of her floor-length *roupoush* coat like a flamenco dancer. Another joined them, clicking her forefingers and gyrating her upper body. The whole bus was soon engulfed by song and dance for the remainder of the journey, interspersed by anti-establishmentarian quips by the silver fox 'toor' host that met with defiant cheers of approval.

Iranians have always been masters of making light of any situation and finding that strain of hedonism in themselves. Here, a busload of like-minded people travelling through a barren wilderness, a micro-phone and a narrow aisle was all that was needed for the party to erupt spontaneously. The three hours to Kashan dissolved in an orgy of sing-ing, dancing, joking and general merriment.

★ ★ ★

Kashan is an old city built on top of a yet older settlement. Tappeh Sialk is the site of an archaeological dig in the town's suburbs that has unearthed traces of one of the earliest human settlements, dating as far back as 6000 BCE in the early Neolithic period. A team of French archaeologists led by the legendary Roman Ghirshman in the 1930s uncovered what they suspected to be the remains of a 7,500-year-old ziggurat – a tiered struc-ture originally thought to be of Mesopotamian origin[1] and the earliest form of religious architecture. Mr Toor Host (as I had come to think of him) had, between his singing and dancing routines, given us the potted history of Sialk with such poetic elegance and verve that the entire bus was eager to arrive at what was clearly evidence of Iran's greatness 'while the rest of the world, especially the Europeans, were still swinging from branches. They, with their wretched computers, forget that we have tens of thousands of years of civilisation behind us.' In his agitation, he clearly needed one of those computers, or at least a calculator, but all the ladies were now nodding earnestly.

Their reaction when we arrived at Sialk was one of unbounded disap-pointment. All of Mr Toor Host's temples, pools and grand avenues were now nothing but a huge mound of rubble. The odd wall had been pains-takingly excavated and, with a bit of imagination, the tiers of the ziggurat could just about be made out, but this did little to assuage the disgruntle-ment of our party. At one stage it looked as though mutiny was brewing, but Mr Toor Host managed to stave off the rebellion with an impas-sioned – and presumably largely imagined – re-enactment of how the ritual procession would walk up the large central walkway and on to the 7,500-year-old bricks of the highest tier where the ziggurat's altar sat.

From Sialk it was a further short ride to the Fin Gardens, a luxurious, leafy pleasure garden and bathing complex originally built for the Safavid shahs. The walled enclosure is known to have existed in 1504, when it was used as a meeting place by Shah Ismail, but it was in the reign of Shah Abbas in the early seventeenth century that a royal residence, bathhouses and a central pavilion were built on the site, and it is for one of these bathhouses that the gardens have come to be renowned.

The bathhouse in question found its way into Iranian legend by being the scene of the assassination of Amir Kabir by the Qajar shah, Naser-al-Din (1848–96). Amir Kabir was a progressive minister highly respected for instigating social reform, implementing public services and revising the country's questionable foreign policy by reducing their reliance on Britain and Russia and cultivating relationships with increasingly powerful states such as Austria, France and even the then-fledgling United States, which had no history of difficult relations with Iran. Chief tutor to a fifteen-year-old crown prince, Naser-al-Din Mirza, Kabir was influential in helping the monarch secure the throne. For this he was rewarded with the hand of the king's sister. His innovative ideas, though, had made enemies of some influential figures and his growing popularity was a source of concern for the Queen Mother. Taking advantage of one of her son's famed drinking bouts, she persuaded the inebriated monarch to have the statesman killed, claiming that he intended to usurp the throne. The Shah dismissed him from his position as prime minister, stripped him of his titles and banished him to Kashan.

After forty days of confinement, a royal messenger came to summon Kabir to Tehran for an audience with the King, leading him to believe that he was being reinstated in his previous position. Being a highly respectful man and deeply loyal to the King, he deemed it only right to bath before this royal audience. This drive to hygiene proved fateful. The envoys confronted Amir Kabir in the bathhouse with a very different kind of message. The Shah showed his gratitude for all that his old friend, childhood tutor and brother-in-law had done for him by magnanimously allowing him to choose his means of execution. The wily Kabir asked for his wrists to be slit, thinking that the king's men might leave him to bleed out, thus giving him a chance to staunch the flow and escape his fate. His ruse failed and he bled to death on the floor of the bathhouse under the watchful gaze of his executioners. This event is commemorated in all its gruesome detail by a series of papier-mâché figures displayed in the low-roofed brick building.

Though the Fin Gardens have gone down in history as the site of the Amir Kabir assassination, the gardens themselves are noteworthy as being typical of traditional Persian garden design, involving the careful planning of dialogues between greenery, shade, flowers and flowing water. The Fin Gardens are a classic example of the famed *chahar bagh* layout, with their 2.6 hectares split into four (*chahar*) distinct gardens (*bagh*) by intersecting runnels flowing from a number of pools down the middle of cypress-lined walkways. These pools and runnels are fed by a large cistern outside the garden walls, filled by melt-water carried from the mountains to the west of the city in underground water channels called *qanats*. In a land of scarce water, the tranquil sound of life-giving flows can induce a near-poetic state and when this is accompanied by redolent flowers and respite from the sun under the canopy of a towering cypress tree, it is easy to understand the ancient Persian love for the garden.

The inhabitants of Iran were billed as 'the great gardeners of antiquity' by Xenophon, and the garden has been an inextricable part of Iranian life for thousands of years and is still a great source of pride to modern Iranians. Not long after settled communities sprang up, the nomadic hunter-reliant habits of the tribes having been traded for the more efficient and reliable agricultural means of food production, early inhabitants of the country began to cultivate the lands around their dwellings, irrigating them with intricate systems of water channels. These plots provided much-needed food, water and shade in the often harsh environment of the Iranian plateau. A favourite fact amongst Iranians and one they do not tire of repeating is that these early plots, the first gardens in history, were called *pardis* in the early Iranian language of Pahlavi.[2] This is translated as 'around the house' and is the root of the Indo-European word 'paradise': 'The Greek word *parádeisos* was first used by Xenophon to describe an enclosed park, orchard, or hunting preserve in Persia', claims the *Chambers Dictionary of Etymology*.[3] The legendary hanging gardens of Babylon, one of the seven wonders of the ancient world, were, according to myth and fascinated historians such as Strabo and Diodorus, built by the Babylonian king Nebuchadnezzar II around 600 BCE to please his wife Amytis, a Median princess who had grown homesick and hankered for the idyllic gardens of her Persian homeland.

The longer you linger in the Fin Gardens, the more the place seems to take hold of you, so it was with some reluctance that we all clambered aboard the bus for the short ride into Kashan itself. On arrival at the aptly named Amir Kabir hotel, when room keys were distributed in the lobby, a frisson of excitement ran through the gathered ladies. Our engaged couple were sharing a room. Conspiratorial whispers of approval rippled through our little group.

'These young ones certainly have balls,' one of them said to me excitedly, gripping my forearm with a wrinkled hand.

'Not both of them, I hope.' The old lady gave a giggle.

★ ★ ★

The clunking and groaning of the air-conditioning unit in the corner of my room was driving me around the bend but with the mercury pushing 40°C in the midday sun, there was no choice but to get used to it. Out of my hotel window I could see the domed roofs and crumbling mud-walled bungalows of the old town, seemingly seared into a state of timelessness by the relentless desert heat. Reaching up from many of the roofs were *badgirs*. The *badgir* is a simple but ingenious age-old form of air-conditioning. A tower reaches skywards with openings to catch even the slightest breeze that is then funnelled down into the house, often over a shaded pool of water, thus cooling the air – a much quieter and no doubt more efficient means of regulating the temperature of a house than the straining grey box taking up a large part of my hotel room.

Not all of the town is so stuck in the past, though. Kashan has long been famous for its hand-woven carpets but the large number of mechanised carpet-weaving factories it now boasts, although maintaining its status as a renowned manufacturer of textiles, is threatening its long and illustrious history of artisanship – a history integral to the town's fortunes. From the end of the Seljuk period in the latter half of the twelfth century right through to the end of the Safavid period in the early eighteenth, Kashan flourished, its artisans gaining worldwide renown for their glazed earthenware tiles, many of which can today be seen in the British Museum. These tiles, or *kashi* in Persian, were of such great repute that they came to give the town its name.

★ ★ ★

After feeding on distinctly average kebabs I was shepherded back to our rather narcissistic yellow tour bus, anointed by big letters stuck to its windscreen as the 'Golden Chariot'. As we headed from Kashan to a village called Abiyaneh, Mr Toor Host triumphantly described it as the last village to succumb to the Arab Muslim army in the seventh century. The elderly ladies were suitably impressed, but I would visit many towns and villages that claimed to be the last to fall to the invading Arabs. If nothing else, the high number of 'last bastions' was a measure of the confusion and contradiction so often found in Iran: on the one hand a fervent nationalism and anti-Arab sentiment, on the other fervent devotion to the greatest legacy that the Arabs bestowed on Iran – Islam.

The bus drove past a graveyard with triangular gravestones. This, Mr Toor Host informed us, was a Zoroastrian burial site. The triangular shape of the stones was a symbol of the tripartite tenet that is the cornerstone of the Zoroastrian faith: good thoughts, good words, good deeds. The fact that this was a cemetery indicated it was a modern Zoroastrian site, because the adherents of this ancient faith would, up to the middle of the twentieth century, dispose of their dead in a completely different way. They would deposit the bodies of their deceased on top of Towers of Silence, where they would be left to decompose and feed scavenging birds. To Zoroastrians the earth was considered a sacred element whose purity would be polluted by a decomposing body, as mankind is tainted by Ahriman's darkness.

Abiyaneh's most famous resident is Keshvar Khanoum, a Yoda-like figure under a metre tall with a voice that makes her sound as if she runs on helium. Short on stature but big on character, she guided us through the village's immaculate main thoroughfare, which runs alongside a small stream. The dwellings were predominantly built in the traditional mud-brick fashion but given a red hue by the local soil and ground pomegranate skin.[4] Since it's a hillside village, many of the houses were built atop one another, the roof of the house below acting as the garden of the house above.

An old man tottered down the road carrying a bundle of sticks under one arm. White-haired women sat in soft-red doorways, huddled under colourful, floral-patterned chadors, quickly pulling them across their faces as soon as a camera was turned on them. The village was populated only by the very young and the very old; a fact due, a proud villager told us, to their middle-aged children being doctors, lawyers and engineers in Esfahan, Tehran and even abroad. It seemed hard to believe, looking at the weather-beaten faces that betrayed a lifetime of toil in the open air. The urbanisation of younger generations has been severely threatening rural life in much of Iran but here, thanks in large part to the income generated by tours such as ours, the village was thriving.

Leaving the hilly oasis settlement, we wound our way back down into the arid plain that made up the 30 kilometres back to Kashan. As the bus bumbled its way through the darkness, I noticed the members of our tour getting excited about something to our left. We were passing Natanz, described by Dr Arthur Upham Pope as 'one of the loveliest mountain towns in Persia'.[5] A picturesque town roughly 50 kilometres south of Kashan, it was until recently best known for its fruit orchards and its twelfth-century mosque. Now, of course, Natanz has earned a distinction – or rather a notoriety – of a very different sort. It is the site of the infamous nuclear facility at the heart of the global controversy. The side of the road bristled with anti-aircraft guns pointing expectantly heavenward. Meanwhile, at this very moment, I imagined a stealth bomber and its payload of a 'controlled nuclear device' flying high over our heads, its crew chattering away to a controller somewhere in Nebraska or Nevada. In the darkness of night the compound looked like a small town, lit up like a giant birthday cake. 'Makes it a hard target, doesn't it,' one of the elderly ladies said wryly.

'May God put a curse on them,' said another lady, looking glum.

'Who?' I asked.

'All of them – Americans, Iranians, Israelis, Palestinians, Chinese, Mexicans – the lot. They're all rotten.' Everybody nodded quietly in agreement. One of the ladies began a mournful song about the folly of love but gradually the pace and the mood picked up and it was not long before the bus was in full swing, with Mr Toor Host once more fully in control.

* ★ *

The next day was to be a special day, the reason for my trip to the Kashan area: the rosewater ceremony. We were all ready to set off before sunrise and clambered drowsily into the Golden Chariot to be driven to the little farming village of Ghamsar, famed for its *Mohammadi* roses. Some of the ladies were clearly not enjoying having their much-needed beauty sleep cut short but the early start was necessary. These flowers lose their scent once the sun's rays hit them so they are harvested at first light. After a half-hour drive during which the denizens of the coach were eerily silent, we arrived at a small estate and drove into the grounds. The village itself had clearly prospered from the rosewater trade and the accompanying tourist interest.

The *bagh* seemed more overgrown than idyllic. Teeming with flora, it was dominated by leafy bushes dotted with fragrant pink *Mohammadi* flowers, smaller than normal roses and different in form. An old man and woman were dexterously picking the flowers and tossing them by the handful into burlap sacks hanging from their shoulders. The scent of the flowers, the sound of nature slowly rousing itself with the first rays of the rising sun and the backdrop of bold mountains glistening with the last remnants of snow on their peaks against the diaphanous blue of a cloudless sky was truly breathtaking. I sat on the ground to drink in the peaceful, pastoral scene. The people around me disappeared, time stopped. I was planted in a landscape painting, in a dream. A quick double tap on my shoulder snapped me out of my reverie. A rural accent warned me not to sit on the ground. Responding to my quizzical look, the man simply said, 'Scorpions'.

Scorpions and their terrifyingly sinister reputation make up only a small portion of Iran's menacing wildlife, the creation of which Zoroastrian cosmogony attributes to Ahriman, the evil influence in the universe. Other animals that fall into this category are snakes, spiders and most other venomous creatures that travel in rural Iran will necessarily throw up encounters with. Prior to my departure on almost every trip, I would be warned by Tehranis to watch out for scorpions, *roteil* and *drakoola*. The *roteil* is a type of tarantula attracted by the scent of blood that bites when falling from ceilings or tree branches. Its sting is located on its underbelly and a bite can be lethal. The *drakoola* is a type of fire-ant especially common in northern Iran. It sprays a noxious substance that causes skin to blister and boil; swiping at one with a hand causes the harmful liquid to spread to a larger area of exposed skin.

The Kashan area is particularly famed for its scorpions thanks to a legend dating back to the Arab invasion of the seventh century. Kashan's thick town walls and solid defences managed to stave off the Arabs longer than most places. Not wanting to become embroiled in a lengthy siege, the Arab commander leading the assault ordered his troops to gather hundreds of scorpions from the surrounding area and pour them over the city walls. This ingenious tactic concentrated the minds of Kashan's inhabitants and persuaded them to flee the city in panic, leaving its undefended gates wide open. Whatever the source of the terror, every Iranian – man, woman and child, young and old – has had the fear of scorpions drummed into them since childhood. I was certainly no exception. That one word snapped me smartly out of my reverie and, in as dignified a manner as possible, I strode smartly away.

A suitable quantity of the flowers having been harvested, we were taken to a large house in whose garden stood four vats. The roses were poured into these vats full of steaming water heated by gas fires underneath, their lids closed and sealed. Two tubes led upwards before plunging back down in an inverted 'v' shape into a smaller tank submerged in a trough of water. The vapours rose through the pipes and, when channelled through the submerged tanks, were sufficiently cooled by the water to condense and drip to the bottom as rosewater. The fumes were inebriating; one of our elderly ladies said that it reminded her of sharing a lift with a family of Arabs. The vast majority of rosewater produced in Iran is exported to Arab countries, where it is used to scent clothes and houses. The highest-quality rosewater is sent to Mecca to be mixed with water from the Zamzam well and used for the annual washing of the Ka'aba ritual. In Iran it is used predominantly for cooking, as are the dried rose petals, or made into jam. The rosewater itself was an incredibly effective cure for migraines, I was informed by another of the elderly ladies in our group, with the assurance that only comes either from firsthand experience or from being an elderly Iranian lady. Another of the ladies sidled up to me and whispered, 'Back in my day it was used to perfume the water from the *aftabeh*.' The *aftabeh* is the now plastic receptacle resembling a watering can found beside every Iranian toilet.

The sweet yet pungent smell, the vibrant pink of the petals, the peace of the well-kept garden, the early morning birdsong, the breeze and the warm rays of the rising sun mingling with each other against the backdrop of the distant mountains slowly turning turquoise in the dawn light – all this created a veritable feast for the senses. Before long, we were led onto a carpeted balcony where the thirty of us were treated to a very different kind of feast: a traditional Iranian breakfast. Boiled eggs, honey, goat's cheese, fresh mint leaves, peeled walnuts and yoghurt were wrapped in floury sheets of unleavened *lavash* bread, eaten and washed down with steaming glasses of freshly brewed tea sweetened by a sugar cube clamped between the teeth.

One of the ladies hoisted herself up and came to sit next to me. 'Why aren't you married?' she asked with a smile.

'He's got a *farangi* [foreign] girl waiting for him back in England. They do things differently over there,' another of the group replied for me.

'Nonsense,' said the woman beside me, taking my hand in hers. 'Why do you think he's really come to Iran?' I shifted awkwardly, beginning to blush under the gaze of the entire group. She patted my forearm as she reached into her handbag. After a brief rummage, she pulled out a dog-eared photograph and pressed it into my hand. 'My niece. She's a real beauty … and a wonderful cook.'

Chapter Eight

The Kurdish people are thought to be descended from an Indo-Iranian tribe that settled the region after the Aryan migration from the Russian steppe-lands in the third and second millennia BCE. Their language is believed to be amongst the closest surviving relatives of Pahlavi or Middle Persian, the language of the Sasanian era. Numbering 35 million, the Kurds' ancestral land these days straddles the mountainous border regions of Iran, Iraq, Turkey and Syria. Fierce looks attest to their reputation as indomitable warriors. As such, the Safavid Shah Abbas (1588–1629) relocated many of them from their ancestral home in the Zagros Mountains to Khorasan to defend the country's north-eastern border from marauding Uzbek tribes. Their struggle for an independent state has long been catalogued and their plight in Iran, where they make up roughly 7 per cent of the country's population, makes up a significant part of that narrative. After the 1979 Revolution, militant Kurdish forces rose up against the new central government, resulting in the deaths of 10,000 Kurds fighting for independence.

Kurdistan is, along with the Azeri-dominated north-west (Azeri Turks make up close to 25 per cent of the country's population), one of Iran's most volatile regions. The Kurds are mostly Sunni Muslims and, like the Azeris, have long been vying for some form of autonomy; both have largely been unsuccessful in their aspirations. The central government of Shi'i Iran, mindful of the region's wealth of natural resources such as oil, coal, copper and limestone, is sensitive to any concessions which would diminish its control over the region and strengthen tendencies towards independence. In 2005 three Kurdish activists were killed by Iranian security forces, sparking a wave of riots and violent protests that swept across the western state and resulting in a number of deaths. Tensions were still high a year later, as I was making final preparations for a trip to the Kurdish hinterland. Their long, turbulent and colourful history has helped to define modern Iran and it is for this reason that I was determined to explore the area despite being advised against doing so. And so, under the hazy early-morning sun of a June day, I set out from Tehran in a car borrowed from a kind neighbour on a 700-kilometre drive west, through vast tracts of arid wasteland, to the province of Kurdistan.

★   ★   ★

The foothills of the Zagros Mountains spring up out of the central Iranian plateau, transforming the horizon of dusty uniformity into one of tawny hills and green fields rolling one into another until swallowed by the handsome faces of the mountains proper. The Zagros are less dramatic than the Alborz along the Caspian rim, softer in contour and colour but no less picturesque. The road I was on meandered through verdant foothills, the emerald-green vegetation undulating gently, rhythmically, as though the land itself was drawing gentle breath. At times I found it hard to believe I was in Iran; the pastoral landscapes resembling the English or French countryside were not something naturally associated with this part of the world and certainly not what I had expected from Kurdistan. Iran's ability to surprise – the fact that after hours and hours of barren emptiness one can suddenly emerge, wholly unexpectedly, into a vastly different world – was, I soon discovered, one of its most enchanting qualities.

My entry into the province was held up by a series of checkpoints that induced, as any brush with authority tends to in Iran, a degree of uncertainty. Here I was, a sole young man, in somebody else's car, with no explanation for my being there that would seem plausible to Revolutionary Guards, blithely driving into a politically sensitive area – suspicious indeed. But it soon became apparent that interrogations and inspections were reserved for traffic leaving the province rather than entering it. Kurdistan is a thoroughfare for smugglers bringing alcohol and other illicit substances through the mountains and over the border from neighbouring Iraq.

By the time I had negotiated the roadblocks, it was beginning to get dark and I still needed to find a campsite. I systematically searched the surrounding area, up every dirt track that led off from the main road winding to a remote village or down a valley. Finding an ideal spot proved too time-consuming so I decided to pitch a makeshift camp on the first relatively flat spot I could find. The long hours of driving, the heat of the day and the darkness of the night had taken it out of me and desensitised me to my surroundings. So it was to be a small campfire, a hasty meal of bread and cheese and sound sleep in my tent.

Early next morning, I wormed out of my sleeping bag, stepped into a pair of trousers and out of the tent. Once my eyes had adjusted to the morning sunlight, I was awed by the beauty of the place I had seren-dipitously stumbled upon. The hill I was perched on rolled down into a gently sloping valley, its grassy sides dotted with the odd patch of forest. To the left was a rocky outcrop of soft yet dramatic peaks and overhangs. The dirt track I had come up meandered left then right, its rich, earthy hues snaking their way to the bottom of the valley and lead-ing to a sleepy village nestled in the emerald hills in the distance. Little grey cottages clambered up the sides of the valley, seeming to float one above the other. An almost complete spectrum of greens lay before my eyes, from the rich deepness of the forest and the sparkle of the grass to fluorescent fields of swaying crops, all crowned by the azure intensity of the sky, lightly dotted with puffs of cotton clouds.

Once I'd brewed up some tea and munched down some more bread and cheese, I packed up and was back in the car probing the various nooks and crannies in search of a second campsite. This search for a site with the necessary prerequisites swiftly became a quest for the ideal one. After a few hours' driving, I arrived at Marivan and its renowned lake. Reflected in the mirror-still body of water was a mountain range beyond which was war-torn Iraq. The Iranian side of the lake boasted a carnival-like atmosphere. Being a Friday, the Iranian weekend and a public holiday to boot, there were scores of families reclining on carpets brimming with food under every available patch of shade. A couple of fairground stalls – bizarre in this setting – added to the fes-tive atmosphere. The usually gloomy scene of shroud-like black chadors was replaced by the whites, gaudy pinks and floral designs of the prov-inces. Families enjoyed a picnic together whilst watching young couples walking by holding hands and sharing an ice-cream, oblivious to the ever-present khaki-clad figures of authority – even they had their caps tilted lazily back on their heads with smiles poking through their stubbly faces. Central authority and clerical orthodoxy were a million miles away from this lakeshore.

★ ★ ★

I soon had my fill of the light-hearted buzz of the lake and decided that some solitude was what was needed in this beautiful mountain setting, so I drove a couple of kilometres away from the built-up shores of the once-beautiful lake to the more secluded shade of a tree beside an *esta-khr* (a pool of water used for irrigation). Plunging my hot, dusty limbs into the cool water, I unfurled my own little banquet – more bread and cheese, this time supplemented by fresh mint and juicy tomatoes. A local farmer spotted me and was soon scuttling over under the weight of a large pail of fresh yoghurt he insisted I accept.

Having revived my spirits and sated my appetite, I set back out on my search through the Kurdish valleys and past the occasional village standing out from an otherwise green background. I was in search of a flat lie and, more crucially, a river or spring to camp beside. My quest whittled away much of the afternoon and just as dusk was approaching and I was considering throwing in the towel, the valley arced away from a little village and flattened out as an alluring emerald river cut through it – at last, the ideal campsite. A fortuitous cloud must have been hovering overhead because I soon discovered that I had unwittingly pitched tent metres away from a freshwater spring. Above the river rose a steep incline on which local Kurds were finishing their day's work, gathering hay into little bundles that dotted the hillside. The women wore flowing robes of bright reds and pinks glistening with sequins in the setting sun. These fairy-tale dresses floated gracefully through the air with their every movement. The men wore Kurdish trousers that bulged out from the waist before tapering down to the ankle, particularly unflattering on a portly man who looked like he might roll down the hillside as he gave me a friendly wave. A black sash was tied around his waist like a cummerbund (*kamarband* in Persian means belt, literally translated as 'waist fastener') and a similar cloth tied to his head with tassels that danced against his brow as he worked the crops.

The searing heat of the following day drove me to spend much of it on the shady banks of the fast-flowing river. Beside the spring was a pool of calm water in which I bathed, fearful of the roaring, writhing rapids. A shepherd boy no more than ten years old appeared on the far bank with his flock. Leaving the sheep to graze a little way upriver, he pulled off his shirt and dived straight off a rock into the churning waters. A second or two later, his shorn head popped out of the bright-green flow and was hurled downstream by the swift current. The boy shot along at astounding speed, avoiding rocks with precise, effortless flicks of his feet. The way he negotiated the jagged obstacle course through flawless knowledge of each little eddy was truly impressive. He made the whole ordeal seem so effortless and, despite his Kurdish trousers ballooning out of the water like a comedy backside, graceful.

He repeated the feat a few times, each as spectacular as the last, before he was joined by his two little brothers, who dived in behind him. He expertly guided them through the rapids and to safety with a few well-timed flicks of his *giveh*-clad foot. The *giveh*, a surprisingly comfortable and sturdy traditional cloth shoe, propelled them either side of the ominous rocks with a wet clap. The middle brother, whose flame-red hair and sparkling eyes complemented the ebullience of his character, then climbed onto a rock poking through the river about a metre away from me and proceeded to hurl himself into the water with a series of somersaults clearly for my benefit. They began gesturing at me, encouraging me to give it a go. Not willing to be upstaged by a few children, I clambered onto the nearest rock and plunged into the churning waters. Flapping and flailing, I barely made it 200 metres downstream before I had had enough and hauled myself onto the riverbank coughing, spluttering and bleeding from a gash to my leg, much to the amusement of the boys.

Having recovered my poise, I lunched on the banks of the river next to a Kurdish family, who, with the customary '*Befarmayid!*', invited me to join them. Despite my dwindling lump of cheese doing little to enhance their spread, they plied me with freshly baked bread, grapes, shelled walnuts and delicious apples. Their three young children, one of whom was a red-headed girl with piercing blue eyes, hung from the boughs of a nearby tree. They watched me with the unflinching gaze that only a village child is capable of – a reminder of my status as an alien intruder in this idyllic world of theirs.

* * *

The next day I decided to break up the long drive back to Tehran by heading to Hamedan and finding somewhere to camp overnight. There was much more of Kurdistan that I wanted to explore, but I was compelled to tear myself away from its unexpected beauty and return to the capital. Touched by the hospitality of the Kurds and admiring the stoic preservation of their cultural identity against all odds, I was already hatching plans to return and delve deeper into their culture, but that was to be for another trip.

The journey to Hamedan was short and the weather bearable and soon I was cruising through the picturesque baked-earth colours of adobe villages with streams of curious kids chasing after my car. I stopped outside a nondescript village to regroup and get my bearings when I was suddenly surrounded by what seemed to be every menacing-looking male the village could muster. The men were polite yet cold; the unspoken yet abundantly uninviting sentiment a far cry from the warmth of the Kurds. My brother, a photographer, had travelled rural Iran a few years back taking portraits of local tribesmen and villagers. He had told me of the frosty reception he had got upon approaching many more isolated settlements. Now, the sight of a burly 4 × 4 kicking up dust from its oversized wheel-arches conjures only one thought in the provincial mind: officialdom. Villagers throughout Iran view the government with an innate sense of mistrust and no small amount of contempt. The state is viewed as a meddlesome threat to their way of life, one that only appears with unwanted news and unsought woe. It often took my brother many hours, sometimes days, to convince the simple folk that he was not such a harbinger of doom, merely an artist interested in capturing their rural charm and faces oozing with character on camera. With this in mind, I empathised with the defensive villagers' reactions to my off-road vehicle crunching through the serenity of their secluded settlement and, assuring them I was merely passing through, was quickly on my way again.

I eventually followed a dirt track up into the hills of Hamedan; surprisingly greener than Kurdistan, more naturally beautiful but less rugged. I set up camp on a flat formed by the convergence of three hills. Within minutes of my tent going up, the curiosity of the locals had been aroused. A village leader had sent a couple of men out on a motorcycle to scout the newcomer and report back on his intentions. Soon after he had roared out of sight another, more numerous, more official delegation appeared. This looked ominous, but I thought it best to take the initiative so I walked out to meet them. Before they had a chance to make their minds up about me, I offered them tea and some of the apples the Kurdish family had insisted I take with me and began showering compliments on their beautiful region and its friendly, hospitable people. Seemingly taken aback, they muttered a few greetings and swiftly left amid the loud splut-tering of motorcycle exhausts.

The next day I sat in the morning sun enjoying a cup of coffee and watched as first one, then another and yet another shepherd appeared over the hilltops with their respective flocks and converged upon my tent. Before long I was surrounded by a sea of bleating wool. One kind-faced shepherd sidled over to me exchanging the customary greetings and informed me that the authorities were on their way back. 'Hide any-thing you shouldn't have,' he said with a conspiratorial smile. I assured him I was 'clean' and bade him a good day.

Either the authorities never showed up or I did not hang around long enough to give them a chance to. Once I had breakfasted, I packed up my tent and was soon back on the road. I decided to take a detour via the Temple of Anahita, the pre-Islamic goddess of water and fertility, at Kangavar. When I arrived at the gate I was reminded by a surly-looking guard that it was a public holiday and so the temple was shut. 'If you're quick though, I'll turn a blind eye to you hopping over the fence,' was his reply to my insistence that I had driven all the way from Tehran just for a glimpse of the magnificent site. The guard was as good as his word, giving me a leg-up right over the 20,000-rial-entry-fee sign.

The temple was first built *c.* 200 BCE, during the Seleucid period that followed the invasion of Persia by Alexander the Great in 334 BCE. The remains of the temple consisted of an impressive yet incongruous stone staircase reminiscent of those found in Persepolis and the toppled ruins of a few stone columns bearing testament to the fascinating mix of Greek and Persian ideas that was born out of this Alexandrian dynasty.

The site was in a truly poor state. It resembled a rubbish tip more than an ancient, sacred temple to a principal deity. The guard agreed with my observations and added that it had been neglected since the ousting of the Shah. Robert Byron's account of visiting the site in the early 1930s informs us that the temple has long been in a state of disre-pair. The late nineteenth and early twentieth century saw many of the ancient stones being pilfered for use in the construction of the rapidly expanding adjacent town of Kangavar. Recently, the Islamic govern-ment's overt lack of interest – even disdain – for anything pre-Islamic has hastened the monument's plight and construction work next to it has further damaged the 2,000-year-old temple.

Chapter Nine

It was a huge relief when, in mid-September, the searing temperatures started to subside. I had been in Iran for nearly seven months and had been riding out the summer hiking through the mountains around Tehran and impatiently waiting for the onset of the milder weather. With autumn on the horizon, I readied my kit and prepared to set out on the road. I was planning on heading north to the Caspian shores once again, but this time towards Rasht on the landlocked sea's north-western shoreline. I had talked through my itinerary – a long trip travelling anti-clockwise around a large swathe of the country – with a well-travelled friend a week previously and was about to set out for the bus station when my telephone rang. 'Are you still thinking of heading north? I have a friend you should meet who can give you a lift,' said Anoush, a resourceful type who saw it as his personal mission to furnish me with as many different experiences and perspectives as he could during my time in Iran.

And so I found myself in the back of a black Nissan Patrol, Franz Ferdinand's bass riffs reverberating through me, staring at a sticker on the dashboard that read in English, 'A good tool is hard to find'. Were it not for the sea of endless, unchanging yet somehow intoxicating dust stretching as far as the eye could see, and the imposing majesty of the Alborz disappearing into a tawny horizon, I could well have been back in England. In the driver's seat was Raam, drumming his hands on the steering-wheel and singing along to the music as we sped west out of Tehran. We were heading towards Karaj and beyond into the wilderness of an ancient road now alive with plastic bottles and bags being swept this way and that by gusts from passing cars, occasionally so thick the earth beneath was lost to sight; Raam to visit some friends near Rasht, and I to set out on a journey of nearly two months that was to take me through some of the most ancient and revered sites of Iran.

Over the course of the next couple of years Raam would become one of my closest friends and an invaluable guide to youth culture in Tehran. He was the lead singer of a rock band, a form of music deemed illegal in Iran – and to make matters worse he sang in English. The underground music scene was thriving, he told me, with so many young Iranians wanting to express themselves through the music they loved and, despite the government's best efforts, had easy access to through the internet. Young musicians would congregate at certain houses and underground locations discussing current trends in international music and jamming with one another, covering everything from classic rock to contemporary chart hits. Slowly, as relationships developed and common tastes were discovered, bands would form. The bigger the reputation of a musician or band, the more talented musicians would seek them out in the hope of joining forces. That is how Raam came to be the frontman of a band named Hypernova.

Hypernova had been playing clandestine gigs for a couple of years and had gained a considerable underground following thanks in no small part to Raam's charisma and his witty, probing lyrics. As we drove to Rasht, Raam told me about the trials and tribulations of being in an illegal rock band in Tehran, about gigs in abandoned factories being raided by the police and about how they were busy recording an album in a hidden basement that had been sound-proofed and turned into a studio. However bleak his tales of life in Tehran occasionally became, they were always punctuated by raucous laughter. Despite his often miserable appearance, Raam was a true exponent of *hal kardan* – the Iranian art of finding the joy in every situation.

Hal kardan literally means 'having a good time' but this translation does not properly convey the idea and feeling behind the Persian words. The concept of *hal* reveals a lot about the hedonistic side of the Iranian character. With implications of living for and revelling in the moment – appreciating it as a Baudelairean moment of spiritual elation that lifts you from the ennui of daily life – the word *hal* (pronounced as an American would say 'hall') suggests experiencing pleasure with mild mystical undertones. Iran has a torrid history full of suffering, and the attraction of pure elation can be easily understood as a psychological counter-measure and traced back to the same source in the national psyche that produces the corrosive, dry humour and ability to make light of adversity which Iranians have perfected.

Raam had spent part of his youth in Canada and thanks to his tongue-in-cheek English lyrics and the healthy online presence Hypernova had developed, the band had managed to attract a certain amount of foreign media attention. They were hoping, Raam told me excitedly, that once they finished recording their album, they would be invited to play at the South by Southwest festival in Texas and try to take on America.

'Everyone buys into this idea that we're all hell-bent on destroying America. The whole Great Satan thing,' the car swerved as Raam convulsed with laughter. 'It's just propaganda. Most people I know love America. They're obsessed by the culture and spend their lives trying to engineer ways to move out there. I've been to the States but the other guys in the band, they've never left Iran. They've got their fantasies about what life is like over there. I just want to get some place where we can actually have a shot at a career in music. And if it works out … well, then the guys may yet get to live out some of their sordid fantasies.' Raam's eyes shut momentarily as he chuckled at this thought.

'I swear this place gets bigger every time I drive past it,' said Raam as we approached Karaj. Originally a small settlement built to house workers building and operating the dam nestled in the folds of the mountains to the north-west of Tehran, it has become a sprawling town well over a million strong and growing by the day. Karaj is typical of the social problems Iran faces as it fails to tackle the rush to urbanisation that threatens many smaller, rural settlements and traditional ways of life. It is not uncommon to come across near-deserted villages devoid of anyone between the ages of sixteen and sixty. The empty promise of money and the prospect of work have caused Tehran and its suburbs to explode, sprawling chaotically in every direction to accommodate a population that has, in a few decades, gone from 2 to nearly 20 million.

After a couple of hours we had arrived at our first port of call, the oasis town of Takestan. Like so many Iranian towns, Takestan just appears out of nowhere. And again, like so many Iranian towns, its sudden appearance out of nowhere is explained by the abundance of water that flows beneath the earth as it runs down from the snow-capped mountains in the distance. Most of the country's small towns have very little to flaunt but what they do have they proclaim with a vengeance. In the case of Takestan the local produce is grapes. Grapes were everywhere; on the town placard, on bumper stickers, on posters in windows, and of course the grapes themselves were being sold by the side of every crossroads in town, piled high on stalls, in wheelbarrows or out of the open doors and boots of cars. Small, round and incredibly sweet, they were delicious to eat and, so an enthusiastic local told us as Raam bought a big bunch, excellent for wine-making.

★ ★ ★

Wine-making originated in the fertile region that straddles modern-day Turkey, Iran, Azerbaijan and Armenia. The history of wine-making in Iran is long and rich despite its current illegal status. It was frequently used in Zoroastrian ceremonies, and monarchs from the ancient Elamites in the second millennium BCE to the Safavids in the sixteenth to eighteenth centuries CE and the Qajars in the nineteenth century CE were famed for their wine-drinking bouts. The famous Shiraz vine also originates from the ancient province of Fars but, as with much of Iranian history, the true origins of wine-making have been clouded by time and commingled with mythology. Zoroastrian cosmogony states that Ahriman made an attempt to sabotage the creation of the world by Spenta Mainyu, the Spirit of Good, by slaying the Cosmic Bull but this attempted sabotage backfired: 'For when the bull expired, its brain and other organs were scattered over the ground and fertilized it, and from its severed members every kind of grain and healing plant sprang up while from its blood the vine arose "from which wine is made".'[1]

A slightly more poetic and less gruesome version of the mythological origins of wine are cited in the *Nowrouznameh* attributed to the celebrated astronomer-poet Omar Khayyam. The ancient king of Herat, Shemiran, was approached by an eagle begging the king for help. A snake had wrapped itself around the majestic bird's neck and was slowly strangling the life out of it. The king ordered his son, an exceptional marksman, to kill the snake. This the prince did with the shot of a single arrow. The eagle, thus liberated from the deadly beast, circled the castle three times in thanks before flying away. A year later to the day, the eagle returned and dropped a few seeds on the exact spot where the prince had freed it. The king ordered that the seeds be planted. Several years later, the vine that grew from the seeds bore fruit in bunches that in autumn 'turned black, juicy and appetizing'. Seeing that the grapes were so full of juice, the king ordered that they be pressed. 'After several days the juice began to bubble and boil, but they waited until it became once more calm and lucid and a rich ruby-red, and they all agreed that this must be the end product.' Not wanting to risk ingesting the unknown liquid himself, the king summoned a prisoner who had been condemned to death and instructed him to drink, stipulating that if he survived he would be pardoned and set free. The prisoner grimaced as he drank a cup of the red liquid with tentative gulps. The moment he finished it, he asked for another. 'Upon drinking the second glass he became very jovial and merry, and began to sing and dance, losing all his bashfulness and forgetting completely the presence of the king.' Again, he asked for another cup, saying 'Give me this third glass for now I do not care if I die.' He drank heartily, 'after which he became very drowsy and fell into a deep sleep, from which he did not arouse until the next day.' Once the prisoner regained consciousness, the intrigued king questioned him on his experience of the previous day.

'When I started to drink at first I found it bitter, but when it reached my stomach I yearned for more. After the second glass I felt a glow of merriment and joviality, and I lost all bashfulness and was unable at this stage to find any difference between Your Majesty and myself. When I drank the third glass I fell into a deep sleep.'[2] True to his word, the king released the man and immediately passed an edict requiring the drinking of wine on all occasions of state and celebration.

★ ★ ★

As with any drive from one side of the Alborz to the other, the scenery gradually became softer and more stunning the closer we got to the Caspian. We left the dusty drabness of Takestan and the identical roadside villages of the plain – each comprising a baker's, two mechanics and a few grocers dangling colourful tat in an attempt to ensnare passers-by – behind us as we moved towards the tiered fields, hexagonal tin hats and yellows, browns and greens of agricultural communities nestling among the mountains. The rolling green hills and a patchwork of fields again felt distinctly European until the road twisted into another valley to reveal a series of trees planted in the shape of the four-pronged symbol of the Islamic Republic, a graphic that reads *Allah*. Next to it was a similar-sized rectangle of greenery that had once depicted the *Shir-o-Khorshid*, the now outlawed ancient royal emblem of the Sun and Lion. Descending through the mountains, we cruised towards Rasht, the principal city along the Iranian rim of the Caspian sea. Like its surroundings, there was a freshness and viridity to the place, a tangible sense of excitement at having outgrown the state of a sleepy seaside town. The city looked much like countless others in Iran, but the atmosphere had a certain relaxed, rural charm to it.

We drove right through Rasht and on into its suburbs. Alarmed, I told Raam that we had passed the guest-house I had planned to stay in. He just laughed. 'Oh, how little you know about Iranian culture, my friend.' This was to be the first of many times I would be 'taken hostage' by Iranian hospitality.

* * *

Having bobbed along a dirt road for a few kilometres, we pulled into a dishevelled driveway and parked in front of a couple of small bungalows. On the porch of one sat Alla, his portly frame supported by a rickety bench straining under his weight. His fingers were stuffed into chunky, stone-encrusted rings. He wore a vest and baggy shorts and, as his sandals flapped towards us, Raam jumped out of the car and ran over to him. Putting one hand on Alla's curly locks and the other onto his sizeable and equally curly beard, Raam shook his head from side to side. 'It's good to see you, my friend. Where's Atta?'

'Here,' came a lackadaisical, nasal voice as a slouching youth ambled around the corner, a rifle with a double-barrel slung over his shoulder. Alla and Atta, two brothers – the first in his mid-twenties and the other his late teens – had been Raam's neighbours in Tehran until they decided to turn their backs on city life and settle at one of their favoured fishing spots. Being natural outdoorsmen they used to flee Tehran to hunt and fish at every opportunity. It was on one of these excursions that they heard about a fishery that was available for rent. Without hesitation they renounced their comfortable urban life for a simple rustic one. Since then, they have been running the 30 hectares and eighteen freshwater pools of this sizeable operation breeding various types of carp: grass carp, bighead carp and silver carp (known locally as *fitofag*).

We were given a tour of the fishery and introduced to their tawny Great Dane before grabbing some rods and indulging in an obligatory spot of evening fishing. They had purchased the dog to chase off poachers; the rumour amongst locals was that the two city boys had tamed a lion. Once we had caught our dinner, our hosts decided it was time to let the festivities begin. We clambered into Alla's rusty pickup and headed to the local *kababi*. There, to my surprise, a bottle of *aragh* – the prevalent moonshine of the region – was ordered. In reply to my bemused look Alla pointed to nearly every table, where people were openly enjoying a drink with their steaming skewers of lamb, apparently oblivious to the fact that drinking alcohol carried a severe penalty in the Islamic Republic of Iran. 'This is the North. Things are a little different here,' Alla explained. 'They've got whisky and vodka too, but I wouldn't go near that.' On the way back we drove past a toothless local standing by the side of the road who gave Alla a friendly wave. 'And that's where to get opium,' he smiled and, with a single outstretched finger, pushed up the peak of his cap in greeting.

As Alla regaled us with the fishing tales that appear to be universal fare amongst angling enthusiasts the world over, we settled down to a meal of expertly filleted and grilled fish and rice back in Alla's bungalow. We ate the meal, hastily prepared by the two brothers, from the traditional *sofreh* spread, off the floor of the room that we all later bedded down on; a pile of cushions and rugs in the corner of the single room that all shared, as was customary – provided, of course, that the company was all the same sex.

The following morning I awoke to find Raam bolt upright, wide-eyed and trembling with excitement. 'You missed them, they were incredible,' he beamed. He had awoken to see three jackals curiously eyeing the bungalow, no more than 6 metres away, and had been waiting motionless, camera in hand, for the past forty minutes in case they reappeared.

★　★　★

When he heard that I was planning to explore the local area, Raam insisted that he accompany me. The road west from Rasht – past Fuman and up towards the lofty heights of Khalkhal – traces its way through valleys of dense forest snaking up the mountainside. Without warning, the compact green of the forest was disrupted by an explosion of soft yellow glowing invitingly from above. This was the mountain village of Masuleh, with its houses arranged neatly so that, as at Abiyaneh (the village near Kashan I had visited with Mr Toor Host), the roofs of the dwellings on one street level functioned as the pavement for the street above. On approach, Masuleh seemed the epitome of the quaint mountain community and yet it all rang hollow when we reached the village streets. They were awash with the tacky tat of a tourist trap. The whole extraordinary array of Iranian confections, from the flapping red pancakes of *lavashak* and the chewy, cake-like slices of *conjed* (sesame, crushed walnuts and honey), right through to the shiver-inducing sourness of *gharaghoroot* (obtained by boiling the water left over from the yoghurt-making process which metamorphoses into a brown substance somewhat resembling fudge in all but taste) – all these and much more were laid out on trays and tables the crowds were herded towards by toothless old women desperate to make a sale.

Then came the village bazaar. The narrow alleys were crammed with dangling wares and postcard carousels. Silver-haired stall-keepers with the weathered hide of mountain villagers, beaten by a lifetime of winter chill and summer heat, occasionally beckoned to us with a half-hearted gesture, as if knowing that these visitors too would not provide salvation. The heavy, knitted socks, the rugs with their bands of vivid colours and simple animal pictography, the roughly hewn copper bowls and trays would remain untouched for another day. Here, like many a mountain village I had visited in the Andes, was a community that had transformed itself from the harsh daily struggle of a self-reliant, traditional high-altitude people to one of complacent dependence on selling worthless trinkets to a dwindling stream of tourists. UNESCO has made this village a protected site to preserve its traditional beauty but the mixed blessing that is the tourism industry at once provided a cure from financial ailments whilst simultaneously compromising the cultural integrity of traditional life. For romantic eyes like my own, the process of redefinition had irretrievably corrupted the soul of this village. Abiyaneh, its terracotta-coloured twin, had thus far managed to embrace the industry with a touch more decorum.

Curiosity had led Raam to carry on driving an hour or so past the village along the old, barely travelled mountain route that led to the hot springs of Khalkhal. We drove up through the clouds until the asphalt road turned into a bumpy dirt track, but so magical was the scenery that we were impelled to keep on going. Our car was briefly engulfed by the mist that swirled about the valley like a raging sea until we climbed through it to be dazzled by the sharp, ethereal light and crisp air beyond. Here, the panorama – rolling hills with alluring, soft curves of emerald-green, the odd tree standing dutifully on guard, its shadow stretching over a carpet of gently swaying grass – suggested anything but the Middle East. At this altitude the colours of the green hilltop poking through the white sea of rising mist like a verdant glacier and the perennial backdrop of the blue sky were so vibrant and alive as to give the whole scene an otherworldly feel.

'Everything's so clean up here ... even the sheep,' chuckled Raam as a lonely shepherd and his flock appeared along the road – the first signs of life we had seen since leaving Masuleh. He was right; the sheep's fleeces had the pure sheen of fresh-fallen snow, the dirt road somehow lost the appearance of dirt and even the shepherd, a mountain-dwelling nomad, looked as though his clothes had been freshly washed and pressed. We pulled over and basked in the beauty of the place as low-hanging clouds drifted so close we could reach out and touch them.

As we drove on, still near Masuleh, we happened on an isolated roadside inn that our stomachs dictated we stop at. Here, reclining on carpet-covered *takhts* (raised wooden platforms with stiff cushions for backrests, found in most traditional restaurants and many homes for *al fresco* dining), we ordered an array of kebabs, rice, garlic yoghurt and fresh bread. I asked Raam for a sip of water from the bottle he had just set on the table. 'Help yourself,' he replied, 'only you may want to order something to mix it with,' he added under his breath. So it was that we feasted on kebabs and moonshine in a remote mountain village deep in the heart of the Alborz Mountains; I sheepishly, my companion with admirable gusto.

The intoxicating mixture of tender lamb, moonshine and the idyllic surroundings soon set my mind drifting and, as Iranians so often do, reflecting on this country to which I at once belonged and was alien. As I looked around me I knew that, at that moment, for all its fatal flaws and contradictions it most decidedly was mine – the overt opulence of old royal chambers, the daunting grandeur of past palaces, the imposing scale and occasionally exquisite skill of its ancient bas-reliefs, the sensuality of its architecture and its landscapes, the refined delicacy of its miniature paintings, the intense spirituality of its poetry, even its maddening people and their uncanny skill at not meeting their capabilities – all these were mine. This was a land of opulence and sensuality, a nation as decadent as it was devout; able to tolerate, to borrow a line from the poet Hafez, 'preachers who from the height of their pulpits sparkle in their sermons, when back at home devote themselves to business of a different sort'. No amount of austere Islamic fervour could hide this reality. Iran is a land of contradiction; of snow-capped mountains and arid salt plains, of lush jungle and interminable desert. Its people are as schizophrenic as the land they inhabit, torn by the cosmic struggle of light and darkness – of Ahura Mazda and Ahriman – that has been fated to rage within their souls.

★ ★ ★

The following morning it was time for Raam to return to Tehran with the car, leaving me to carry on my journey north. As we said our good-byes, Raam grabbed my head with both hands and landed a wet kiss on my forehead. With that, he clambered back into his car and drove off in a cloud of dust and laughter.

I boarded a local bus driving past Gisoun, a beach Alla had recom-mended I visit. After about half an hour I was dropped off at a T-junction and watched the bus trundle off, trailing thick plumes of black smoke from a dangling exhaust. Opposite me sat a battered cart resting on two warped wooden wheels, an empty bottle of water resting on the impro-vised counter and a bag of potato crisps hanging from a wire, bobbing in the gentle breeze. 'How do I get to Gisoun beach?' I asked the heavy-set vendor sporting a straw hat perched languidly on his head and with very little to sell. He raised a podgy finger and with a silent nod pointed to a road that led deep into the thick forest. I had not been walking long when a passing car slowed down. The young driver, in Ray-Ban shades, Nike T-shirt and blue jeans, eyed me curiously and offered me a ride. He was a recent graduate attempting to make a living selling real estate in the region to those newly enriched in Tehran. The 6-kilometre drive went by in a flash of high-speed machismo as the young driver regaled me, a complete stranger, with lurid tales of past conquests which com-peted with blaring German Trance music, negotiating the twists and turns of the road with a casual palm as his other hand, elbow perched on the open window, ran a comb through his gelled hair.

Gisoun beach was not the quiet, sandy strip of secluded seaside jungle I had anticipated. A *chadori* woman sat perched on the steps of one of the dilapidated iron shacks generously described as 'villas', thick brows sur-veying her eight screaming children busy chasing an innocent chicken while their vest-clad, mustachioed father fanned flaming coals in prep-aration for meat-laden skewers. Colourful, circular cafés with thatched roofs catered for loud, littering crowds. A forlorn young woman stood ankle-deep in the sea, staring wistfully at the soft spume of breaking waves, her chador flapping in the salty breeze. It did not take much to induce me away from the crowds, moving along the beach in search of a suitable, more secluded spot to camp.

In the fast-fading light I stumbled upon a boy no more than twelve years old. The faint fur of his top lip was the first sign of impending adolescence. His slow, rural drawl, slightly oversized tongue and disproportionate features, along with a lackadaisical amble, all conspired to give him the impression of being a touch slow. But this was far from the reality. Armin informed me that the sizeable farmhouse above was his, that his uncle was away tending to business in another village and that he might not return for a day or two. He offered me a room in the house and breakfast for 5,000 *tomans* (roughly five dollars at the time). I declined, explaining that I had my heart set on camping. He insisted a number of times before eventually agreeing to let me camp on his lawn for 3,000 *tomans*. I suspected he was more desperate for the company than the money. Just as I had set the tent up on the beachfront, Armin reappeared with a rug and some eggs for the following morning. I thanked him but explained that I had no pan. He then insisted I join him at the house for breakfast before disappearing into the night, paying no heed to my feeble objections and eventual thanks. Ten minutes later he had returned with an excessive pile of fire-wood and lit a fire. He sat down with me, this time upon my insistence, for a simple meal of bread, cheese, onions – which he bit heartily into like an apple – and tomatoes.

One glance at the English scrawl in my notebook had Armin very excited at the prospect of trying out his handful of English words. He noticed my surprise at his easy recognition of the foreign script. A saturnine look overtook his youthful features as he launched into the story of his grandfather who not so long ago owned the entire stretch of beach until he was stripped of it by deceitful developers. They duped him into making his mark (he was an illiterate farmer) on a document that entitled them to develop the land and, once certain specified conditions were met, forced him to sell it on to them at an extortionately low price. This was the sad plight of countless villagers the world over but here, played out between the lush verdure of the Alborz and the melancholy grey Caspian Sea, the story seemed all the more doleful. It was made even more depressing by the detritus of modernity which was taking over the seashore – the cans, bottles and plastic wrappers that outnumbered the shells and driftwood. More depressing still was Armin's indifference to all this.

The pleasant sea air and soothing sound of gently breaking waves ensured a good night's rest. My slumber was momentarily disturbed, though, by an invisible old man who, from the darkness beyond my tent-flap, warned me of lurking 'cutthroat' thieves. The thoughtful comment spurred me to hurriedly pull my bag into the already cramped tent, zip it shut and lie coiled, pocket-knife in hand, until my anxiety was overpowered by fatigue and I again drifted off.

I awoke to the clucking of chickens busy strutting around my tent. Poking my head out, I saw a line of cows ambling across the beach silhouetted against the morning sun twinkling on the surface of the ocean. A solitary bull eyed my tent quizzically, its snout poking over the rickety fence between us. Armin soon came to fetch me for the promised breakfast and the news that my nocturnal visitor had been none other than his uncle, who had returned from his business late last night and who, in Armin's own words, 'enjoyed a drink as much as he did a joke'. After a hearty breakfast of fried eggs and tomatoes, fresh flat bread, cheese and mint leaves washed down by glasses of tea, I bade Armin farewell as he washed our dirty dishes with water from the adjoining well, humbled by the hospitality of my young host. As I turned to leave, he noticed the plastic bag full of rubbish I had in my hand. 'Let me take that for you,' he said, 'the dogs'll eat it.' He emptied it on the lawn metres away from his front door and turned back to the dishes.

★ ★ ★

The heat and humidity dissuaded me from walking the 6 kilometres back to the main road I had left yesterday. It did not take long to find someone willing to drive me to Hashtpar, a village that straddles the main road leading north. From there it was a short but heart-stopping ride in a *savari* taxi to Astara. I stuffed myself and my backpack into the back of a tired looking Paykan, next to two passengers and behind two others – six passengers in a four-seater. Before I had managed to press myself into the back of the already cramped car, the driver slammed his foot down on the accelerator and we lurched forward. As I tried to disentangle myself from my unamused co-passengers, the car wove in and out of traffic indifferent to which way it was going, overtook on blind corners and occasionally screeched to an unannounced and very sudden halt to drop off and pick up passengers, oblivious to anything else on the road. *Savari* drivers as a breed consider themselves masters of their fate, unassailable by mishaps and quite oblivious to the death toll amongst them in a country with the highest car-crash fatality rate in the world. My fingers were slowly burrowing deeper and deeper into my thigh with every terrifying kilometre of the journey. However terrifying *savaris* may be, I came to learn that they are almost always the fastest, cheapest, easiest and quite often only means of getting from one place to the next in Iran.

★   ★   ★

Astara is tucked into the northern tip of the western shores of the Caspian. It is both a port and a border town. Shopping malls, the bazaars of the twenty-first century, have mushroomed all over the place, displaying the flood of cheap Russian goods that have saturated the market from across the Azeri border. Neon signs and strip-lights hummed characterless arcades into life as groups of shoppers floated idly between small shops disgorging surplus stock out of their doors. Chaotic piles of jeans, shirts, trainers and sunglasses tottered precariously, labels displaying the Cyrillic script of their country of origin. From out of the dreary folds of chadors strutted legs clad in faded blue denim, imitation designer frames sat on heads draped in black and the latest smartphones were pressed to every ear. These sights are familiar in Tehran, Shiraz and Esfahan but were surprising in a distant provincial town the size of Astara. The profusion and prices of DVD players, wide-screen televisions and digital radios showed that the god of consumerism had pervaded even the far reaches of the Islamic Republic.

Other than discount shopping and illicit black cans of imported vodka, Astara has little to offer the traveller. After dark, I decided to wander towards the border. Until 1991, this had been the border between Iran and the Soviet Union, between the so-called 'Free World' and the dark, sinister empire (as it was then portrayed) of communism, when – until the Islamic Revolution in 1979 – Iran was a staunch ally of the Americans in the Manichaean struggle between the West and the Soviets. After the fall of the Shah in 1979, the new Iran created an uneasy friendship with Moscow, but with the dissolution of the Soviet Union in December 1991, this became the border with the Republic of Azerbaijan.

'Don't loiter or you'll get shot by the guards,' advised the friendly man I had stopped for directions. A 3-metre-high concrete wall complete with razor wire, turrets and searchlights ran along the bank of the river that separates Azerbaijan from Iran. A heavy gate blocked access to a bridge leading to foreign soil. A shuffle in a guard tower above was enough to send me scuttling back through what resembled a seedy dockyard. I had seen enough to persuade me that there was little worth seeing.

★ ★ ★

The Astara–Ardebil road, through the Gardane-ye-Heyran, a meandering drive over forested foothills and through fertile valleys, is famed for its beauty. Sir Roger Stevens compared it to the English South Downs and the friend in Tehran who had suggested the route called it 'a slice of heaven' – both comparisons proved justified. Somewhat immunised by the *savari* experience of the previous day, I hired a *savari* '*dar bast*' (literally closed door), meaning I took the taxi exclusively for myself.

We sped along the valley floor beside a barbed-wire fence the other side of which lay the Republic of Azerbaijan. The forest covered both sides of the border in a rich, leafy canopy. My driver, his wrinkled face red with excitement, extolled the virtues of Iran whilst pouring abuse on all other nations he had visited – always for the purpose of pilgrimage. No journey through Iran would be complete without a vitriolic rant from a cab driver on the woes of modern life. This particular man's social analysis was quite straightforward and delivered with considerable gusto. It went something like this: there are no jobs for young men, which means they cannot afford their own places, which means they cannot marry, which invariably leads to laziness and loose living, meaning promiscuity and drug use (disturbingly prevalent in Iran and on the increase, with some statistics claiming it has the highest percentage of addicts of any country on the planet).

'Work and marriage are the mortar that holds together the bricks of society,' he yelled, swivelling around to thrust a clenched fist bearing his wedding ring millimetres from my nose. When he asked about my life, I quietly muttered that I was not married, nor did I have a job to speak of. He took a long look at me in his rear-view mirror before swearing that he would work until the day he died. I fell silent, trying to decipher the meaning of this last sentence as we sped towards Ardebil.

Chapter Ten

Tracking down Mr Djavadi's car parts shop proved easier than anticipated. Mr Djavadi had been my father's driver over thirty years ago and had remained in warm and friendly contact with my family. Twice a year, at *Nowrouz* and on my father's birthday, he would telephone, most of the twenty-minute conversation taken up by both men enquiring about the other's health and the health of their respective families. When, in their last conversation, my father had told him that I was in Iran and was planning on visiting Ardebil, Mr Djavadi insisted on coming to Tehran to pick me up and had only with great difficulty been dissuaded from doing so. Now, standing in front of his shop wearing a smart but ill-fitting suit, his fingers adorned with large rings, he had more the look of a local dignitary expecting to receive a government official than someone in the car business. I was formally welcomed by the whole family and within minutes was sitting at the back of the shop with a glass of fruit juice, listening to the customary social compliments about my family whilst shoppers rummaged through bins of spark plugs and drawers full of bolts. Very much the patriarch now, Mr Djavadi sat at the back of his shop holding forth whilst the younger Djavadis, all boys, scuttled around making a fuss over the two of us with friendly smiles for me and unwavering respect for the *hajj agha* (*hajji* being the honorific title given to those Muslims who have performed the Hajj to Mecca).

During our conversation I mentioned that I was keen to visit the mighty Mount Sabalan, described by Sir Roger Stevens as 'the most haunting of all the mountains of Iran'. Before I knew it, I was rumbling through busy streets inside Mr Djavadi's white Nissan Carryboy, watching the bustle that was Ardebil slide past the window. We drove west out of town towards the towering branch of the Alborz mountain range dominated by the near 5,000 metres of extinct, perennially snow-capped volcano that is Mount Sabalan. 'It is not surprising,' Stevens writes in *Land of the Great Sophy*, 'that according to legend, Zoroaster compiled the Avesta on its summit; nor yet that Sheikh Seifuddin [*sic*] meditated at its base.'[1]

Sheikh Safi al-Din was a thirteenth-/fourteenth-century founder of a mystic order based in Ardebil. With the collapse of the Mongol Empire around it, this order grew from strength to strength, its leadership being passed down through Sheikh Safi's bloodline. Amongst the followers of the order were a tribe of Turkoman origin renowned for their bravery and their savagery. These were the Qizilbash, named for the distinctive red headgear they wore, with twelve points representing the twelve Imams of orthodox Shi'ism. Rumoured to have considered themselves invincible and to have indulged in cannibalism, they were feared warriors fanatically loyal to their sheikh, whom they viewed as benefitting from divine favour.

It was with the help of this semi-nomadic warrior tribe that, in 1501, the fourteen-year-old Ismail, descendant of Sheikh Safi, claimed the throne of Iran in Tabriz. By 1509 he had unified the country under his rule, establishing the Safavid dynasty. Although Twelver Shi'ism had existed in little pockets of Iran for some time, it was Shah Ismail who declared it the official religion of the realm. This conversion to Shi'ism was a calculated political move designed to make clear the division between Safavid territory and the Sunni Ottoman Caliphate looming to the west. This new faith was forced first upon Tabriz, a largely Sunni city, and then slowly and violently upon the rest of the country. Fearing for their lives, many Sunni scholars fled south to Arabia or west into Ottoman territory.

A large number of Shi'i scholars came the other way, imported to Iran from Syria and South Lebanon (today's Hezbollah stronghold) to help establish the new national faith by more peaceable means. It was the power granted to these jurists that set the precedent for the growing influence of religious figures in Shi'i Iran and resulted in their being recognised as living representatives of the Imams. It was in the Qajar era, though, that the hierarchy of *mojtaheds* – a high-ranking group of religious scholars deemed sufficiently enlightened to interpret the *hadith* – became fully established and the titles of *Hojjat-ol Eslam* (Proof of Islam) and *Ayatollah* (Sign of God) came into being, the culmination of which is the *Velayat-e Faqih* (Guardianship of the Jurist), the system of Islamic governance conceived and implemented by Ayatollah Khomeini since the Islamic Revolution of 1979.

Despite Shah Ismail's aggressive tactics, Shi'ism was not fully established as the nation's faith until the reign of Shah Abbas I (1588–1629) and it was only at the end of the sixteenth century that Sunnism was, for the most part, eradicated in Iran.

★ ★ ★

The new Alvares ski area, developed on the foothills of Mount Sabalan and proudly but spuriously claiming to be north-western Iran's largest resort, is perched in the vertiginous folds above Sarein. A once sleepy village, Sarein has recently metamorphosed into a thriving town thanks to the busloads of ailing, superstitious or simply curious tourists that flock there to bathe in its sulphurous springs. Dull, grey concrete skeletons herald yet more apartment blocks to join the disorderly jumble of hotels and holiday homes. The streets are awash with garish colour: burning neon signs and strings of coloured bulbs signalling restaurants and ice-cream parlours; multi-coloured beach balls emblazoned with Disney cartoon characters and the colours of every major European football team hang outside crammed shops waiting to ensnare the occasional hovering tourist.

The 'vast ski area' turned out to be one rickety two-man chairlift that might have seen better days in an Eastern European resort two generations earlier. But it was all enough to fill Mr Djavadi with wonder as he swept the air with his cigarette-holder to invoke suitable utterances of awe from me. The rusty chairlift creaked and groaned, heaving its empty chairs up the slope and down again past a moth-holed Iranian flag. My guide deftly twisted another cigarette into its waiting holder as he looked at me expectantly. 'Incredible mountains,' was all I could offer the ever-cheerful Mr Djavadi, who seemed to have discovered in the chairlift a source of great awe and pride.

We took a different road back through mud-walled villages, piles of straw stacked onto roofs next to menhirs of manure stockpiled to burn as fuel through the coming winter months, particularly harsh in these parts. The livestock-based mountain villages gave way to the fields and furrows of agricultural communities as we descended the mountain slopes. Much of the land we drove through belonged to the prolific Iranian footballer Ali Daei, a local who, rather improbably, holds the world record for international goals scored, ahead of such footballing juggernauts as Pelé, Ferenc Puskás and Maradona.

* * *

Despite my best efforts, Mr Djavadi thwarted all my attempts to pay for the various historical sites we visited and our lunch in Sarein. He had even arranged to pay for my room in the local guest-house unbeknown to me, batting away all my protests with a dismissive swipe of his cigarette-holder. I was a guest and that was the end of the matter. As we visited the fourteenth-century mausoleum of Sheikh Safi al-Din, known as the *Allah-Allah* on account of the repetition of God's name adorning the sky-blue mosaic-work of the salt-cellar-shaped tomb, Mr Djavadi became subdued. Here, in the presence of a holy name from the history of Iran, he deemed it necessary to refrain from interjecting his own persona into the scene. Gone was the ebullience, the arm-waving and the cigarette-holder. Here Sheikh Safi must be allowed to rest undisturbed.

Mr Djavadi's endlessly welcoming manner, his brushes of wit and his air of mannered authority were endearing. I was sad our encounter had to be so brief, but my schedule was unrelenting, so with an '*Ensha'llah*' I promised I would return for a longer stay.

Ardebil had been described by al-Moqaddasi, the eleventh-century Arab geographer, as 'one of the latrines of the world', but with me the town had left a favourable impression. With a population of just over 350,000, its relatively small size made the place a poor cousin to Tabriz, the regional capital. Still, Ardebil, its streets littered with history and its people full of stony charm, watched over by the protective presence of Mount Sabalan, had managed to retain much of its original character.

* * *

Tabriz, the capital of East Azerbaijan province, lies some 220 kilometres due west of Ardebil. As I approached Tabriz and left the verdant Caspian shoreline further and further behind me, the landscape became increasingly arid. The picturesque green scenery gradually gave way to majestic near-desert splendour, decorated by dusty soft-brown fields sweeping down from the ever-present Alborz Mountains. Tabriz lies in an airy plain encircled by mountains and, as my *savari* wound through a final mountain pass, I caught a first glimpse of the industrial city. Having skirted its entire length on a ring road, we pulled into the mayhem of the main bus terminal. Rows of battered buses were surrounded by a swarm of rusting yellow cabs. The hubbub of raised voices yelling destinations, scolding children and arguing over fares was deafening. Even before I had pulled my backpack out of the trunk of the car, I was engulfed by stained shirts, sandals and moustaches pulling and poking me, haggling over prices with one another and attempting to swat away competition with a swipe of the *tasbih* prayer beads. The scrum for my custom was complicated by the (to my ears) strange sounds of Azeri Turkic. Here the Turkic dialect reigned supreme and Persian was spoken only grudgingly, as if to emphasise the distinctions of this part of Iran from its political centre of gravity, Tehran.

★   ★   ★

The early history of the city of Tabriz is opaque and, like much of Iran's ancient history, tinged with mystery and myth. Historians believe that the earliest reference to the city can be found on a stone tablet dating back to the reign of the great Assyrian king, Sargon II (721–705 BCE). A Seljuk settlement may have come into being in the eleventh or twelfth century but Tabriz only really flourished as the seat of the Ilkhanid throne in the thirteenth and fourteenth centuries following the Mongol invasions and again under the Safavids in the sixteenth to the eighteenth centuries. Situated at the north-western corner of Iran, at a point where many great empires of the past converged, the city has had a turbulent history littered with sackings and invasions. This, coupled with the region's susceptibility to earthquakes, has ensured that nearly all of the city's historical monuments have been destroyed. The Arg-e-Tabriz, a fourteenth-century brick citadel with two large arches, is one of the few to have survived but otherwise Tabriz is typical of so-called modern industrial cities in the developing world: architecturally soulless, ugly, built up with no vision other than securing the financial interests of low-grade developers.

It is for its recent history that Tabriz is better known these days, and for two very different episodes in Iran's history. By the early twentieth century, Iranians, who had largely remained culturally and politically isolated from the rest of the world, were beginning to become aware that arbitrary absolute power was not the only way to organise the governance of a country. Notions of pluralism and accountability began to seep into the consciousness of the literate few who constituted the country's elite – the merchants, the clergy and government officials – and who had access to Persian writings from abroad highly critical of the political order in the country. Exacerbated by memories of foreign commercial concessions granted for a paltry sum by Naser al-Din Shah in the late nineteenth century, and by resentment towards the quasi-colonial British and Russian interventions in the domestic affairs of Iran, the clamour for a constitutional reordering of the country's politics grew rapidly. By 1905 public disapproval of Iran's political order had resulted in protests culminating in the closure of Tehran's bazaar. Mozafar al-Din Shah's heavy-handed reaction, violating the sanctity of the mosque protesters had taken shelter in, only served to galvanise the dissidents and further alienate the general population.

The ageing Shah agreed to a constitution drawn up in 1906, after thousands of people camped out in the British Embassy's gardens as a form of dramatic protest, but the old king died soon afterwards. His son, Mohammad Ali Shah, was less sympathetic to the constitutional cause and sought to wrest power back from the nascent parliament. In the summer of 1907, unrelated to these events, the British and Russians, now beginning to become concerned by growing German power, decided to end their rivalry in Asia. In this arrangement between these two great powers terminating 'The Great Game', Iran was divided into two 'spheres of influence': the Russian sphere to the north and the British sphere in the south, with a neutral buffer zone in the middle. This effective carving up of the country only stoked the flames of rebellion and strengthened the resolve of the reformists. In June 1908 the new Shah invited the leaders of the constitutional movement to a meeting, promptly arresting all but four of them in an effort to quash the uprising. This he followed by bombing the *Majles*, the seat of the newly formed government.

Fighting soon broke out in pockets across the country, but it was in Tabriz where the battle to end the institution of absolute monarchy was fought, an institution that claims to stretch back as far as recorded history in Iran. An unlikely hero of the Constitutional Revolution was a man named Sattar Khan. This mercurial figure rose to local prominence as a brigand before joining the armed guard of Crown Prince Mozafar al-Din, before the latter became shah. Sattar had soon grown weary of his official duties and reverted to brigandage. But a devout Shi'a and now politically incensed, he marched to Tehran to defend the *Majles* against the monarchist troops, fighting a tyrannous king in the name of social justice – always a powerful incentive among Shi'i Muslims.

As the fighting continued to escalate back in his native north-west, Sattar Khan was quick to leave the capital and return to help the rebels of his hometown. Tabriz underwent an eleven-month siege in which Sattar established himself as a folk hero, famously scurrying through the besieged streets of the city removing the white flags of surrender that his fellow constitutionalists had raised at a particularly dispirited, hunger-stricken point in the stand-off. It was thanks to his bravery and recalcitrance that the constitutional cause survived the siege. After the abdication of Mohammad Ali Shah in July 1909, Sattar Khan was made governor of Ardebil, a post which he resigned two months later. His fame and success were reputed to have gone to his head and, despite his privileged position, he frequently indulged in often violent drinking bouts and turned to his favoured pastime of brigandage.

Sattar Khan, who has become an Iranian cult hero, embodies two defining traits in Iranian culture. The first is that of the archetypal Shi'i underdog hero fighting for social justice against a tyrannical figure or institution. The other most Iranian of traits is the incongruity found in his character: a devout Muslim with a weakness for alcohol; a champion of the people with a penchant for banditry; a proclaimer of the popular will with autocratic tendencies. From an Iranian's romantic, metaphysical point of view these characteristics are not contradictory, simply human. Rather than the clear-cut Islamic sense of right and wrong, the Iranian psyche still tends towards a more forgiving, flexible, Zoroastrian interpretation of the human condition where good deeds and evil deeds are weighed against one another in deciding an individual's eternal fate.

★ ★ ★

Another even more unlikely hero of the Constitutional Revolution was a young Nebraskan missionary born in 1885. In 1907, Howard Baskerville, a Princeton graduate, was sent to the Presbyterian school in Tabriz as a teacher. Swept up by the fervour and progressive vision of the reformist movement, Baskerville joined the constitutionalists in 1908. He was soon the leader of a militia of 150 people fighting to break the siege that was strangling the life out of the rebel city. On 19 April 1909, aged just twenty-four, Baskerville was shot through the heart by a monarchist sharpshooter. His body is buried in the Christian Armenian cemetery in Tabriz and his contribution to a movement that was fundamental to shaping the modern era in Iran is commemorated with a bronze bust in the city's Constitution House. 'The only difference between me and these people,' Baskerville said, in a statement with particular poignancy for my own situation, 'is my place of birth, and this is not a big difference.'

★ ★ ★

The second episode which propelled Tabriz into the centre of modern Iranian history occurred immediately after World War II, when Iran became a flashpoint in the lead-up to the Cold War. At the start of World War II, Iran had declared itself neutral. The then king, Reza Shah Pahlavi, was unwilling to back the Allies, which would have been an unpopular move given the anti-British resentment at the country's continued interference in Iranian affairs. At the same time, to have backed the Germans would have been foolhardy given Britain's continuing influence in Iran and its control of the country's oil industry. In 1941, following the Soviet and US entry into the war, it was essential for the Allied war effort that a supply corridor into the Soviet Union be created. Iran was the obvious choice. So on 25 August 1941, British and Soviet troops invaded the country, summarily deposed Reza Shah, sending him into exile, and installed his son, Mohammad Reza Shah, a young man of just twenty-one, as his successor. For the remaining four years of the war, the British and the Soviets dominated the affairs of the country with a nominally independent Iranian government supposedly in charge.

With the end of World War II, the British and Americans withdrew the bulk of their forces from Iran. The Soviets did not. Instead, they backed the independence movement in Tabriz that, in November 1945, declared the province of Azerbaijan separate from the central government in Tehran and installed Jafar Pishevari, an Azeri Turk born in Khalkhal and founder of the Communist Party of Iran, as its prime minister. This was to be the first of many confrontations between the Soviet Union and the West over the next several years. The US government, keen to test the effectiveness of the nascent United Nations in the 'maintenance of international peace and security', appealed to the UN Security Council, which, on 30 January 1946, passed Resolution 2 declaring the continuing Soviet military presence in Iran illegal. It took two more official complaints, lodged by Iran and supported by the USA, to result in Resolutions 3 (4 April 1946) and 5 (8 May 1946), for Stalin, who had used the occasion to probe Western determination to uphold the post-World War II settlements agreed at the conferences in Tehran (1943), Yalta (February 1945) and Potsdam (July 1945), to get his answer and pull back Soviet troops. As a result, the Pishevari government in Tabriz collapsed, he and his cabinet fled to the Soviet Union and Tabriz's brief moment in the international political sun came to an end.

★　★　★

From Constitution House I headed to the bazaar. Originally built in the eleventh century but largely rebuilt in the fifteenth, it had a high vaulted-brick roof and arches suspended above narrow alleyways awash with activity that linked the various caravanserais and mosques in its environs. The buzz and movement had the feel of an ant colony perpetually in motion. Old men, as threadbare as their tattered clothes, hauled hefty cartfuls of carpets and other wares, rumbling over the cobbled ground, whilst the younger, visibly more prosperous stall-owners put their imitation-Gucci-shod feet up and watched little television sets with clothes-hangers as makeshift aerials. A customer's query would be answered with an uninterested nod or nonchalant gesture without a break from the gaze on the screen. Every now and again the aroma of grilled lamb or liver would waft along the warren of alleyways, drifting over the clothes, carpets, sacks of nuts and colourful herbs and spices of the stalls.

★　★　★

The day had been unexpectedly hot and the night was delightfully mild. I had noticed plenty of fruit juice bars and ice-cream parlours along the obligatory Imam Khomeini Street a short walk from my hotel. After dark, similar establishments in Tehran would be teeming with packs of adolescents and students busily flirting, frolicking and exchanging phone numbers. But here in Tabriz the white plastic chairs and tables were empty. In search of some verve, I decided to take a half-hour taxi ride to Elgoli, an affluent suburb of the city housing a luxury hotel, theme park and large artificial lake. I was dropped off at a large square swirling with traffic. Rough-looking youths lay languidly across the bonnets of Paykans, talking, laughing and smoking while stands offered a variety of street food. The place was busy, but noticeably different from Tehran was the relative absence of young women. The laughs, the jokes, the banter all came from clusters of young men. Provincial Tabriz obviously seemed a step or two behind metropolitan Tehran and its devil-may-care youth culture.

The flaring lights and wailing music of a fairground beckoned to me and I walked around in search of an entrance. I noticed an open gateway leading to a large hut-like structure and wandered in. The place was filled with men in scruffy suits and a few women in full-length black chadors. Then I noticed the closely-shorn, khaki-clad figures of soldiers distractedly tapping their bulky black boots to the martial music being piped through a PA system. The men, with their suits and tell-tale beards of Iranian officialdom, together with their wives were staring intently at life-sized posters of Khomeini, Gaddafi and Arafat. Here and there were images of Uncle Sam being crushed in the fist of a Revolutionary Guard or a John Bull being kicked in the balls by a machine-gun-toting *chadori* woman. Along one wall a bank of screens flickered with the all-too-familiar black-and-white images of the Revolution, along with the large banners brandishing anti-imperialist, anti-American slogans, the largest of which read (loosely translated): America Can't Do a Damned Thing (*Amrica hich ghalati nemikhore*). I had unintentionally stumbled into an exhibition celebrating the successes of the Islamic Republic of Iran.

Having spent some moments respectfully admiring the images on display, I slipped out and came across a staircase leading up to a series of softly-lit walkways winding around an artificial lake that dated from the Safavid era. Little clusters of youth, again mostly boys, perched on benches or ambled along the walkways as colourfully lit fountains cascaded into the rippling water. I could hear the neon noise of the Lunapark over the fence but I was now more drawn to the open-air restaurant. A bowl of *ash-e-dough* (a very tasty kind of hot yoghurt soup) later and I was reclining on a *takht*, enjoying the smooth comfort of a *ghalyan* water pipe washed down with piping hot tea as birds chattered in the cool night air.

The journey back into town was given a bizarre twist when my young cab driver decided to bring a friend along for company. His friend, who by my count possessed no more than two teeth, was already in the passenger seat with his seatbelt fastened before I realised what was going on. Sticking his head out of the open passenger window, he would let out a loud, lupine yelp at every passing car. Each time he yelped the cab driver would land a playful but firm smack on the back of his head before giving his earlobe a tug. When we arrived at my hotel and I paid the fare there was no explanation, or even mention, of the young man. The driver thanked me, his companion smiled and off they went. As I watched them disappear into the distance I saw the friend's head pop out of the passenger window and howl loudly up at the moon as a hand reached out and yanked him back in by the earlobe.

The following morning I awoke early, packed up my gear and headed downstairs sheepishly to ask whether breakfast was being served. It was the first day of the month of Ramadan, the Islamic month of fasting and I had no real idea what to expect. Even the less religious element of Iranian society simply pay heed not to smoke, drink or eat in public until after the evening call to prayer: the closed and curtained doors and windows of every teahouse and restaurant, the threat of a fine or flogging from the police or, worse still, a beating at the hands of an irate *Basiji* act as effective deterrents. Travellers, I had a vague notion, were within their rights to break the fast for the duration of their journey but I was not sure exactly how this would apply to me. To my relief, I was served tea and eggs without a fuss and was soon back on the road. I had again opted for a *dar bast savari* (private taxi) so that I could visit the village of Kandovan, an hour's detour from my route to Lake Orumiyeh. This would allow me to take the ferry across the middle of the lake rather than the longer, less picturesque bus route around its northerly shores.

★ ★ ★

The turning off the main road to Orumiyeh led through sleepy little villages of old men in misshapen, discoloured jumpers and hardened women wrapped in colourful, floral-patterned chadors, through their leafy fruit and nut groves and out onto a fertile plain irrigated by the melt-water of the Sahand Mountains. Mount Sahand itself is an inverted pudding-bowl shape and its outline was beautifully silhouetted against the unblemished blue sky. In his book *Legend*, David Rohl postulates that this may have been the biblical Mountain of God in the book of Genesis, a theory in line with many a scholarly opinion that the Garden of Eden is located somewhere in the region.

Kandovan is a small village hewn from the fantastical natural rock formations of the very mountain on whose stony side it rests. Stalagmitic ovals reach up from the mountainside like a forest of menhir-like rocks. Homes have been hewn into every one of these menhirs, each with a sky-blue metal door. Some historians believe that these troglodytic dwellings were first used as shelters by soldiers on military campaigns over 800 ago, although archaeologists have suggested that pre-Islamic, possibly even prehistoric settlements existed in the area. These cave-like abodes were scattered around the steep, scraggy slope that somehow served as streets cluttered with cats, clucking chickens and the odd village woman cowering behind her chador at the sight of a camera as she went about her daily chores. As I clambered between the tall rocks, a woman emerged from her home and gave me a stern rebuke for taking pictures of her front garden. 'Can you not see this is someone's private garden?' she bellowed, gesturing at the metre-wide strip of rubble on which I was struggling to keep my footing.

The teahouse sold locally produced honey, nuts and bottles of supposedly healing water from the village's spring. 'Especially good for kidney stones,' the shopkeeper insisted, pointing to his stomach. A busy clanging came from the next-door construction site; a luxury hotel was being built in the mountainside. The most startling of this primitive village's little quirks was the web of black electrical wire that ran from the top of one rock-dwelling to the next and the obligatory antenna that jutted clumsily out beside it. Nearly every one of these caves, no bigger than 2.5 metres in diameter, one naked bulb dangling from a ceiling like an incandescent stalactite, a hearth-stead as a kitchen and a hearth-rug as the only piece of furniture, had a television.

★ ★ ★

The westerly road leading to Orumiyeh was a two-lane strip of asphalt that stretched through the middle of an immense, boggy basin encircled by the brooding volcanic rock of the westerly Alborz range. Only a few years earlier the plain we were driving over had been a small lake. A fractional but seemingly permanent climate change in the region leading to lower rainfall and a marginal increase in temperature had caused this lake simply to evaporate. 'It was God's will,' said my taxi driver through a thick, silver moustache. Once out of the plain, the road swung around the base of the low mountains to reveal the brilliant white shores of Lake Orumiyeh shimmering in the sunlight. The level of salinity of the lake is too high to sustain anything but primitive crustaceans. This is due to the lack of any outlets for the many radial, salt-bearing streams that feed into it. Like the Dead Sea, it is indeed dead to life. The lake is 140 kilometres long and 55 kilometres wide at its broadest point but across its narrow, pinched neck a bridge was under construction.

'They've been building it for twenty years,' said the taxi driver. 'It will never be finished. It is God's will.'

The short drive between Lake Orumiyeh's western shore and the town itself was lined with fragrant, walled gardens exploding with mulberry, pomegranate and cherry trees. It was a relief to have left the 2-million-strong sprawl of Tabriz behind for what seemed like an attractive town of manageable proportions. When I said as much to the hitherto laconic driver, he exploded in a diatribe of abuse at the city authorities, their ineptitude, their unwillingness to produce low-cost housing, their corruption and their lack of any qualification for even existing on this earth. 'It is God's will,' I ventured.

Having been enchanted by the glistening white shoreline of the lake and notwithstanding the ills of the city fathers, I decided to spend a night in Orumiyeh, the supposed birthplace of the prophet Zoroaster. The precise date of his birth is, as previously mentioned, the subject of much debate amongst historians and academics, with anything from 600 BCE to 1800 BCE having been proposed in recent times. It had long been assumed that much of the mystery and confusion surrounding the prophet Zoroaster's dates and origins had stemmed from the fact that his teachings were passed down through oral tradition for many centuries, only being transcribed by the Magian priesthood as late as the fifth century CE. These records had been the basis of much modern research into the era, but it is only recently that historians have unearthed certain glaring inconsistencies that suggest a somewhat more creative cataloguing of the religion's early history in an effort to legitimise the Magian priesthood of the Sasanian era's interpretation of the ancient faith.

Despite his disputed origins, Zoroaster in different ways and at different times gave ancient Persia its religion before the arrival of Islam in the seventh century. The Zoroastrian faith, often erroneously misconstrued as fire worship, sees the world as organised between two poles: good and evil, light and dark, fire and earth. As such it is not unrelated to the Judeo-Christian-Islamic notions of God and Satan; the essence of good living being to secure as much positivity in life as possible in the face of temptation and negative impulses. It is a religion well suited to an Iranian temperament which values flexibility and discourse. Many an Iranian, though true to the precepts of Shi'i Islam, expresses a longing for the true Persian spirit as reflected in Zoroastrianism.

Orumiyeh proved a town full of surprises. Its position at the delta of converging civilisations was evident in its ethnic makeup of Anatolian

Turks, Azeri Turks, Armenians and Assyrians; even the odd Kurd could be seen walking proudly around sporting his characteristic tasselled turban, cummerbund and baggy trousers. The town is divided into ethnic neighbourhoods; some, like the Armenian area, tangibly more affluent. Well-groomed pedestrian shopping streets housed faux-designer boutiques, internet cafés and electrical goods retailers which nudged up against the metalworkers' bazaar nearby, with its incessant hammering on copper bowls and silver dishes. On every corner dates, sweet bread, tea and various other traditional *eftar* foods were doing a roaring trade. *Eftar*, the break of the fast at dusk, is a festive time in which the family and the community in general, so important in the Islamic tradition, come together for the first meal of the day. Restaurants and the odd random house handed out steaming cups full of *ash* soup to passers-by – a custom that lasts the duration of the month throughout the country and the Islamic community as a whole.

* * *

The following morning I set off straight for the busy alleyways of the bazaar, amassing all I needed for a long-overdue night or two under canvas. My spirits were dampened on arrival at Lake Orumiyeh with the discovery that the western shoreline of the lake was noticeably different from its eastern counterpart. The desolate black rock and crystalline salt beaches had given way to a small, uninhabited village in front of which lay a vast boggy wasteland. The road running through the village was bordered with large rectangular enclosures in which tens of thousands of white grapes had been spread on white sheets and left in the sun to slowly shrivel into raisins.

An impossible wind whipped salty specks up from the surface of the lake and into my eyes. A few pathways spread off the road, leading to a large, blue water tank on stilts, a little workman's hut and an unlikely car-park with two Paykan cars and their three passengers who seemed to be mining salt. The grey surface-layer of salt and mud gave under foot in places, like thin ice, plunging my shoes into deeper mud. These were no conditions in which to pitch a tent. Having watched my taxi drive off into the distance, I blew about in the wind, shielding my eyes, scratching my head and wondering what I was going to do. On the drive over I had noticed a cluster of buildings further up the shoreline. With a slow, wind-beaten plod, I set off in their direction hoping to find shelter, or at the very least a telephone to call for a ride back to town, my mobile phone predictably out of service. The cluster of buildings I had spotted turned out to be a couple of hotels.

The Flamingo was a far cry from its Las Vegas namesake but it was the smartest hotel I had come across thus far. The lights were off and the place was empty but the door was unlocked. As I barged into a grand but gloomy reception hall I startled a body slumped over the reception desk into life. Outside, packs of wild dogs lolled shaggily around as tumbleweed blew across the deserted streets. 'You wouldn't believe we were full just over a week ago, would you?' the receptionist said after exchanging the customary greetings, rubbing the sleep from his eyes. It was hard to imagine the lifeless foyer and deserted sweeping staircase anything but eerily empty. A bin rattled incessantly against its metal frame in the wind outside. This, I was informed, was a government hotel and therefore stayed open all year round to cater to the odd passing delegation and the occasional conference. The rest of the area only opened for the summer period popular with tourists and in the spring for the flocks of ornithologists drawn to the lake by the annual invasion of migratory birds. A raucous guffaw met explanations of my intention to camp. 'You would have woken up on the lake bed,' he snorted before giving me a bargain price for a *veela*, a small self-catering bungalow I was grateful to take shelter in.

★ ★ ★

Having shaken the salt out of my hair and eyes, I laid a spread of tomatoes, cucumbers, bread and goat's cheese on the floor and washed it down with a pot of tea which the by now fully awake caretaker brought me. After this simple meal, I grabbed my camera and a bottle of water and wandered out into the howling wind and empty streets, the occasional plastic bottle rattling across the asphalt. Following the shoreline, I came across a road that led to a big blue water tank elevated on two concrete breeze-blocks. 'Hot water shower' read the unlikely hand-written scrawl under a rusty showerhead poking from its side. Next to this, six or seven metal frames resembling goalposts were scattered around. Long strips of tawny fabric danced and flickered from them in the gale; these threadbare ribbons all that was left of what, in a previous incarnation, were awnings providing shelter from the sun.

As I wandered along this desolate, wind-swept landscape, I came across an empty open-air stadium planted, for no apparent reason, in this middle-of-nowhere. I clambered silently around the empty seats bathed in soft afternoon sunlight. Closing my eyes, I tried to imagine a roaring crowd but the scene was too unlikely in the lonely silence broken only by the soft howl of the wind. I made my way back to the lakeshore in time to catch a slow, smouldering sunset, admiring the little pools and rivulets that burned in the mud with golden reflections of the dwindling sun. Flocks of small white birds swept low over the salty basin. Bright pinks and explosive oranges seemed to burst out from a solitary cloud that hung shrouding the sun as if only to enhance the view.

Sitting in that glorious desolation, mountains on all sides – some near, some just visible in the twilight over the far side of the lake – a little bubbling pool of mud between me and the inky blue waters, it was impossible not to be at once exhilarated and humbled by my natural surroundings.

But the exhilaration did not last long. In the fast-fading light, thick swarms of mosquitoes began to buzz in the air like menacing predators. There were so many that I was forced to snort and spit them out of my mouth as I ran back to the hotel manically slapping myself as I went. When I arrived back at the bungalow I was horrified to discover that I had left the light on. The glass door was alive with thousands upon thousands of mosquitoes. Trying to shoo them off would be disastrous so I braced myself, opened the door just enough to squeeze through and slammed it behind me as fast as I could, but not fast enough to prevent a thick, buzzing cloud spilling in behind me. The next hour was spent frantically chasing around the room, swiping a rolled up notebook to and fro. Hitchcock and his birds had nothing on me.

The following morning, with the clouds of mosquitoes gone, I wandered over to the reception area to find that the caretaker had prepared a breakfast of bread and cheese and was brewing up a pot of tea. The television set in the dining area was tuned into a cleric taking questions from callers about correct Ramadan procedures. A young man from Kerman rang in to ask about the acceptable way to burp during the holy month. 'You must exhale the burp,' intoned the priest. 'To re-swallow the gassy emanation is consumption and is therefore a violation of your sacred fast.' More questions followed about defecation, fornication and the accidental swallowing of a fly during Ramadan, a question very pertinent to my experience of the previous night. Each inquiry was followed by the stony-faced yet kindly response of the mullah, who treated every questioner as a curious and well-behaved child worthy of a pat on the head.

Chapter Eleven

I awoke frozen to the bone and disoriented. I was on an overnight bus heading south along the border with Iraq towards Sanandaj, the capital of Iranian Kurdistan. The bus driver had his window wide open and the icy desert air was blowing straight onto me. The gentle autumn climate of the north had been left far behind, replaced by the harsh bite of the mountains.

Stoically resigned to the cold, I cursed myself for not having a blanket or even a jumper to hand. But at least the blast of cold air was keeping the driver well awake and all the passengers alive through the treacherous, winding mountain roads. I watched enviously as the driver poured a steaming glass of tea from a flask beside him. 'Don't get too jealous. It's laced with opium.' I turned to see a young soldier sprawled over the two seats next to me, his heavy boots lolling in the aisle between us. 'Small doses keep you alert. It's only a full dose that sends you off,' he responded to my look of alarm.

Striking up a conversation with the soldier, I discovered that he was halfway through his obligatory two-year stint of military service and was on his way back to his posting in Sanandaj, having just returned home to Tabriz for his grandfather's funeral. 'It's not so bad here in Kurdistan,' he replied when I asked what military service was like. 'Half the time we're training. The rest of the time we seem to be here just to make our presence felt.'

As descendants of the ancient Medes – who first fought against the Persians and then amalgamated with them when Cyrus the Great's father, Cambyses I (600–559 BCE), married Mandana, a Median princess – Kurdish communities, whether in Iran, Iraq, Turkey or Syria, have always striven to preserve their Kurdishness, determined not to be assimilated or absorbed by the central authorities of the countries in which they live. As a result their relations with central governments in these countries have always been uneasy, if not downright hostile. Iran has been no exception. In the 1920s and 1930s, Reza Shah arrested many of the Kurdish tribal leaders and ordered the wholesale transportation of many Kurdish communities, some several hundred kilometres away from their traditional tribal lands. This was Reza Shah's heavy-handed attempt to quash tribal power, to preserve national unity and to undermine any talk of autonomy, let alone secession from Iran. But all this did was to produce enormous resentment among Kurds. During the later reign of his son, the shah who was deposed in 1979, the Kurdish areas did not benefit from the investment and economic prosperity which the boom in oil prices and production brought to the rest of Iran. This was a deliberate attempt to encourage migration by Kurds and thus integration into the larger pool of Iranian society. In other words, what Reza Shah did on a small scale by force, the later regime of his son attempted to achieve by stealth and economic manipulation. The early days of the Islamic Republic saw a revival of Kurdish aspirations, which were ruthlessly put down by the new central government. Now we were in a period of uneasy peace again, but the region was prone to flare up from time to time. The number of soldiers garrisoned in the province was clear evidence of this latest instability.

'You hear some nasty stories, though,' the young soldier continued, discussing military service. 'I think I got pretty lucky with my stationing. When my cousin came back he was a different person. To this day, he's never talked about what happened.'

On arriving in Sanandaj in the small hours, I emerged from the bus stiff and sleepy and bundled myself into the back of a particularly rickety Paykan taxi. I had decided to stay in the centre of town and my young taxi driver took me to a dingy little *mosaferkhaneh* (traveller's hostel) near the *maidan* (town square) that was run by a cousin of his. This young man's bearing and attire were distinct from what I had come to expect from the usual provincial youths. I soon discovered that Pejman had lived and gone to school in Tehran for a few years in his late teens, that he had recently graduated from the local college and that he was now driving a taxi in the absence of any work as a teacher, which was his vocation. He had a gentle and refined manner and we were soon chatting very openly about a whole host of subjects – all very unusual in Iran, where everybody is automatically suspicious of strangers. Arriving at the little hostel, Pejman parked and came upstairs with me to instruct his cousin to give me a friendly rate. 'I'll be back this afternoon to show you around town. Let's say three o'clock.' With that he slipped off before I'd had a chance to thank him properly.

★ ★ ★

As promised, Pejman picked me up at the appointed hour and drove me up into a poorer part of town past a large building; a *hamam*, or public bathhouse. He winked and whistled at various shifty characters skulking around the building, a few of whom came over to the car, had a quick chat with Pejman in the local dialect and left, shaking their heads. Slowly, it dawned on me what Pejman was trying to do. Although this was Sanandaj, far away from the watchful eyes to be found on every corner in Tehran and other metropolitan centres, Pejman displayed caution. He was telling me, in great detail, about the severe beating he endured in jail for trying to buy alcohol during Ramadan a few years previously – whilst trying to buy alcohol during Ramadan. This did little to set my by now twitchy mind at ease. Drawing a blank at the bathhouse, Pejman phoned a friend, whom he arranged to meet a couple of hours later. To kill time he drove us up to Abidar Park in the hills above the city.

Sanandaj is hugged by the foothills of the westerly Zagros Mountains, and their gently swelling slopes of light brown are a spectacular sight dappled by the soft afternoon sun. The city sweeps over natural contours of the valley in which it nestles amid patches of green. Sanandaj wears its heart on its sleeve: it is about two things – Kurds and contraband – and both are proudly displayed on the streets. The baggy, ballooning trousers and matching jackets, the *kamarband* and tasselled cloth of the traditional Kurdish headdress is worn by nearly all men and chadors are nowhere to be seen amongst the women. In the proud, gaunt faces and light eyes, at once friendly and fearsome, the warrior tradition of this people is ever manifest.

The porous border and relative lawlessness of Iraqi Kurdistan make Sanandaj a major smuggling hub. Hashish, opium and heroin continue their journey west from Afghanistan and Pakistan, and alcohol (illegal), soap and fabrics (regulated) flood into Iran. The city's bazaar openly displayed stall after stall of fabrics of all textures and colours whilst the smell of cheap, perfumed soap suffused the air. Wandering through the bazaar I was surprised to see a row of booths crammed full of Kurds of all ages, each sitting close to large television screens. As I got closer I saw they were frantically tapping the buttons of Sony PlayStation controllers. My attention was drawn to a particularly fearsome-looking middle-aged Kurd, brow furrowed with concentration, tongue clamped determinedly between his teeth. I peered into his booth to see what it was that had so engrossed him. He was playing Britney's 'Dance Beat'.

★ ★ ★

Later that evening, a bottle of 'Jack Williams' whisky having been successfully obtained, Pejman took me to meet a friend of his who owned a buffet. This turned out to be one of the octagonal glass teahouses with *takhts* outside that line the roads in certain parts of the country. We walked in to find three young men busily puffing out twisting clouds of heavy, fruit-scented smoke from a series of *ghalyan* water pipes of different shapes and sizes. Another *ghalyan* was readied and put in front of Pejman and me when it dawned on me that I was going to have to hold my own amidst some extremely aggressive smokers whose faces frequently disappeared behind billows of grey smoke. It was not long before I discovered that smoking was not the only thing I was going to have to keep up with. Three *estekan*, small tea glasses, were put in front of us by Pejman's friend and discreetly filled with our bootleg booze.

'Just pretend it's tea,' he said, noticing me looking sheepishly at the group of people who had just walked through the door, one of whom trailed a pet monkey sporting a fez behind him on a leash. I asked the owner, who was obviously very pleased with his charge, if he had taught the monkey any tricks. He looked at me contemptuously before tutting and turning away. By this stage a small crowd had gathered around the monkey, who was hoisted into the air and held aloft by its beaming owner, as though the proud father of a new-born baby. Then, with impeccable timing, the monkey unleashed a stream of piss all over the man.

'It definitely knows one trick,' said Pejman, howling with laughter as the man's face glowed as red as the coals of our water pipe. As soon as our *estekan* were empty, Pejman refilled them and just as quickly emptied his with a single gulp, urging me to do the same. After seven or eight large shots that tasted suspiciously like rubbing alcohol and a lot of flavoured tobacco, we got up to leave rather shakily. Pejman insisted on driving me back to the hotel and brushed aside my attempts to pay him. 'Friends don't pay each other,' he said. '*Man behet hal dadam*, I showed you a good time. You will do the same for me if we meet again in Tehran.' Here again was this concept of *hal*, but in this instance it was being given as the most precious gift Pejman could have offered me.

★ ★ ★

Giddily, I returned to the guest-house, inebriated as much by the ephemeral friendship I had made as by the heavy smoke and liquor. I collapsed onto my bed and just as my eyes were coming together, my mobile phone rang and brought me round.

'Mr Massoudi, why are you not at the ceremony? Where are you?' The voice belonged to a Mr Karimi, whom I had heard about in Tehran. In my unexpected whirlwind encounter with Pejman, I had managed to completely forget about going to the traditional weekly Sufi ceremony performed in the *khaneghah*, the Sufi place of worship and a shelter for wandering dervishes. Mr Karimi had arranged the visit and excitedly informed me that the *sheikh* (also known as a *pir*), the Sufi spiritual leader, had recently returned from England, where he studied and was looking forward to meeting me. And now I was already forty minutes late.

I leaped from my bed and stuck my head under the cold tap before hurriedly brushing my teeth. This was a unique opportunity, one that I had been looking forward to as much as anything else I was to do in Iran. Rapidly coming around from my Jack Williams-induced haze, I cursed myself and stumbled about the room in a tottering panic. After a few more minutes, I hurtled out of the guest-house and into a taxi. Of course he knew the *khaneghah*, the driver insisted dismissively, but it was only having driven in circles for twenty minutes before eventually swallowing his pride and asking a passer-by for directions that we eventually found the place.

I hurried through a courtyard and was greeted by a smiling young man who took my shoes and led me into a room full of people sitting on a large carpet, transfixed by the sermon of the *sheikh* standing before them in flowing brown robes. It was one thing to be late to a religious ceremony that I was privileged to have been allowed to attend, it was completely another matter to arrive drunk to a Muslim ceremony – and of all times in Ramadan, the month of fasting and abstinence.

I sat on the floor at the back of the room, as far away from the next person as I could manage. I could not understand the sermon being delivered in Kurdish, but then a few glaring words jumped out. 'Ramadan,' I heard, '*mashroub*' – meaning alcohol and specifically 'whisky' – were thrown out in that order by the *sheikh*. I stifled my breathing as much as I could, exhaling through my nose to mask the fumes. I had images of a frenzied crowd insulted by the evidence of alcohol chasing me for dear life out of the place and along the streets of Sanandaj.

The *sheikh* wrapped up his sermon and the expression of intense concentration on the faces around me soon broke into smiles as everyone rose to their feet and slowly formed a square, one side of which was made up by a row of chairs. On them sat four long-haired and bearded dervishes, each armed with a *daft*, a large tambourine-like drum which they began to beat to a slow, steady rhythm. The rest of the congregation then began chanting to the rhythm of the *daft*. The beat of the drum, combined with the chanting, created a heady and hypnotic rhythm to which the dervishes swayed their heads up and down like a row of human metronomes. As this *sama* spiritual dance went on, the pace picked up until the once-harmonious soft chanting became a mix of wild yelps and breathless gasps, all the time repeating one of the ninety-nine names of God. I was now witnessing an orgiastic fit of trance-like spirituality in which people threw their heads about wildly, as though possessed. The beating of the *daft* and the chanting had succeeded in producing a state of transcendence in which the congregation had induced itself into a communion with God and the ecstasy that went with it – a *hal* of a very different sort from that which I had experienced only hours earlier with Pejman.

★   ★   ★

Different Sufi orders come with different traditions and practices. In the ceremonies of some orders, once this transcendent state is reached, Sufis pierce their flesh with swords or pick up burning logs and swallow fire, all seemingly unharmed, before carrying on chanting the name of God. In this state the material world is temporarily left behind, the body is an empty vessel filled with the Infinite and pain is simply non-existent. It is thus that Sufis explain the incredible feats they perform. Of the many different schools of Sufism, each with its own rites and rituals, those that perform the intoxicating *sama* dance are known as Drunken

Sufis. The most renowned of these are the Mevlevi order – also known as Whirling Dervishes, reflecting their actions as they achieve their heightened state – based in Konya, south-eastern Turkey, and founded by the mystic poet Rumi. Many Sufi orders frown upon these actions, whether the self-harm or the trancing, and prefer to reach their state of spiritual transcendence through study and contemplation.

The basic tenets of Sufism closely resemble many other types of mysticism. Though this form of worship may seem a far cry from the Christianity that we are familiar with today, many people from saints and early Christians to prominent personalities of the modern world practised similar and frequently more bizarre rituals to achieve a state of spiritual consciousness. Biblical names such as John the Baptist and St Paul and historical figures like St Francis of Assisi and Joan of Arc right through to William Blake and T.S. Eliot are a few familiar examples.

Mysticism, the search for ultimate Truth that lies beyond the logic of the physical world around us, a quest for the infinite, for a return to godhead, is a concept that by its very nature is pantheistic. 'I am neither Christian, nor Jew, nor Gabr, nor Moslem. I am not of the East, nor of the West, nor of the land, nor of the sea,' wrote Rumi.[1] It is this kind of universality – the breaking down of faith to its simplest reality – that has threatened many a religious institution into often violent suppression. The Islamic Republic of Iran is no exception. A few months earlier in Tehran, I had been shown a grey ponytail displayed defiantly on the wall of a dervish I visited. He had been beaten and his hair cut with a knife simply because he was a dervish.

Sufism is currently undergoing a surge in popularity, particularly amongst the educated urban youth of Iran, who see its spiritual and metaphysical qualities as more representative of true Iranian culture than the stringent interpretation of Islamic law being enforced by the current regime. I often found myself at gatherings in which young people recited their favourite passages from the revered mystic poets of Iranian literature. On many occasions a *tambour* player would begin to pluck the strings of his long-necked lute as someone grabbing a reed flute called a *nay* would start up in accompaniment. Soon a whole congregation would keep rhythm with *daft* hand-drums or simply by clapping as someone sang the verses of Hafez or Rumi to the music.

The Sufi Path, like the path of any mystic, begins with the shedding of the ego which shackles our spirits to the material world and imprisons our minds in a cage of logic and rationality. Sufis, in their purest form, attempt to rid themselves of any attachment to material existence, from physical possessions right through to abstract notions of pride. The word Sufi comes from the coarse woollen cloth worn by the dervish (which itself means roaming mendicant). Another word frequently used to describe these holy wanderers is *faqir* (meaning poor in the Persian language), commonly recognised as 'fakirs' in India. It has to be acknowledged that the world of Muslim mysticism is not devoid of its charlatans and freeloaders. As in any country and with any religion, there are many who exploit the power of faith to their advantage. Just as religious relics and pardons have been readily peddled throughout the history of Christendom, so too have many posed as roaming mystics only to profiteer from the credulity and generosity of society, ready to give and wonder at bizarre masochistic rituals, many of which may have a deep religious provenance, but which are just as often nothing more than hollow showmanship for personal gain.

The Iranian youths who attend these impromptu gatherings are not true Sufis, they have not turned their back on the material world, but neither are they charlatans. They are merely tapping into an emotive and ancient part of their culture, a part that gives them a sense of identity they cannot find elsewhere in the world around them.

★   ★   ★

Back in the *khaneghah*, as the chanting wound down people slowly snapped out of their elevated states and once again became aware of their surroundings. Again they sat and listened to Sheikh Mokhtar with utter devotion as he spoke. Even though his Kurdish words meant nothing to me, his mellifluous tone and the look of beatitude on the faces of his congregation was striking. A short sermon was followed by another round of chanting and swaying to the steadily increasing beat of the *daft*. This cycle of sermon followed by *sama* was repeated once more, each time the pace and purpose of the chanting and swaying becoming more fervent. By this stage, some were stumbling around in wild spasms, as though completely incapable of controlling their movements. Most eyes were closed and all expressions distant, devout. The *sheikh* suddenly took centre stage as he reached a hand to the back of his head and released long black locks that he began to spin round and round with every impassioned flick of his head, whirling occasionally, effortlessly, as the tempo mounted. Cries of '*Allah! Allah!*' punctuated the chanting. One middle-aged man was forcibly restrained by an attendant on hand to help control those that have lost themselves to the trance.

The Sufi congregation was made up only of men, since women were deemed not to have the intellectual capacity to reach God in this way. Female Muslim mystics have always existed but have not made their mark on the practice of Sufism. Women in certain Sufi communities chant whilst going about their daily chores and have been known to achieve transcendental states in which they 'eat fire' but they are still excluded from the *khaneghah*. As the attitude towards women rapidly evolves in Iran and other parts of the Muslim world, no doubt Sufi congregations will begin to accept women into the fold, but for now it remains an exclusively male environment. Boys of no more than eight or nine years of age were swaying side by side with elders whose long, greying locks flicked back and forth in a graceful tangle. It was a breath-taking display of collective human energy and faith. The setting, the drums, the chanting and intense atmosphere were intoxicating and I found myself disarmingly swept up by it all.

A signal from the *sheikh* brought the ritual to a climax, after which smiles and hugs were shared amid bewildered expressions. The men and boys looked moved and exhausted, propping themselves up against one another or the wall, eyes welling with tears. The *sheikh* rounded things off with a short speech during which glasses of tea were being passed around. I was desperate for a glass to snap me out of the stupor of the proceedings and my previous indulgences, and to help mask the smell of my booze-laden breath before talking to Sheikh Mokhtar. But just as the tray was reaching me, I was called up to sit beside him. He was cross-legged on the floor with a circle of people around him, wishing him well, offering their devotion and passionately kissing his hand. One old man with a pock-marked face was moved to tears by his personal audience with the *sheikh* and seemed unable to let go of the holy man's hand. I sat on the periphery of the circle when with a tap on my shoulder tea was finally offered. Its warming, waking powers had just taken effect when the *sheikh* called me over.

I knelt down in front of him and was very quick to apologise in Persian for my tardiness and to express my gratitude for the opportunity to meet with him. 'Let us speak in English,' he said in a broad Northern English accent. We talked of his study in the United Kingdom. He was completing a PhD in hydro-engineering at Newcastle University which he intended to put to use improving conditions in his native Kurdistan. I spoke to him of the purpose of my trip and of my hopes to present a side of Iran with which those in the West were less familiar. I had a million and one questions for him but, alas, I knew time was not on my side and that, since it was Ramadan, the *sheikh* was yet to break his fast for the day despite it being almost midnight. My interview was brief but rewarding and as he gave me his contact details he pointed out that his email server was Yahoo; 'hoo' being one of the ninety-nine names of God which Sufis chant and 'ya' the common prefix for invoking the name of God (*ya'llah*) or the Imams (*ya Ali, ya Hossein*). I left feeling I had witnessed an expression of pure faith unlike anything I had previously seen.

★ ★ ★

Back at the hostel I sat on my bed feeling inspired by my experience and, as the exhilaration wore off, suddenly slightly empty and alone. Polishing off the dregs of the Jack Williams that Pejman had left me with, I settled into writing up the last couple of days in my journal. Flipping distractedly through my notebook, I came across a quotation from Freya Stark that seemed particularly apt at that moment:

> Solitude … is the one deep necessity of the human spirit to which adequate recognition is never given in our codes. It is looked upon as a discipline or a penance, but hardly ever as the indispensable, pleasant ingredient it is to ordinary life, and from this want of recognition come half our domestic troubles … Modern education ignores the need for solitude: hence a decline in religion, in poetry, in all the deeper affections of the spirit: a disease to be *doing* something always, as if one could never sit quietly and let the puppet show unroll itself before one: an inability to lose oneself in mystery and wonder while the world develops around us.[2]

Chapter Twelve

The *savari* taxi driving me the next day through the foothills of the Zagros to Kermanshah was packed full of fierce-looking Kurds with chiselled faces, all in the traditional dress which they wear as much as a symbol of cultural identity as through habit. Once in Kermanshah, I found a suitable room to rent and, it still being Ramadan, feasted illicitly on a banana. Refuelled, I set off for the city's northernmost point and the series of bas-reliefs known as Tagh-e Bostan.

A large pool fed by a spring considered sacred by Zoroastrians reflects the dramatic cliff-face and its two arched alcoves standing side by side, one taller than the other. Inside these alcoves are incredibly well-preserved 1,700-year-old rock carvings, considered amongst the finest and most intricate in Iran, commemorating the coronations and hunting feats of some of the great Sasanian kings, including the 3-metre figure of Shapur II (309–79 CE), the longest-ruling monarch of the dynasty. His reign was defined by wars on every frontier of the empire. Around 325 CE, he marched south to subdue the Arabs who had been attacking the Gulf coast from Bahrain and successfully drove them back into the Arabian heartland. To the north, Armenia's conversion to Christianity under King Tiridates III, supported by Rome, posed a grave problem. Shapur led a campaign against Rome in 337 CE, when Constantius II was proclaimed emperor. Despite initial successes, he was forced to leave this campaign in a stalemate in 350 CE because central Asian nomadic tribes had invaded the east of the empire. With these Hunnic tribes successfully subdued by 359 CE, Shapur turned his attentions back to Rome and the West by launching an attack on Syria. In 361 CE Rome, now under the rule of Emperor Julian, retaliated, winning a number of battles with the Sasanians. These victories culminated in the Romans laying siege to Ctesiphon, but, with victory seemingly in their grasp, they contrived to lose the city thanks to the disorganisation and pillaging of their own troops.[1] The Persians rallied and, now equipped with elephants, defeated the Roman Army in June 363, mortally wounding Julian in the process.

The larger of the two alcoves houses a bas-relief depicting four figures whose identities have been a source of much debate amongst historians. It is now believed that they depict Shapur II and his successor, Ardeshir II (379–83 CE), with a figure thought to be Mithra standing on a lotus flower. The two Sasanian kings are trampling on the figure of a vanquished foe thought to be the Emperor Julian. It was Ardeshir who ordered these rock carvings alongside one of the main caravan routes of ancient times, with the presence of Shapur and the sacred figure of Mithra designed to demonstrate the legitimacy of his succession, the vanquished Roman emperor underfoot to lend it glory.

★　★　★

The streets of Kermanshah had been deserted when I had left my hotel shortly after arriving in the town. Hardly a soul stirred and all the metal shutters of the shops were pulled down throughout the daylight hours of the fast. I returned several hours later to find the same streets awash with activity. The shutters had been thrown open, various honeyed delicacies were being carefully stacked on stalls or in window displays, industrial vats of *ash* soup were being heated and sweet breads and dates seemed to appear from every angle as shopkeepers braced themselves for the wailing of the evening *azzan* call to prayer, especially sweet to a Muslim's ear in the month of Ramadan, for the hour of prayer signals the setting of the sun and the end of the day's fast.

My wanderings in the heat of the day had been draining, especially so because of my reluctance to eat or drink. Despite being exempt as a traveller, it is disrespectful to break the fast in front of others. I had repeatedly been warned that tempers would be short during Ramadan and such perceived irreverence could lead to a severe beating. As I was on the road for the entirety of the month-long fast, I, for the most part, adhered to its strictures. But while most Muslims rest during its days, my schedule obliged me to be out making the most of the daylight hours. By the time I was ready to settle down for a meal, hungry fasters had cleared out nearly every restaurant and snack bar. Luckily there were street vendors aplenty, barbecuing skewers of liver or corn on the cob, selling pistachios so fresh they still had their skin on and plenty of other Iranian treats that I gorged on before washing them all down with a glass of fresh melon juice.

★   ★   ★

Bisotun is a small, light-industrial town 30 kilometres from Kermanshah. I made my way there by means of a string of *savaris* and a minibus ride with a sinister-looking driver who would have looked more at home in a black cape and armed with a scythe than in his ill-fitting brown trousers and sweat-stained shirt. The passengers also looked fit to be crossing the Styx but in place of their two pieces of silver, this ragged collection of rural antiques handed over a grubby 2,000-*rial* note to their Iranian Charon.

Being left at a crossroads seemingly in the middle of nowhere, I was baffled as to where to go. I had assumed, this being one of the country's major tourist sites, that there would be a sign or at least some visible evidence of a place of major historical interest. As an old man ambled into view, I approached him with a big smile and hands raised in greeting. I asked for directions and his answer was literally startling – he slapped me three times in the face. The first slap was intended as a friendly pat on the cheek but age and faulty sight had thrown his aim and the second blow bent the arm of my glasses and another left my nose smarting. He then grabbed my wrist firmly and dragged me towards the cliff-face I had come to see that lay on the road from the Mesopotamian plain to Ecbatana (modern Hamedan), a road thought to have been in use for more than 10,000 years. My new friend said he would show me all I had come to see. For the next hour or so he revealed all about his erectile shortcomings, feeling the need to animate his pained monologue with frequent, unedifying and wholly unnecessary hand gestures. Having sympathised with his predicament, I insisted he tell me something about the sites I had come to see. With a sweep of his hand he declared, 'These carvings are very old. They were made about one hundred years ago.

And that sitting in the middle is an old shah.' Then, undeterred, he proceeded to bemoan how unsympathetic his young wife – his third, whom he had only recently married – was to the woes of an old man.

The 'one-hundred-years-ago' immense rock carving had in fact been chiselled into the side of the mountain nearly 2,500 years ago. It is arguably the first manifestation of massive political propaganda and certainly the most dramatic expression of barefaced power in the ancient world, dwarfing that of Ardeshir at Tagh-e Bostan. The 'old shah' was Darius I, depicted in this ancient bas-relief being honoured as king by both his subjects before him and by the winged Zoroastrian symbol of the *Fravahar* above his head representing divine accreditation. In the foreground is Gaumata, a Magian priest who spuriously presented himself as Bardiya – son of Cyrus and heir to the Achaemenian throne – who had in fact been surreptitiously slain by his brother Cambyses. As a result partly of the size of the boots he had to fill and partly of incompetent campaigns in Egypt, Cambyses has come to be thought of as the weak link in the Achaemenian dynasty. In one of the most dramatic episodes of early Iranian history, Gaumata, posing as the murdered Bardiya, usurped the throne whilst Cambyses was on what proved to be the last of his ill-fated campaigns in Egypt. The dethroned king died whilst attempting to conquer the African kingdom, leaving the Magian imposter as undisputed ruler. At this point Darius, an Achaemenian but not of Cyrus's direct lineage, burst onto the scene and overthrew Gaumata, claiming the throne as his, declaring: 'The kingdom which had been taken away from our family … I re-established it on its foundation, as before.'[2] Whether these events are historically accurate or whether this was one of the most elaborate propaganda campaigns in history – the 15 metre by 25 metre inscription dominating one of the key ancient trade routes like a giant stone billboard – designed to justify Darius's claim to the throne, we will never know. What we do know is that the rule of Darius I (522–486 BCE) combined imperial expansion with serious state-building and is considered the pinnacle of the Achaemenian dynasty, earning him the moniker 'the Great'.

It was a truly memorable experience to be awestruck by the mighty mountainsides and their 2,500-year-old carvings, history coming to life 100 metres above my head, whilst having a decrepit Don Juan declaring it had been twenty years since he had had any semblance of an erection, 'And probably another ten before that since uunngh …' he said excitedly, ramming his right arm, fist tightly clenched, into the air in an unmistakable gesture of virility.

'Youth is not appreciating what you've got; old age is regretting not having appreciated what you had,' said he, shaking his head dejectedly as he contemplated his lyrical pearl of wisdom. As we parted company he gave me a bawdy smack of the lips farewell, pinched my backside excruciatingly hard and threw in a wrinkled wink for good measure.

★ ★ ★

I left Kermanshah for a day and a night's detour to Khorramabad, the capital of Lorestan province. I could not resist a foray into Lorestan, having been beguiled by Freya Stark's account of her daring archaeological adventures in the region. In the early 1930s Stark left her adopted home of Baghdad, clandestinely crossed the Iranian border with a forged passport and swept through the Lorish mountains in search of buried bronze and hidden gold. Her inspiring book *The Valleys of the Assassins and Other Persian Travels* had painted a picture of wild mountain tribes and cutthroat brigands roaming areas where even the police force of the mighty new shah of the time, Reza Pahlavi, feared to tread. Even today Lors retain their reputation for savagery and banditry, hence my mother's warning that I would be decapitated there. 'A mule track leading into the heart of Luristan from the north,' writes Sir Roger Stevens, 'passes two mountains named Chia Dozdan (the hill of thieves) and Pir-e-Dozd (the old thief [or 'the thieving old man']). "There is no-one like us for stealing in the world," Freya Stark's guide told her proudly; and she describes "their expressive way of sucking their forefinger and holding it up to illustrate the complete destitution in which one is left" after receiving their traditional attentions.'[3]

★ ★ ★

The town of Khorramabad is nestled in the bosom of the Zagros Mountains, dwarfed by dramatic rocky peaks and hemmed in by dark-green rows of firs doing their best to climb the rugged slopes. The town was bigger and more prosperous than I had expected and I was instantly taken by its vivacity. The open-air bazaar was abuzz with black-clad *chadori* women busy with their evening shop, old men pottering aimlessly whilst fingering prayer beads, peddlers offering unbeatable prices 'just for you' and caged chickens clucking pleadingly at passers-by. Younger men were hosing down the pavements in front of their shops and houses to settle down the dust. A dwindling river cut through the lively streets and meandered past the Falak-ol-Aflak fort, originally built in the third century CE by the Sasanian king Shapur I, which to this day keeps a watchful eye over the river valley.

The Lors have their own dialect that, to my untrained ear, resembled Persian much more closely than the Kurdish language, which, despite having been traced back to ancient Persian origins, sounded more guttural and similar to Arabic. The Lors are no newcomers to the Persian table either; their origins can be traced back to the Kassites – an ancient tribe that settled in the region between 4000 and 3000 BCE, coming to prominence in the eighteenth century BCE with a daring attack on Babylonia.

Looks were wild yet refined, hard yet attractive. Young boys had a steely countenance that added to their years and attractive young women strode purposefully through the crowds. I was surprised by the quantity of *manteaux* and fashionable headscarves on parade, not having seen such a concentration of these since Tehran. I soon discovered this was thanks to Lorestan University and its thriving campus. Khorramabad was just one of the many remote towns I visited that housed a recently opened or expanded university campus to cater for the dramatic surge in people seeking higher education. Many of these students hail from Tehran and its suburbs and have started to bring the modern ways and attitudes of the capital to these more conservative areas of the country.

As I reached the entrance to the fort I saw that the gate was padlocked shut. A group of soldiers was lounging on the grass under the shade of a stone wall that spanned the fort's perimeter. I approached them to ask about opening times and was soon ensnared in a long conversation during which all the usual questions were fired at me about my origins. In these parts tourists were enough of a curiosity in themselves, but to have one who looked like an Iranian and spoke Persian but was clearly a foreigner caused quite a stir. In no time a crowd of passers-by had joined the soldiers, swarming around the foreign curiosity. One old man kept prodding me as if to make sure I was present in the flesh. I was surprised to have drawn so much attention so quickly and so inadvertently. It was a bizarre, slightly uncomfortable feeling, being the centre of such scrutiny, but the friendly, fascinated nature of the crowd and the encouragement for the nature of my trip soon had me feeling slightly more at ease.

As was so often the case, the interrogation turned from amusing questions such as 'Can Western women cook?' and 'Is it true they drive as well as the men there?' to some of the more sensitive topics of Western liberalism. The young soldiers were soon asking nervously, between giggles, questions like: 'Do ladies show their hair in the streets?'; 'Is it true that boys and girls kiss in public?'; and 'What else do they do before they get married?' Even though they were conscripts, young men just like me who had been forced into military service and not *Basij* or *Pasdars*, the feared draconian enforcers of Islamic morality, I was reluctant to indulge them too much. I was acutely aware of saying the wrong thing, which, in staunchly conservative provincial towns like this, could land me in hot water.

When eventually released by my interrogators I strolled around town, taken in by the infectious energy of the townspeople going about their daily lives. As with Kurdistan, though, I could sense a distinct tension in the air. With the Kurds it was politics, whereas the Lors simply seemed untamed – as though beneath the veneer of a prosperous, modern town still beat the heart of a fearsome mountain tribe. Here conventions seemed to function as a constraint. Below the surface, I got the impression that every male Lor I came across had the capacity to switch his joviality into a deadly confrontation if slighted or not shown the right respect. These people certainly seemed to have far less time for the restrictions and policing that were taken for granted in other parts of the country. Another passage from Freya Stark kept coming to mind:

> [The tribesman's] treasure is the freedom of his spirit: when he loses that, he loses everything. And if civilization is that state in which the unshackled mind bows voluntarily to Law, freedom and discipline are the two wheels on which it runs. The tribesman does bow to a law of his own, but his apologists must admit that discipline is in him the less developed of the two fundamentals: his freedom is more lawless than it should be. It is, however, genuine; it emancipates his being.[4]

* * *

The following morning I made it to the Late Antiquity-era Falak-ol-Aflak fortress, where construction was started by the Sasanians in 226 CE but which was only completed in its present form more than four centuries later. Its commanding position and towering walls gave it a sense of grandeur not reflected by its interior. Its most intriguing internal feature was a dehumidifying system that the Sasanians had engineered to keep the stone and wood foundations dry. A network of metre-deep trenches runs underneath the fortress, designed to channel air currents that create a dehumidifying effect, and it was for this reason, along with the more usual defensive benefits of an elevated position, that the fortress was built on the highest point of the city.

Access to much of the fortress was limited. As with many buildings of this type, it had been taken over by the local government and was being used simultaneously as office space and as an anthropological museum. What piqued my interest in the museum were the extensive photographs and reconstructions of traditional Lori tribal life, including a three-part model of a traditional wedding. The groom, sporting what looks remarkably like a kimono, waits in the village as the mounted bride is led to him by her father at the head of a procession. Once in the village, she is handed over to the groom amidst a chorus of cheers and festive cries from the crowd. With the wedding ceremony completed, the newlyweds are then escorted to a partitioned circle which the villagers swarm excitedly around whilst the bride and groom do their best to consummate their marriage.

★　★　★

At dawn the following morning, I took a cab to the town's bus terminal to hunt down a *savari* bound for Ilam province, Lorestan's westerly neighbour. I pulled up at the terminal to find it swamped by a large, surly crowd. My cab driver muttered something about Ramadan, heat and short fuses and left me to 'God's will' with a wry smile. Pulling on my backpack, I took a deep breath and stepped into the mêlée of hirsute brawlers just as a scrawny little guy stepped in to break up the fight only to receive a fist square on the jaw. When he picked himself up and shook himself down, he did the only obvious thing: he steamed back into the crowd with flailing fists, attempting to land a few blows of his own.

In the meantime I managed to navigate the throng unscathed and stood on the other side of it, unsure what to do next. For the first time in my travels I had arrived at a town's terminal and not become the subject of squabbles among all the drivers around bidding for my custom. Everyone was so engrossed by the fight that I was left scratching my head, stranded in a sea of unmanned Paykans.

I then spotted a lanky young man watching the whole scene unfold from a distance, perched James Dean-like on the bonnet of his car. His oversized white collar, flared jeans and long, pointed shoes tied in perfectly with the thick, stylised sideburns he was sporting. I sidled over and told him I wanted to go to Ilam. He told me to wait, disappeared into the still agitated crowd and returned a few minutes later with a full complement of passengers.

★   ★   ★

The two-hour drive swept us down into plains and up through rugged mountains. Soft fields of golden yellow, nestled between tree-covered hills, gave way to barren stretches of desiccated earth and jagged rock formations. The road wound around the edge of a ridge that reminded me of a sheep's jaw-bone, complete with craggy teeth. Around the other side of this jaw-bone, about 20 kilometres from Ilam town, we drove past a conical mound that I was later to learn was the scant remains of an ancient fort.

Ilam was smaller, quieter and greyer than I had expected. The town is the capital of the recently formed province of the same name that borders Iraq. It is through Mehran, a border town a short journey from Ilam itself, that a constant stream of pilgrims flows into Iraq and on to the holy cities of Najaf and Karbala that house the tombs of the two most revered Shi'i Imams, Ali and Hossein. My young cab driver laughed when I told him I had come to visit Ilam itself. 'You came all the way from Tehran to visit this graveyard?' was his baffled response. It seemed that only those passing through to Mehran and on with their pilgrimage came to Ilam. He dropped me off outside a surprisingly smart hotel in which the receptionist took one look at my scruffy appearance and my backpack with its array of items dangling from it and, before I had even managed to utter a greeting, informed me there were no rooms available. She directed me to a 'more suitable' choice of accommodation. This turned out to be a derelict building with a dilapidated neon sign hanging limply on its side. Through the broken front door held up by an uninviting padlock, I could see a floor carpeted with bottles, cans, crisp packets, syringes and all the other detritus of contemporary urban life. I was wondering whether this really was the only other place in town or whether the receptionist had taken one look at me and assumed I was destitute when a passer-by stopped to tell me that there was one other hotel just around the corner. I promptly headed there and managed to get a comfortable, if overpriced room (steeper prices are a norm on pilgrimage routes and cannot be avoided). The hotel had that air of decrepit grandeur that many of Iran's once fine hotels now languish in.

I asked the receptionist what there was to see in town. He looked at his colleague and they both laughed. When I asked the same question of the scruffy man sitting by the door wearing what was once a white coat – it would be too generous to call him the doorman – he eagerly pointed me towards the park. This turned out to be a concrete square with a couple of grassy banks, a few dusty benches and the obligatory Islamic sculpture of Qur'anic verse that adorns most squares, roundabouts and open spaces in Iran. Unmoved, I continued my walk around town determined to find something to redeem its reputation and self-esteem. It proved difficult. The town of Ilam was as grey and drab as the weather that day, which did not help my mood. I trudged around gloomily until I was once again lost. There is no better way of coming to terms with a town or city than to simply be swallowed up by it. As the strange roads twist and turn in on themselves, parts of the labyrinth start to become recognisable; streets and landmarks slowly fit together like pieces of a vast urban puzzle.

A rudderless wander proved the ideal tonic for my funk and I was soon contentedly observing the characteristics and contradictions of Ilam town. Poverty, provinciality and pilgrims seemed to dominate, yet there was verve about the youth. The boys outdid each other with their various gelled hairstyles as they strutted with purpose through garbage-filled streets. Young women darted smouldering glances from beneath chadors, unblushingly holding gazes and flashing provocative smiles. So, fresh young blood did flow through the greying veins of Ilam. The streets of Tehran are ablaze with youthful energy but there is something far more telling, more exciting about a smouldering look from under a provincial chador; it speaks volumes more than the cosmetic-caked faces and tight *manteaux* of the capital.

★ ★ ★

I was drawn into an internet café by the sound of cheering. A young lad of no more than fifteen was peering at a computer screen through an enormous pair of glasses held together by masking tape. A group of men in their late twenties and early thirties swarmed around him goading him on. As I attempted to peer over the huddle, I felt a hand on my shoulder. 'This guy is a genius!' said a stranger as I was drawn into the crowd. The bespectacled kid had bypassed the government firewall blocking access to any websites deemed unsuitable for a good Muslim. On one side of the screen I could see the gyrations of Shakira in her latest music video and on the other the kid was exchanging lewd quips with a young woman in Canada. His rudimentary grasp of English was not hindering him in getting his point across.

The influence of technology on Iranian society is phenomenal. Nearly every house now has a television, even in small rural communities – and caves, as in Kandovan. Many of these have satellite dishes wired into them. Mobile phones, digital cameras and MP3 players have all played their part in enabling the computer-literate youth of today to reclaim some of the social freedoms denied them these past thirty years and for which they have been pining. Nothing, though, can compare with the explosion of the internet onto the Iranian scene, undoubtedly the most influential event in the country's history since the Islamic Revolution.

Despite governmental restrictions, the internet is an uncontrollable source of global information and culture, and the myriad social networks and chat rooms provide a platform for the social life which has until recently eluded the youth of Iran. It was no surprise to learn that Iranians are among the most frequent users of chat rooms on the planet. The significance of the internet, and more specifically social media, in Iran's struggle for reform was most effectively highlighted by the so-called 'Twitter Revolution' that followed the 2009 elections. Even so, the use of the internet as a political vehicle is still not being maximised either by opponents or supporters of the regime despite the ever-growing number of blogs.

*   *   *

The following morning I went in search of the Ministry of Culture of the Province of Ilam. The Ministry turned out to be two partitioned desks side by side in a ramshackle building some twenty minutes' walk from my lodgings. I was greeted by a beaming Lori woman, delighted that an actual tourist had turned up. With the fierce features of a tribal princess, her aquiline nose framed by strong arched eyebrows and darting eyes, she fired out her words so quickly I was barely able to decipher them. Before I had a chance to ask her to repeat herself a little more slowly, she had thrown a selection of posters and pamphlets into my outstretched arms and sent me on my way. There was, I discovered, a whole host of historical sites and points of beauty in Ilam. All, though, were a considerable drive away from town and there were no organised tours. Dropping pamphlets with every other step, spilling posters as I bent to pick them up, I made my way back to the hotel to try and digest the barrage of information that I had been assaulted with. As I stood at a crossroads waiting for a break in the flow of traffic, a cab driver caught my eye and I spontaneously hopped into his rusty red Paykan.

'Hello, sir, *khaste nabashi*,' I said. This literally means 'may you not be fatigued' but conveys a conventional politeness more like 'I hope you're having a nice day'. 'Could you take me to the dam or the water-fall please?'

'*Ghorbane shoma.*' Literally, 'I'm willing to sacrifice myself for you' but in reality something closer to 'Yes, if you like'. 'The dam is over 30 kilometres away. The waterfall is another 25 or so beyond that.'

We negotiated a price for the trip to the dam and decided to take it from there. That was about as far as our conversation stretched until we were a good fifteen kilometres out of town and in the middle of nowhere on a dirt track winding into the deserted foothills, when the cab driver suddenly slammed on the brakes and sent my posters and pamphlets flying off my lap. He turned to me with an odd look.

'You know you really shouldn't hop into a cab with just anyone and trust them to drive you out into the middle of nowhere. Half the cab drivers in town would cut your throat and leave you out here for little more than your cab fare.'

'So which half do you belong to?' I countered nervously.

This bizarre exchange was the start of one of the most fascinating encounters of my travels. It turned out that my cab driver was a Kurd who happened to double as the town historian. He gave a brief but obviously well-informed synopsis of Ilam's history, explaining that the original settlers in the fourth millennium BCE had split from a lesser Lori tribe to inhabit the other side of a mountain that now straddles the provincial border, eventually making their way down to what is now Ilam town. He listed the four previous names of the town, the various feuds that made up its history right up to the Revolution. He recounted how the townspeople fled to the mountains where they camped for years during the war with Iraq, watching as bombs rained down on their homes, reducing them to dust and rubble. He informed me that the conical mound I had spotted just outside the town was in fact a fort known as the *Ghaleh Ghiran*, lengthily expounding a theory of twin forts and the various systems of defence used against maraud-ing tribes. He recounted historical fables involving local rulers I had not come across, donkeys ringing bells and magic trees. All this he did eloquently and passionately.

As he span out his information, he suddenly switched from history to the present without a second's respite, pouring advice on me about life, my project, marriage and children. He explained to me the importance of seeing things through to their completion using the allegory of a pomegranate tree. I followed him down this path for a while only to lose him completely when, five minutes into his musings, he was comparing the price of pomegranates with the fictitious stall-owner next door in an imaginary bazaar. Though I had lost track of his metaphors and allusions I was charmed by the man and grateful for his company. I reflected on my good fortune thus far on my trip, including such chance encounters. 'You are a good person trying to do a good thing. Providence is smiling on you,' he pronounced. Whether providence or serendipity, I was certainly thankful for it.

We wound our way along a dusty road and through some barren hillsides. The car strained its way up a final climb, barely making it to the peak. At the top of the hill we stopped, to give the engine a break as much as to take in the breathtaking view. Opposite was the dam nestled in the folds of a series of cliffs straight from a lunar landscape, perfectly reflected in the cyan-coloured water. My new friend relished the chance to reel off countless statistics about the dam. Seeing my bewildered expression, he replied, 'I should know all this. I spent four years working on it.'

This man's pride in his hometown was touching. 'Ilam is a good town, a traditional town, a religious town,' he said furrowing his brows. 'It has kept its values when the rest of the country is becoming an increasingly alien place. The women here all keep the chador and their modesty. I have heard all about the girls in Tehran, may God have mercy on their souls.' I asked about the young blood I had seen in town. 'We have four universities now. The two big ones have brought in 6,000 new students this year alone.' He stressed, above all else, the importance of history and cultural awareness. To this end he was pleased that such a fast-growing number of the youth attended university but pointed out the fact that traditional artistry and handicrafts were suffering as a result, as was rural life in general. 'There are not enough jobs for all these graduates and someone with a university degree is not going to sit down and make carpets or weave baskets for a living. It is below their expectations, below their dignity. All of these traditional skills will die out in a generation and with them a large part of our heritage.'

This sudden increase in further education has had many a knock-on effect on Iranian society. It has certainly contributed to the rapid urbanisation of the country, leaving rural communities made up entirely of children and elders struggling to cope with the daily strains of agricultural life. This gravitation towards urban centres began with the last shah's failed White Revolution, in which land was taken from the landowning elite and redistributed to the farmers themselves. Although well intentioned, this was a myopic move destined to fail. Without money the newly propertied farmers were unable to effectively farm their land, so many of them ended up selling their plots back to the landowners and taking the money to town with them. With such an unbalanced population, the jobs-to-graduates ratio is worsening by the year, creating both unemployment and a brain drain as the best students stream abroad in search of better opportunities.

The desire to flee to *kharej* (abroad) is endemic in Iranian society. Anywhere outside Iran is viewed as the Promised Land where all woes magically disappear. This false image is perpetuated by the myriad American television shows and Western movies beamed into households by satellite television. So caught up in the idealised world outside Iran are they, full of its apparent freedoms and opportunities, that Iranians automatically dismiss the world they live in. This attitude even stretches to consumerism. *'Kharejiye ya Irooniye?'*: is it foreign or Iranian, they ask of everything from hairbrushes to headache pills. An obvious question in a culture in which everything Iranian is deemed second class.

Conversation with my historian-driver eventually and inevitably turned to life in England. He listened carefully to what I had to say about the place: security, stability, a pleasant, predictable life. He looked sceptical. 'They say it rains a lot there and everything is expensive. You are Iranian. You belong here. You have family here. This is your country.'

Chapter Thirteen

I rumbled away from Ilam in a battered old Mercedes bus heading for Ahvaz but hopped out at a crossroads to await a lift to Shush. Shush is a small town in Khuzestan province roughly 200 kilometres from Ahvaz, the provincial capital and ultimate destination of the bus. Khuzestan is famous for and positively dripping with two things: history and oil. It has been the capital of key civilisations stretching back some six millennia that we know of and almost certainly more. The first traces of habitation in the region have been dated even earlier, to 7000 BCE. It is believed that a lost civilisation going back to the fourth millennium BCE developed the area, making it one of the oldest known settlements in the world. In the middle of the third millennium BCE Shush, or Susa as it was known in the ancient world, became the capital of the Elamites, who conquered much of Babylonia at the height of their powers in the second millennium BCE. The renowned biblical king of Babylon, Nebuchadnezzar I (*c.* 1126–1103 BCE), defeated the waning Elamite civilisation in the twelfth century BCE, plundering Susa's riches – most notably the statue of the Babylonian sun god Marduk that had been taken from its homeland during earlier Elamite conquests. Susa was again sacked and almost completely destroyed by the Assyrian king Ashurbanipal between 645 and 640 BCE, just prior to the time that the biblical figures Daniel and Nehemiah lived in the city during the Babylonian captivity of Judah. The ancient city's fortunes were revived in the following century by Cyrus the Great (*c.* 559–529 BCE) and his son Cambyses II (529–522 BCE) in turn. After Cambyses's death, Darius I chose Susa as the site of his winter palace. The city saw Alexander and his successors the Seleucids come and go, enjoyed a renaissance under the Sasanians, who ruled Persia between the third century BCE and the seventh century CE, and was again sacked by the invading Arab armies marching under the banner of Islam in 638 CE. Susa was again rebuilt and enjoyed a bout of relative peace for a few hundred years only to be lost in the murky tracts of time after Genghis Khan swept through the region in a grim wave of destruction and bloodshed in the thirteenth century, making it another one of the many victims of the Mongol invasions that devastated Iran and many other parts of the Middle East.

For centuries the great ancient capital of Susa lay buried, forgotten by one and all until just over 150 years ago when a British archaeologist by the name of W.K. Loftus unearthed the remains of the lost city in 1852. The archaeological baton was then passed to the ever-fastidious French, who constructed the Château de Morgan, a fortress that still lords over the small town, behind whose sturdy walls they could carry on their work unperturbed by the wild tribesmen beyond. Modern-day Shush has since re-emerged as a small town thriving from tourism and the agricultural produce of its fertile land.

Oil had long been known to exist in the region, since it was often seen to seep to the ground's surface. Occasionally, when ignited, it would provide a bed of gentle flames, which was always regarded as an auspicious sign by Zoroastrian priests and worshipers, who revered light and fire as a sign of probity and good. This surface oil would often be harvested and used by Zoroastrian priests for ceremonial purposes, providing their temples with light and the symbolic flame which lay at the heart of their religion. But it was not until the turn of the twentieth century and the industrial world's sudden and unquenchable thirst for it that oil began to play such a fundamental role in the economic and political fortunes of Iran.

It was in Khuzestan province that the fateful discovery of oil was made by a British entrepreneur named William Knox D'Arcy in 1908. D'Arcy had negotiated an exclusive sixty-year concession to explore and obtain Iran's minerals which, after several false starts, had resulted in oil being struck at Masjed-e Soleiman in Khuzestan. The country was to be for ever changed by this discovery. Within a year the Anglo-Persian Oil Company (APOC) was formed and was to define Iran's relations with Britain and the rest of the world for nearly half a century, until the nationalisation of Iran's oil industry in 1951. This discovery of what would prove to be one of the largest oil reserves on the planet was particularly significant to the British government in the early 1900s, coinciding as it did with the Royal Navy's planned conversion of its fleet from coal to oil. With World War I looming, a steady supply of Iranian oil was vital to British interests.

★ ★ ★

The issue of oil has played such an important part in Iran's modern history that it is worth providing some further explanation of how this has come about.

By the end of the nineteenth century and into the early twentieth century, a weak and inept Qajar-ruled Iran had collided with the expansionist interests of the British Empire, which, above all in this region, felt the need to safeguard access to the jewel in its imperial crown – India. For the British, therefore, it was crucial to exercise some degree of control over Iran without the added burden of actual administrative responsibility. They achieved this by insinuating their influence through inducements, flattery and outright payments to the Iranian court and the country's elite. This indirect control and exercise of power which the British achieved in Iran brought with it added economic and strategic benefits for them.

A string of concessions and renegotiated agreements – starting with a grant to Baron Julius de Reuter in 1872 by Naser al-Din Shah and followed by another grant by the Qajar shah's successor, Mozaffar al-Din Shah, to D'Arcy – culminated in the stand-off between Reza Shah and the British government in June 1932 when the APOC famously announced that the Iranian government's royalties for the oil exported in the previous year totalled £366,782 while APOC paid the British government close to £1,000,000 in income tax alone for the same period. The result was another renegotiation of the oil concession, this time somewhat more favourable to Iran.

From this point Iran was, under Reza Shah, on a march towards modernity. With ambitious plans for agricultural and industrial development launched in the late 1940s, revenues from the oil industry once again became a bugbear for the Iranian government. This prompted the *Majles* (parliament) to demand improved concessions, looking for a fifty-fifty profit-share with the now renamed Anglo-Iranian Oil Company (AIOC). The more the AIOC held out, the stronger nationalist feeling grew, inspired in part by Dr Mohammad Mossadegh and the intransigent stance the veteran politician took on the matter. Under growing pressure, the AIOC finally agreed to the fifty-fifty profit-share in February 1951 but by this stage Mossadegh and the wave of nationalist feeling had grown so strong that one month later, on 15 March 1951, the *Majles* voted to nationalise the Iranian oil industry. Shortly afterwards, Mohammad Reza Shah, who had two years earlier replaced his father on the Pahlavi throne, grudgingly named Mossadegh Prime Minister of Iran.

The excitement and fervour at this apparent victory were to be short-lived. Britain pulled its technicians out of the country and enforced a global ban on Iranian oil. Iran's economy was hit hard, and even though the AIOC once again agreed to improve its deal with Iran, in large part thanks to pressure from the oil-hungry US government, Mossadegh and the *Majles* felt that they had the winning hand and held out for an even better offer. Mossadegh's hard-line stance on this issue was a challenge to the young Shah, whose relationship with the eccentric Prime Minister had been fractious from the outset. When, in 1952, Mohammad Reza Shah refused Mossadegh's demands for what amounted to more power, the Prime Minister resigned, prompting riots to break out. Mossadegh was soon, once again, reluctantly reinstated by the Shah.

On 3 August 1953, prompted by a spate of parliamentary resignations, Mossadegh dissolved the *Majles*. The US government, who until this point had encouraged (if not wholeheartedly supported) Iran's nationalist movement, now under the presidency of Dwight D. Eisenhower and with growing fear of the spread of Soviet influence, became suspicious of Mossadegh and his relationship with the communist *Tudeh* Party, suspicions fanned by Britain, which much resented the nationalisation of its Iranian oil interests. Encouraged by Britain and aided by the USA in the shape of CIA operative Kermit Roosevelt, the emboldened Shah attempted to remove Mossadegh with a military coup, replacing him with General Fazlollah Zahedi. Mossadegh refused to step down and the coup seemed to have failed. The Shah fled the country, first over the border to Iraq and then on to Italy. But in his absence, thanks in large part to the efforts of Kermit Roosevelt, whose operatives liberally dispensed dollars in central Tehran, pro-Shah troops rallied and support for the exiled monarch grew. On 19 August 1953, after street fighting and some thuggery on all sides, Mossadegh's supporters were defeated and the Prime Minister was arrested, tried in a military court and banished to his country estate until his death in 1967. The Shah was returned to the throne, accompanied by Major General Norman Schwarzkopf Sr (father of General 'Stormin'' Norman Schwarzkopf Jr, who nearly forty years later became commander of the American and Allied troops which invaded Iraq in the first Persian Gulf War of 1991). Schwarzkopf Sr, who had had earlier experience in Iran training the Iranian military, had many contacts among the Shah's generals and was seen as a useful support in the Shah's attempts to reassert his authority. His brief included the training of an effective security force that came to be known as SAVAK, Mohammad Reza Shah's infamous secret police. On 19 September 1954, a Consortium Oil Agreement was signed and shortly ratified by the *Majles*, now firmly controlled by the Shah's supporters. Shares of the consortium were split between a number of international oil companies – 40 per cent of which were held by the AIOC, now rebranded as BP – including Royal Dutch Shell, the Compagnie Française des Pétroles and five American oil companies. The agreement saw, for the first time, equal profit-sharing between the oil companies and the host government. This prompted the economic boom that was to see Iran flourish for the next twenty-odd years. It also resulted in Iran becoming a focal point of international attention.

★ ★ ★

As I sat at the lonely crossroads waiting for a ride to Shush, I watched the sun disappear behind green fields of sugar cane swaying gently in the breeze as a dust devil swirled its way down the road when, as if out of nowhere, a maroon Peugeot 405 crunched to a halt beside me. The window wound down smoothly with its electric buzz.

'Cyrus?'

'Yes.'

'What you waiting for then? Get in.'

I got up off of my dusty backpack, slung it onto the back seat and climbed into the car.

'I am Dinarvand, Mostafa Dinarvand.' A big smile on top of a lumbering physique welcomed me to Shush from behind clouds of cigarette smoke. Mr Dinarvand, another person I had been put in touch with by a friend in Tehran, was an agricultural engineer who managed the vast fields of corn, sugar cane and cucumber in the area.

When I first contacted Mr Dinarvand from Tehran and again from Khorramabad a couple of days before my arrival, I was sceptical that he would show up at all but here he was, greeting me like a long-lost brother. When I had spoken to him on the phone he had agreed to help me find a hostel for the night prior to my departure for Haft Tappeh the next day. Now that I was in his car he would have none of it. This, so I was beginning to realise, was not the Iranian way.

'You are staying with us.'

'But I thought we agreed I would stay at a hostel?'

'Hostel? We never spoke of any hostel. There is no hostel!' The obstinacy and determination behind Iranian hospitality can at times be quite trying. But when we arrived at Mr Dinarvand's house and I was shown to my clean and attractive room with its shower, air-conditioning, fresh towels and new bar of soap, I was quite happy that this aspect of the national character was still very much intact. Mr Dinarvand's family consisted of his wife – demure, headscarved, seemingly shy – and two boys, eight and ten – charming, polite, in awe of their father and respectful to their mother.

Their home was a typical middle-class Iranian household. The house itself was a bungalow with a smallish, paved garden/courtyard with a few rows of rose-beds and large pots of jasmine, all encircling a small pond in the centre. Inside, floors were covered by large, overlapping Persian carpets. A reception room was equipped with enough seats to accommodate the frequent onslaught of relatives and other visitors. A few stiff, rectangular cushions covered in a firm, deep-red, floral-patterned material were tidily leaning against the wall as backrests for the many Iranians more comfortable sitting on the floor. Tables were adorned with bowls filled with nuts, fruit and various sorts of local confectionery, all meticulously arranged next to small vases of fresh flowers. The centre-piece of the house was a large sitting-room whose focal point was a widescreen LCD television. Opposite were ranged two large, heavily stuffed sofas. A ceiling fan whirred noiselessly above. Next to the television sat a hand-carved silver frame with an oversized photo-portrait of the man of the house, his expression thoughtful and earnest. The message was clear: the patriarch rules. A small office lay just off the sitting room, equipped with computer, fax machine and the rest. The kitchen and bedrooms lay behind a door that remained shut to guests – the inner core of the house was private.

The Dinarvands seemed to be the model of a perfect Iranian family: the working father, the provider; always impeccably turned out with a straight parting and smart shirt tucked into chinos held up by a black leather belt as his role of *mohandess* (engineer) required. Certain professions are held in great esteem in Iran; engineers, architects and doctors being the most notable. They are so respected that even their wives are granted the title of 'Mrs Engineer'. The obedient, well-mannered and helpful young boys and the beaming mother, the house-manager of the family – her headscarf a constant, usually backstage busying herself with domestic chores – all functioned in harmony with one another, all impeccably mannered, constantly hospitable and irrepressibly good company. I was touched by the fuss they made over me on the first night, scurrying around dismantling and reassembling a bed and waiting on Mr Dinarvand and me as we – the men of the house – ate dinner *tête-à-tête*.

★ ★ ★

My host loaded his car with fresh dates and a thermos of piping-hot tea, bundled me in too and, with a crick of the neck – pulling his sizeable head first left and then right with his palms – set off for a tour of the local sights. He slid a cassette into its berth in the car stereo with an out-stretched finger. 'Shajarian,' Mr Dinarvand announced as a dreamy look came over his face. The first gentle strums of the *santour* (a hammered dulcimer with seventy-two strings) swept through the car before the voice of Shajarian (the master of Persian classical singing, known only by his last name) burst upon us with his melancholy dirge, which in many an Iranian can produce a trance-like response where memories of lost love, sadness and the iniquities of life swell over the listener. The distant look in Mr Dinarvand's expression as he drove his car at full speed did not inspire much confidence in Shajarian's influence on driving, but this reverie was soon brought to an abrupt end. As we hurtled past a police checkpoint the officers gave chase, lights flashing and sirens wailing in competition with Shajarian. When we finally stopped, two officers strode over and Mr Dinarvand slid down his window.

'What can I do for you, *jenab sarhang* [Excellency colonel]?' In fact the officer was only a lieutenant but Iranians grant an automatic promo-tion to any official they have dealings with – a form of flattery to help oil the discussion.

'Brother,' said the officer, 'aren't you a Muslim? I saw you smok-ing just now and I can smell the fumes in the car. Don't you know it's Ramadan?'

'Excellency colonel, what can I say? I have promised my wife I would stop smoking but I'm having difficulty and on this glorious day I could resist no more.' As he was speaking, Mr Dinarvand reached into his trouser pocket, discreetly slid out a bank note and, with great expertise, folded it neatly with the fingers of one hand which he lifted through the car window as if to shake hands with the officer.

Looking Mr Dinarvand straight in the eye, the man said, 'Brother, it is as well you listen to your wife and to the laws of God,' at which point he shook Mr Dinarvand's hand, saying 'God be with you,' and strode back to his car. Mr Dinarvand gripped the steering-wheel with his now empty hand, looked at me with a shrug and drove off as Shajarian's voice again filled the car – only now a couple of notches quieter.

This episode struck me as somewhat incongruous with the values that the month of fasting promoted. Mr Dinarvand was not a fervently pious man but he was a believer and a respecter of religious doctrine. His bendable moral boundaries – including slipping a little bribe to the officer – provided yet another example of the flexibility of the Iranian attitude towards religion. My host took part in the fast, though out of politeness he occasionally broke it for my benefit. He prayed regularly, brought his children up as good Muslims – even banning them from the Dubai cable channels he had beamed to his large television, deeming American sitcoms and music videos a corrupting influence – yet without a second thought he smoked constantly through the month's fast. This, in his eyes, did not make him any less devout. Islam is a religion of total surrender, there is no room for compromise, yet Iranians and their philosophical nature seem to have incorporated the idea that, as long as one's heart is pure and one's intentions good, little indiscretions are immaterial. Here again, it is Iran's pre-Islamic past that seems to provide the answer. This malleable outlook which rejects the dogmatism often found elsewhere in the Islamic world is directly traceable to the three principles of 'good thoughts, good words and good deeds' championed by Zoroaster.

* * *

As we made our way towards Chogha Zanbil we drove through endless fields of sugar cane, cultivated here since 226 CE, and past a run-down factory. 'Sugar factory,' said Mr Dinarvand in his laconic manner. 'Closing down. Government imports cheaper sugar from Cuba and India. First sugar factory in Iran. Shame. Shame. Seven thousand locals worked in these fields, in this factory. Many are now without work or money. Two-thirds of the sugar cane sits there, wasting away. Shame. Other sugar-producing regions, they grow beet, not cane sugar.' This was a complaint that I had heard often – produce was being neglected for cheaper foreign options, slowly killing off local industries.

Beyond the sugar fields lies Chogha Zanbil, a city built around 1250 BCE by the Elamite king of the Anshanite dynasty, Untash-Napirisha (1260–1235 BCE). The city is built around what is now widely recognised as the largest and best-preserved ziggurat in the world. The ziggurat, from the Akkadian word *zaqaru*, meaning to build high or upwards, is thought to be the first effort of mankind's to reach up to the heavens through architecture; these 'earthly towers reaching up toward the sky to mingle with the divine towers of Heaven' were an important step in our spiritual evolution. 'It was the permanent office of architecture, both physically and symbolically, to bridge the awesome gap between the material world and the heavens', writes Dr Arthur Upham Pope, widely regarded as the foremost expert on ancient Iranian architecture.[1] The ancient city, comprising an area of roughly 100 hectares, housed eleven temples and various palace complexes under which a number of tombs have been discovered.

The ziggurat itself, a stepped, pyramid-shaped temple that 'in form and meaning represent the mountain',[2] is built of mud bricks, 5,760 of which are covered in cuneiform script – the world's first written alphabet. These primitive bricks stand as firm as the day they were made nearly 3,300 years ago, glorifying the great god Inshushinak and defying time and the elements. The temple was originally excavated by the French archaeologist Dr Roman Ghirshman in the 1950s and 60s. It consists of five tiers reaching a combined height of over 50 metres. The individual tiers do not sit one on top of the other, but are each built from the ground up with each inner tier becoming progressively taller. Although some of these tiers have collapsed in on themselves, they have not affected the other tiers. The fifth and tallest tier of this extraordinary structure, still largely intact, is thought to have housed an altar on which ritual sacrifices were made to Inshushinak.

★ ★ ★

As we trundled along on the dirt track to Chogha Zanbil, the car's dusty trail had us coughing and spluttering despite closed windows and a straining air-conditioner. Eventually a metal shack appeared in the midday haze, standing lonely and decrepit in the desolate wilderness. A single bony hand drooped out of an opening that had once been a window, fingering a string of turquoise prayer beads. A profusely perspiring man sat staring at us through large, lightly tinted glasses. This was the guardian of Chogha Zanbil and the guide for any visitors who happened to show up. He seemed less than enthused to see us. In the time-honoured Iranian way, Mr Dinarvand asked after the man's health and the health of his family. In the ensuing conversation, he pointed to me and said this young Iranian had just returned from *farang* (abroad), anxious to see all the glorious sights in his country and how fortunate we all were to benefit from such dedicated and learned men as he who were able to hand down our rich history from generation to generation.

The man beamed and said, no, it was nothing. He was only doing his humble duty as an Iranian and the keeper of knowledge. By then we were out of the car and Mr Dinarvand was giving the man the customary handshake. When the man felt the folded note, he took it and smilingly handed it back. Mr Dinarvand then laughed and said, 'But we are friends, you and I. How can you do this to me?' Thrusting the note into the man's shirt pocket, he added a final, 'Let's hear no more of this!' The man gave the sheepish smile customary for such occasions and invoked God, the Prophet and the Twelve Imams to grant prosperity and health to Mr Dinarvand and of course to the young man who had come all the way from abroad to be here today.

With these rituals out of the way, our VIP tour of the complex could begin. Clambering over the ancient bricks themselves, our guide passionately recounted fact after fact: more than 4 kilometres of wall protected the city; it housed some of the oldest standing arches in the world; possibly the first ever water-purification device using limestone as a filter; the underground vaults, unusually for that period, contained only one body each; there was evidence of cremation as a means of disposing of the deceased. Processions came to life with frantic hand-waving as we were drawn around the four corners of the temple, through the main gateway once guarded by winged griffins and bulls, and up the main processional staircase. From the top of the structure where the sacrificial altar had once stood, the River Dez could be seen arcing towards the ancient city. Fields of wheat, sugar and corn stretched off into the horizon, disappearing in a shimmering haze as the relentless heat rose up from the scorched earth below. It may have been autumn but it was still well into the forties in this, the hottest region of a hot country.

That such an ancient monument was so well preserved after more than three millennia was astounding: the sturdy stone door-hinges perfectly intact; the cuneiform script of the adobe bricks and the imprint left by the scampering foot of a young boy as the clay floor was hardening in the sun all those centuries ago both still perfectly clear. This, coupled with the guide's passion for the site, made it hard not to feel humbled in the presence of such antiquity.

★ ★ ★

From Chogha Zanbil we drove on to Haft Tappeh, meaning 'seven hills'. In fact, there are fourteen mounds that rise gently above the surface of the plain on which they sit, the largest of which is about 17 metres in height. Underneath these hills are the ruins and archaeological treasures of another ancient Elamite city still waiting to be discovered. The Elamite civilisation dates from *c.* 2700 BCE to 640 BCE. The architectural remains excavated so far date this particular city at Haft Tappeh to the period between 1505 BCE and 1350 BCE, a period in Elamite history about which very little had been known until the discovery of this site. These ruins were discovered under one of the many sugar plantations of the region when a baked brick wall was unwittingly uncovered during the construction of a new road. Excavation commenced shortly after, in 1965. A step trench has revealed twelve archaeological levels, the first of which dates back as far as the sixth millennium BCE.

To date, finds include the tomb of the Elamite king Tepti-Ahar, constructed in the fifteenth century BCE, that boasts the oldest standing arch in Iran and – according to a dusty placard next to it – the world. The form and design of the arch is more primitive than those found at Chogha Zanbil, which were constructed at least 150 years later. Stone tablets with cuneiform script, some of suspected Babylonian origin, have given archaeologists vital insights into the workings of this period in Elamite history, and one of the most intriguing discoveries is that of an artists' workshop with a large number of arrowheads and other bronze items, bowls with dried plants and the sawn skeleton of an elephant.

I clambered down into an opening in the thatching covering a trench (early excavations had damaged the site, so many of the trenches have been filled with clay to prevent further damage), intrigued by what I might find. Lowering myself into a crypt-like chamber, I tried to imagine the solemn scenes as the body of an Elamite king was lowered ceremoniously into it. My feet had barely touched the earth inside when a growing buzz reverberated around the gloomy chamber. My first thought was that the intrusion had unleashed an ancient curse like those said to guard the tombs of the Egyptian Pharaohs, but then I suddenly recognised the noise and beat a hasty retreat, chased out of the opening by a swarm of very large, very angry hornets.

'An omen,' said my host, mopping the nape of his neck with an already sodden handkerchief. 'Too hot. Let's go home and eat.'

★ ★ ★

In the evening Mr Dinarvand took me to see a friend of his, a one-eyed Arab dressed in an airy white *deshdash*, a *chafieh* coiled around his head. 'Khuzestan's population is about fifty-fifty Lor and Arab. I am a Lor, he is Arab.'

'I am Arab. An Iraqi,' confirmed Abu Hassan, my new acquaintance, in a thick, guttural accent. 'I have lived here since the Gulf War. It is safer here.' Official statistics show Arabs as making up some 2 per cent of the population of Iran, roughly 1.5 million people, with close to a quarter of the population of Khuzestan being of Arab ethnicity. Some were forcibly settled here as long ago as the fourth century CE by the Sasanian king Shapur II after his successful campaign against coastal raiders from Bahrain, but many more like my new acquaintance have fled over the border in recent times to escape the wars and instability that have plagued Iraq in the last quarter of a century.

We made ourselves at home on the carpeted floor and were handed steaming tea from a samovar in the corner of the room. Soon a *ghalyan* appeared in the hands of a young man. 'My son,' said Abu Hassan grabbing the shorn head of this waif-like boy as, with his other hand, he fished out a couple of pieces of charcoal from the *manghal* brazier we were sitting around and placed them on the foil-covered bowl of the water-pipe. 'How long is our friend staying in Shush?' enquired Abu Hassan between thick billows of scented smoke.

'Until I let him go,' Mr Dinarvand grinned at me. One must be released from true Iranian hospitality. I was then subjected to the usual interrogation on *kharej* (abroad): freedoms and constraints, the cost of living, alcohol, the education system and, invariably, sexual relations. Utter disbelief swept across both faces, all three eyes almost popping out of their respective sockets when, having been more frank than usual with my responses, I informed them that unmarried sixteen-year-old couples would sometimes sleep together under the roof of consenting parents. I was worried that my comfortable surroundings had lulled me into a terrible *faux pas*. For all the wonder and esteem with which many from this part of the world regard

Western culture, to a provincial Iranian Muslim father certain aspects of the West remain intolerably crude, unthinkable even, and I had inadvertently stumbled upon one.

Sexual exploits at university got the nod from both men, provided, of course, protection was used. I had been continually surprised by the omnipresence of our little latex friends since first setting foot in the country – a country with severe laws against extra-marital intercourse. Not only were they spilling off the shelves of pharmacies, the full spectrum of shapes, sizes and savours were also readily available in most grocery stores. Age was not the concern, nor, I discovered, was the sexual act itself. What my two curious counterparts had been so taken aback by was the fact that parents would happily consent to this. 'So it's fine for it to happen as long as it's without the knowledge of the parent?' I asked trying to pin down moral boundaries.

'If a son is caught in this situation he brings shame on himself. If a father is complicit in the act he disgraces his whole family, his ancestry. People get stoned for this sort of thing here, you know. It is no laughing matter.'

★ ★ ★

Later that evening we returned to Mr Dinarvand's for dinner, where we caught the second half of a weight-lifting contest in which Hossein Rezazadeh, the veritable Iranian man-mountain, effortlessly wiped the floor with his competition, being rewarded with three gold medals to add to his already impressive haul. The medals hung from his ample neck as though punctuating the '*Ya Abolfazl*' emblazoned across his vast, barrel chest, thus invoking the memory of a holy martyr of Karbala, which for all pious Shi'a was bound to provide added strength and divine favour. This ogre Rezazadeh was my age, could lift nearly four of me clean over his head and probably eat two of me for dinner. In a land filled with great pride for its *pahlavan* (hero-champion) heritage, inspired by the great Rostam figure of Persian mythology, this extraordinary young *shirmard* (lion-man) was amassing quite a following.

The following morning progressed at the leisurely pace dictated by the searing temperatures of the south. My ever-gracious host took me to a museum that proudly but blandly displayed the heritage of Iran. Dusty glass cases were strewn with various archaeological findings dating from the Sasanian era (224–651 CE) right back to the Proto-Elamites (*c.* 3200–2700 BCE) and beyond to nameless lost civilisations. Many of the wares from the Achaemenian Empire (550–330 BCE) seemed immaculately well preserved, especially the glazed tiles that once adorned Darius the Great's palace at Susa.

Lorestan bronzes sat dull, dusty and brooding in their display cases: tools, weapons, animal and human depictions superbly wrought all those millennia ago. My mind tried to picture Lori warriors, famed for their horsemanship (Freya Stark found evidence that suggests a tradition of Lori warriors being buried with their horses), charging their steeds at the advancing Elamite Army, or a warrior of Akkad from Mesopotamia, further west, firing the very bronze arrow-tip in front of me at his Elamite enemy.

Various bowls, plates, jars and necklaces were on display; some, according to the tatty scraps of paper in front of them, dated back nearly seven millennia. What stood out most was a simple earthenware mug with a handle. By no means the oldest item on display, but hardly recent either at 5,500 years of age, its condition and the intricate pattern that adorned its lip were remarkable. As I marvelled at its ancient artistry, I was struck by the timelessness of the artefact and its design.

* * *

Leaving the museum we drove over what seemed an uninspiring, hurriedly constructed bridge. Four sets of three concrete columns held up wooden beams supporting sheets of corrugated iron that acted as a road. 'It was put up during the war,' Mr Dinarvand explained as if reading my thoughts. 'They had to be pragmatic in those days.' He pulled the car off the road and onto a dirt track that curved back round on itself as he parked in the shade of the bridge. To our left two men were washing down a tractor they had driven some way into the flowing green waters of the Karkheh River.

'Iraqi soldiers advanced right up to these banks during the war. Shush was abandoned to the bloodshed for three years. Machine-gun post right here,' he said as his two hands jerked back and forth imitating the action of the weapon. I was taken aback by just how far into Iranian territory Iraqi troops had advanced before being pushed back by sheer numbers and blind resilience. Emboldened by the internal weakness of Iran after the 1979 Revolution and by the assurances of exiled Iranian generals from the Shah's regime that the country was on the verge of collapse, Saddam Hussein, in September 1980, had sent his forces marching into Iran. After initial advances and success, the Iraqis were faced down by a massive popular resistance in which the new government in Tehran managed to mobilise wave after wave of Iranian counter-attacks, often spearheaded by completely untrained youths mesmerised by the pro-spect of martyrdom and a quick and free entry-pass into heaven. And it was on the site of just such a blind but successful counter-attack that I now stood.

At my host's urging I sheepishly took off my shirt and trousers and bathed in the cooling waters of the life-sustaining waterway, more to honour the memory of the young men – often no more than boys – who had fallen here, than to swim.

★ ★ ★

Some towns and cities are fated to see more than their fair share of war and suffering, usually as a result of their position on or near geopolitical fault lines. Shush, being in the oil-rich region that straddles Iran and Iraq, is one such place. The ancient city of Susa (the historical name for Shush) was no different, being the seat of power of the Elamites as they warred against the neighbouring kingdom Babylon for centuries. Like most of these war-ravaged cities, it is their geographical position that lends them their appeal both as places to inhabit and to invade. Susa, sandwiched as it is between the life-sustaining Karkheh and Dez rivers, its soil fecund with alluvium, has been rebuilt as many times as it has been destroyed.

Although Susa was used as a winter residence by the earlier Achaemenian monarchs, it was Darius I who truly resurrected the for-tunes of the old Elamite city around 521 BCE by constructing a vast palace complex that was used in tandem with the more famous palace at Persepolis. This ancient capital lasted nearly 200 years before falling in 330 BCE to Alexander the Great during his Persian campaign, which also saw the destruction of Persepolis. Rebuilt after it was conquered by the Sasanian king Ardeshir in 224 CE, Susa thrived as a trading centre for nearly a millennium before being sacked by the Arab Muslim armies in the seventh century. Again, the resilient town recovered and enjoyed 600 years of relative peace until it was once more ravaged by the ruthless Mongol hordes in the thirteenth century. This last wave of violence spelt the end of the ancient palace for some 600 years, until it was excavated first by the British under W.K. Loftus in 1851 and then the French under Jacques de Morgan in 1892.

De Morgan's efforts were so constantly harassed by marauding tribes and raiders that he used the ancient mud bricks commissioned by Darius all those centuries ago and the yet more ancient bricks unearthed at the nearby Chogha Zanbil – the very bricks he was there to excavate – to build a fortress, in the style of a French medieval castle, from which to work in peace. The Château de Morgan was off limits to tourists but Mr Dinarvand made a few calls and arranged for me, accompanied by the whole Dinarvand brood, to be taken on a tour of the site. Although the castle sustained heavy damage during the war with Iraq, it has now been restored by the government, more keen to save this bastardised part of Iran's heritage than the pre-Islamic palace that lies just beyond its walls.

The royal palace commissioned by Darius was built to the north of the city on what is known as the Apadana mound, a vast platform raised 15 metres above the height of the outlying plain. The southern section housed the royal residences, whilst the northern section comprised the Apadana itself, with its central hall dominated by thirty-six columns, each weighing over 5 tons according to our excitable guide. The roof of the Apadana, some 20 metres high, was held in place by the twin heads of the kneeling-bull capitals that are such a distinguishing feature of Achaemenian architecture. Our guide was trying his best to enthuse the younger Dinarvands with his descriptions of the scale and grandeur of the palace but he was fighting a losing battle. Now, all that is left of the once great palace are delineations of where these walls and pillars once stood so tall and so proud, the odd remnant of a hefty column or bull capital strewn amongst them. Against the appeal of firing imaginary guns at one another from the burly ramparts of the nineteenth-century castle, there was only ever going to be one winner.

Our guide may have lost the interest of the children but he was doing a good job of engrossing the adults. The foundations of the palace complex were built on a pit dug into the ground and filled with gravel, he informed us, so that the loose gravel would shift and absorb the worst of the vibrations from the earthquakes that plagued the region. This technique was known to the Elamites and was, along with the proximity of the River Dez, one of the key factors in the position of Chogha Zanbil, built as it was on a natural sand bed.

A brick pavement led from the royal city through a vast covered passage and up to the Gate of Darius, the official entrance to the palace complex. This gateway was itself vast, measuring 40 metres by 28 metres and with walls up to 15 metres high. On each side of this imposing gate-way towered two 3-metre-tall statues of the Great King himself. These, the cuneiform inscriptions in the folds of his robe tell us, were ordered to be made in Egypt. Darius declares in another inscription found at the site:

> The excavation and the fill and the sun-dried molded bricks were the work of the people from Babylonia. The cedar timber was brought from a mountain called Lebanon. The people of Assyria brought it to Babylonia, and the people from Karkha and Ionia brought it from Babylonia to Susa. The wood called *yaka* was brought from Gandhara and Karmana; gold came from Sardes and Bactria and was wrought here. The precious lapis lazuli and carnelian were brought from Soghdiana, and the turquoise from Khwarezm. The silver and ebony came from Egypt. The decoration with which the walls were embellished were brought from Ionia, the ivory from Ethiopia, from India, and from Arachonia, but was wrought here. Stone, here wrought into columns, was from a town called Abiradu in Elam. The stone cutters and sculptors who made them here were Sardians and Ionians. Those who worked in gold were the Medes and Egyptians. Those who made the mosaic in ivory were the Babylonians and the Ionians. Those who decorated the walls were the Medes and the Egyptians.[3]

Much like Persepolis, the scale and grandeur of this palace com-plex were designed to reflect the might and indomitability of the Achaemenian Empire. The fact that the finest materials and artisans from across the empire were used was again intended to reflect the pervasive-ness of the king's power. The opulence of the palace was renowned all over the ancient world and is referred to by many of the great historians of antiquity such as Herodotus and Strabo. Unlike Persepolis, it is even mentioned a number of times in the Bible as 'Susa the citadel'.[4] It would have been known thus in the ancient world because of the citadel built to the west of the complex that towered over the palace and was the first thing the eye would see upon approaching the great city.

As I tried to piece together the ancient palace in my mind – recon-structing its scale from what was left of the columns and capitals strewn at my feet, and its finery from the glazed brickwork depictions of royal guards, winged lions and griffins I had seen displayed in the museum in Shush and at both the Louvre and the British Museum – the scene was made yet more spectacular by a glorious sunset of deep reds, fiery oranges and shimmering yellows silhouetting the palm trees and bungalows that dotted the horizon. Mr Dinarvand suddenly hoisted his sizeable haunches onto a collapsed pillar, a bull capital prostrate at his feet. With great panache he swept his arms regally towards the west, 'It was from this very palace that Darius ordered his troops into battle, from here that Xerxes set out on his unprecedented campaign against our old adversary, the Greeks.' As he hopped down from his pulpit with surprising agility, he crunched his foot into the earth, 'This ground under our very feet is yet to be excavated,' he continued theatrically. 'Not just Achaemenian remains two and a half thousand years old, but under those lie the ruins of Elamite cities thousands of years older and under them yet more remains of nameless civilisations lost in time.'

★ ★ ★

Shushtar is the larger, less prosperous neighbour of Shush, lying some 75 kilometres to its east. For many years it took over the mantle of regional capital after Shush was decimated by the Mongol armies in 1218 CE. The suffix *tar* in Persian means moist or wet and a quick visit to the town will reveal why it is called 'wet Shush'. Water positively explodes from rock-faces at the site of an ancient hydraulic dam originally built by the Achaemenians for irrigation purposes but developed into its existing form by the Sasanian king Shapur I (239–70 CE) in the third century CE. Shushtar was at that time an island city surrounded by the mighty River Karun, Iran's largest, which was channelled around it to form a defensive moat. Al-Moqaddasi, the tenth-century Arab geographer and traveller from Jerusalem, declared that there was no finer or more beautiful town, surrounded as it was by rivers, gardens and date palms.

The river pours water into channels cut through sheer rock that are then diverted through this staggering complex, or what is left of it. Much of the structure was left destroyed following the Mongol onslaught until the latter part of the nineteenth century, when it was restored nearly 1,700 years after being built by Shapur I. Shapur purportedly used captives from his successful campaign against the mighty Roman emperor Valerian, whom he defeated at Edessa (in modern-day Turkey) in 260 CE, as workers on the bridge which he aptly named *Band-e-Qaisar*: Caesar's Bridge. These water channels powered flour mills that were still in use 'until very recently,' I was told vaguely by a prune-faced old watchman.

The Ministry of Culture, he told me, was planning to repair the mill to operational standards to attract more tourists.

Despite the cooling effect of the churning waters, the midday heat was visibly beginning to bother Mr Dinarvand. I was in no better state, cowering in the shade of a cool grotto inside the copper-coloured rock of the dam as gallons of water roared around me and cascaded back into the waiting River Karun. It was well over forty degrees and the sun soon drove us back across the searing asphalt to our car. The clanging and banging of a construction site could be heard just beside the ancient dam. Shushtar had been a rapidly degenerating city until the last Shah attempted to resuscitate it with building projects that commenced in the early 1970s only to be interrupted by revolution and war. The present government has recently renewed efforts to breathe new life into this ailing city, as evidenced by this construction site. Defeated by the heat, we clambered into Mr Dinarvand's air-conditioned Peugeot and were soon heading back through the endless fields of sugar cane, corn and watermelon.

For his final trick, the indefatigable Mr Dinarvand took me from the ancient dam to a modern one. He had pulled a few more strings to arrange an exclusive tour of the Dez dam complex, roughly 100 kilometres north-east of Shush. The reservoir is 60 kilometres long and 200 metres deep, producing a shimmering cobalt-blue surface. The dam itself is hewn into the sheer rock-face of an old canyon, smoothed into a lunar landscape peppered with caves by its sub-aqueous past. Through an intricate system of tunnels bored into the sheer rock, countless tons of water pass each day, channelled into the River Karun and on to irrigate the many fields of Khuzestan – Iran's south-western province, rich in oil and abutting Iraq. On its way through the dam, the water churns and turns eight enormous turbines that were, at the time of writing, responsible for an eighth of the country's electricity.

An engineer at the dam (who just happened to be a relative by marriage of Mr Dinarvand's) acted as our tour guide for the day. The reinforced concrete dam wall is 27 metres thick and is, the engineer declared boastfully, indestructible. As proof of this bold statement he pointed to a few pockmarks on the wall's surface. 'An Iraqi fighter jet swooped through the river valley and tried to bomb the dam,' he said referring to the Iran–Iraq War. 'This is all that happened,' he declared with a wry smile. What he pointed at looked much more as if it had been caused by machine-gun fire than a bomb blast and seemed paltry proof of the dam's indestructibility, but being neither an engineer nor a fighter pilot, I refrained from judgment.

Pylons sprouted out of the cliff-face at impossible angles carrying web-like wires that curved up and over the cliff like a giant industrial caterpillar, streaming electricity into millions of homes, offices and factories around the country. I am not often impressed by industrial machinery and engineering, but this dam, in its own way, left just as big an impression on me as the ancient remains that littered the region.

As we drove away from the dam towards the bus station in Shush, it hit me that my time with the Dinarvands was drawing to a close. I had been treated to faultless hospitality and unwavering kindness. I had been plunged into the rich history that seeps out of the region's sun-drenched soil and, more than once, was able to confront my own belonging to this place, for all its absurdities. All of this I experienced in the irrepressible company of my chain-smoking companion, Mr Dinarvand. As we stood in front of the bus to Shiraz, our goodbyes were short but heartfelt. 'When I take someone in to my house, under the same roof as my family, they are no longer a friend. They – you – are my brother.' I thanked him and promised that one day I would repay their hospitality and warmth in kind. '*Ensha'llah*,' he said as he turned and walked away.

★ ★ ★

The bus, classy from the outside, cramped on the inside, ferried me the fourteen hours overnight to Shiraz. An uncomfortable journey was made yet worse by a group of eighteen loud teenage boys who made up the bulk of the passenger list. They had clearly drawn their own conclusions about me. My by now thick beard had, I presumed, identified and condemned me without question as a *hezbollahi* regimist. As a result I was served up an inordinate amount of knee-poking and prodding from the seats behind, accompanied by sniggering and laughter as they passed up and down the aisle 'accidentally' bumping into my seat. At one particularly cold point in the icy nocturnal desert crossing, I noticed five of the six air nozzles that could not apparently be turned off very deliberately aimed at my neck. I got off the bus shattered, with heavy eyes and stiff neck.

Chapter Fourteen

I tried to revive my cold, aching body with a hot drink in Shiraz's unexpectedly clean and modern bus terminal. Curiously, the coffee shop
sold neither tea nor coffee so I settled for a couple of hot chocolates and
waited for the sun to come up before disturbing my new host. A family friend had arranged for me to stay with her father, a native Shirazi.
I had traded a lumbering Lor for an obliging octogenarian aristocrat
named Mr Lashgari, a retired agricultural engineer and the founder of
the Agricultural College of Shiraz. He lived in a leafy, well-to-do suburb of the city, rattling around in a large house with creaking wooden
floors and a spacious interior as aged as their owner. Mr Lashgari lived
on his own, but for company had an invasive driver called Mr Zeydabadi
and a toothless old cook who had been in his employ for long enough to
know the strictures of the old man's routine inside and out.

Mr Lashgari's short stature, disarming smile and gentle voice added
to a kindly air that endeared him almost instantly. After a quick glass
of tea, he suggested we head out to see the sights of Shiraz. We strolled
through some of the city's famed gardens in the gentle morning sun.
These *baghs* – leafy compounds in which grand old houses once sheltered the country's gentry – have now mostly been seized, opened to the
public and often the buildings restored and converted into museums or
headquarters for the military or *Basij* militia.

These gardens with their intricate water channels, geometric flow-erbeds, vibrant hues and tree-lined walkways bathed in the shadows of lofty cypresses created a deep sense of calm and repose which contrasted with the relentless heat of an Iranian summer, reflecting how the whole aesthetic of a Persian garden is grounded in a celebration of water and the ways in which this precious liquid sustains life. The plan for the modern garden can supposedly be traced back to the *pairidaeza* of Avestan, the ancient language of Iran. Having mastered irrigation techniques with their system of *qanats*, Iranians transformed the arid earth around their settlements into life-sustaining enclosures which provided opportunity for cultivation and produced their own special idyll. These gardens and walled enclosures were often used as pleasure gardens by the monarchs of the past.

Many cultures and religions use a garden setting to depict heaven, from the Greek Elysian Fields to the Islamic conception of Paradise. The Garden of Eden, the ultimate paradisiacal setting, was theoretically situated somewhere in the border region of present-day north-western Iran, south-eastern Turkey and southern Armenia. Given the aridity and barrenness of the land, it is easy to understand the coveted status of the garden and the Iranian obsession with it.

Shiraz has retained much of the charm and beauty for which it has long been famed. Not only are its gardens constantly preened and pruned to remain in peak condition, considerable thought and effort has obviously been put into the aesthetics of town planning, something which cannot be said for many of Iran's rapidly growing urban centres. There is more to Shiraz than its beauty – the city was excitedly described by the British scholar E.G. Browne over a hundred years ago as 'the home of Persian culture, the mother of Persian genius, the sanctuary of poetry and philosophy'.[1] For many Iranians a visit to the tombs of Hafez and Sa'di is a spiritual pilgrimage, now rendered even more magical by the recent restoration of their gardens.

★ ★ ★

Poetry is pervasive in Iranian culture. Until the end of the nineteenth century, when an Iranian spoke of literature he was referring exclusively to poetry. Iranians of all ages recite lines from their great mystic poets on a near-daily basis. These verses are reference points to which people still not only relate but feel a deep connection. Ferdowsi (*c.* 940–1025

CE), Sa'di (*c.* 1210–92 CE) and Hafez (*c.* 1315–90 CE) are the three most celebrated poets in Iran, but others such as Rumi, Khayyam, Rudaki and Nezami are also greatly loved, not just in Iran but around the world. The rhythmic flow and cadence of the poetic language is intoxicating and perfectly suited to being sung, as the verses of Hafez and Rumi often are in traditional Iranian folk music and as I had often witnessed at social gatherings in Iran. But Persian poetry is so much more than a lyrical, timeless message; it is the perfect encapsulation of the national character. It is philosophical and emotive yet playful and packed full of wit, it is introspective and lofty yet sweeping and self-deprecating. It is a lyrical expression of the love of beauty and sense of aesthetic so apparent in the country's art and architecture.

Probably the most quoted work of Persian poetry is Ferdowsi's *Shahnameh*, The Book of Kings. This eleventh-century epic took the great poet from Tus, near modern-day Mash'had, nearly thirty years to complete. It recounts the history of Iranian monarchy from the mythical first kings of proto-history (having worked their way into the country's folklore from Zoroastrian cosmogony) and their centuries-long reigns to the last Sasanian king, Yazdegerd III (632–51 CE), who was defeated by the invading Arab Muslim armies in 651 CE. These histories, which include many a tale of ancient heroes like Rostam and Sam (pronounced with a long 'a', as in 'arm') and their legendary feats in defending crown and country, weave fact with the myths and stories passed down through the oral tradition. 'The result,' writes Sir Percy Sykes, the soldier, diplomat and author of a weighty history of Persia, 'is a poem which appeals to Persians as nothing else does in their language; which makes them glow with pride at the valour of their forebears and unites them in their intense pride of race.'[2] In its day, Ferdowsi's epic tapped into a resurgent wave of what today would appear like nationalism and a desire to reaffirm an Iranian identity that had been missing since the Arab Muslim conquests of the seventh century. It was not only the tales themselves that restored pride in Iranian history and culture, but also the fact that Ferdowsi famously used only 984 Arabic expressions throughout the entirety of his near 60,000-couplet epic poem. This has been regarded as an amazing feat given that for 300 years the Arabic language had insinuated itself into the native language of Sasanian and post-Sasanian Persia, leaving the local language as a kind of hybrid of Arabic and Pahlavi Persian. What Ferdowsi is therefore credited with is the triumphant rebirth of the Persian language, which has survived essentially intact to the present day.

Sa'di is these days best known for the United Nations' use of his verses on the entrance to the New York headquarters building,[3] but in his time he was renowned and celebrated throughout the Islamic world. This widespread fame was as much down to his itinerant life as it was to the wit and verve of his poetry. He left his hometown of Shiraz to escape the Mongol invasions of the thirteenth century, spending the next thirty years travelling far and wide, experiencing firsthand one of the most harrowing periods in world history as the Mongol trail of destruction seemed to follow him around. Swapping tales of suffering and atrocities with other travellers in teahouses, he journeyed right across the Middle East. Upon his return to Shiraz in around 1257 CE, he released his two most famed works, the *Bustan* (Orchard) and the *Golestan* (Rose Garden). The *Golestan* is a collection of anecdotes and stories that, although not necessarily biographically accurate, are recounted with such wit and alacrity and in such beautifully simple language that their appeal to Iranians is great even to this day. The *Bustan* is a similar collection of tales and anecdotes gathered predominantly from his itinerant experiences but with more of a focus on an ethical or philosophical exploration of the human condition. Sa'di, better than any of the other great poets of Persian literature, captures the absurdity of life that these days so many Iranians can relate to.

Outside the Persian-speaking world, the works of Omar Khayyam and particularly Rumi have enjoyed the most recognition. Khayyam's *Rubaiyat* was first translated by the British Orientalist Edward Fitzgerald in 1859. Fitzgerald took the scattered *rubai* (two line stanzas) of Khayyam's and wove them into a continuous narrative, allowing himself a liberal interpretation of the poet's philosophical ideas. This translation sparked a wave of interest both in Europe and North America that persists to this day.

Rumi is the poet who has most captured the imagination of contemporary Western readers and has even had his verses set to music and sung by stars such as Demi Moore and Madonna. Jalaludin Rumi was born in 1207 in Balkh (modern-day Afghanistan), but, like his contemporary Sa'di, his family were soon uprooted by Mongol incursions from the east and moved to Konya in Turkey. As a young man under the tutelage of his father, an esteemed mystic and the head of a religious school, Rumi had shown an unusual capacity for grasping complex religious ideas. By the age of twenty-four he had taken over from his father and become a highly respected theologian and public figure in his own right.

That was until a fateful day in 1244 when Shams-e Tabrizi, a wandering ascetic – nicknamed 'The Bird' for his peripatetic tendencies – soared into Rumi's life. Shams set Rumi on the path of *erfan,* teaching him to free himself from his ego and the necessary social constraints that his position as both patriarch and preacher imposed upon him. Outrage followed the pair as Shams encouraged Rumi to disgrace himself by appearing drunk in public. Much to the dismay of the great poet's loving family and reverent public, Shams persuaded him to turn his back on them and instead give himself unreservedly to God.

For a long time Rumi and Shams were inseparable, locking themselves in a room for days at a time as they fasted and meditated, trying to rid themselves of the trappings of the mortal world and transcend to a state of intoxicating communion with the divine. Whispers spread through the scandalised community that the two men were lovers or, worse still, that Shams was the devil in disguise come to corrupt the cleric's soul. One day a few years down the line, though, Rumi awoke to find Shams gone without a trace. This mysterious figure had disappeared from his life just as suddenly and unexpectedly as he had flown into it. Rumours abounded that an outraged member of the poet's family or congregation had murdered Shams to free Rumi from his spell, but the cleric refused to believe this and spent many years determinedly searching for his friend.

Although this search was fated to be unsuccessful, it was not in vain. The loss and consequent search for Shams led Rumi to compose the *ghazals* that established him as one of the world's great mystic poets, using his grief and his longing to be reunited with his beloved friend and spiritual guide as a metaphor for mankind's yearning to be reunited with God. It is said that the *sama* spiritual dance performed by many Sufis to help induce a heightened spiritual state originated from Rumi's habit of spinning himself around as he dictated his verses to a student-scribe. The most famous exponents of the *sama* are the Whirling Dervishes, otherwise known as the Mevlevi Sufi order established by the great poet in his adoptive hometown of Konya.

Many mistakenly believed that Shams had led Rumi to turn his back on Islam, but much of his poetry revolved around a more mystical interpretation of the Qur'anic message. Shams opened Rumi's eyes to the fact that the strictures and traditions that had grown up around Islam were mere distractions, acting like a restrictive web. He taught Rumi to see beyond this to the only thing that was truly important: giving oneself completely to God.

Ironically, one of the reasons for the popularity of Iranian mystic poetry in the modern era, particularly the verses of Rumi, is the often overly literal interpretation of the symbolism frequently employed. Love, sex and wine are metaphors for access to and communion with God. Coupled with tales of shady esoteric practices and drunken bouts inspired by Shams, it is easy to see why verses extolling intoxication – meant to symbolise a state of spiritual elation from communion with God – are misconstrued and why Rumi's popularity surged with the hippie sub-culture movement in 1960s America and is still growing to this day.

Rudaki is widely regarded as the father of Persian poetry as he was the first to write in 'New Persian' in the ninth century. Nezami's epic tales of tragic love – the two most celebrated of which are *Leyla and Majnun* and *Khosrow and Shirin* – have singled this Azeri lyricist out as the greatest of Persia's romantic poets. Farid al-Din Attar was another contemporary of Sa'di's and Rumi's during this Golden Age of Persian literature, his allegorical Sufi poem *The Conference of the Birds* being his most recognised work. Jami, who lived in Herat (modern-day Afghanistan) in the fifteenth century, is widely regarded as the last of Persia's great mystic poets.

Of all their poets, though, it is undoubtedly Hafez and his *Divan* that most appeals to the Iranian imagination. The *Divan* is as pervasive in Iranian households as the Qur'an, and its pages are consulted for guidance just as frequently, if not more so. Hafez was famed for his prodigious memory – his name means 'he who knows the Qur'an by heart'. He is viewed as a seer capable of tapping into a collective consciousness out of the reach of ordinary people. His eloquent verses are filled with the imagery of classical mystic poetry – the ecstasy of love, wine and intoxication – and are frequently used as a means of divination known as *faal giri*. But it is Hafez's self-deprecating wit and his determined onslaught against false piety and hypocrisy, particularly that of the authorities and institutional religion, that strikes such a chord with contemporary Iranians. Through his poetic persona he admits that he is far from perfect, that he is (as are we all) only human. Why hide our flaws and foibles under a cloak of false piety when they are the very things that make us human? 'A drinker who is devoid of cant is superior to a piety-seller who practises pretence.'[4]

★ ★ ★

Standing in the shade of a tall cypress tree beside the entrance to Hafez's tomb in Shiraz, a blind man with a shock of brilliant white hair was clutching a wooden box full of folded pieces of paper. A bright-green budgerigar hopped from his hand to the box and, with a few jerky pecks, pulled out one of the pieces of paper and deposited it into the waiting hand of a passer-by. Cradling it carefully in his palm, he studied it with intent; his lips moving silently to the words of the *Divan* as he tried to decipher their meaning and apply them to his own situation. Inside the grounds of the tomb located on the north bank of the Dry River, plenty of young couples lay languidly in the shade of fragrant bushes, holding hands, whispering tenderly, enjoying what would surely be considered one of the most romantic cities of the world were romance not considered an illicit indulgence.

Mr Lashgari and I walked slowly through the fragrant garden, past an old man sitting on a bench reverently thumbing the dog-eared pages of a *Divan*. My host paused as he stared wistfully at the reflection of the great poet's tomb in the mirror-like pool at its foot. As we approached the octagonal pavilion with its domed roof, I noticed a few people kneeling beside the tomb, their hands pressed tenderly against its cold stone, their heads bent in prayer, their cheeks streaked with tears. Iranians have been making the pilgrimage to Hafez's resting place since the fifteenth century and their love and reverence for him show no sign of abating.

★　★　★

The Safavid dynasty that ruled from 1502 to 1736 – and was responsible for the country's conversion to Shi'ism, with the help of imported Muslim legal scholars from South Lebanon – saw Persia re-establish itself as one of the great empires of the world, the apogee of which was the reign of Shah Abbas I (1588–1629). But all great and prosperous periods in a country's history eventually must come to an end. More often than not, the final chapters of these periods are ones of stagnation and steady decline that are all too often the precursor to periods of extreme instability and upheaval as rival factions vie for the seat of absolute power. The Safavid era was no exception.

With the loss of Esfahan to invading Afghan forces in 1719, the dynasty that established Shi'ism as Iran's national religion was irreparably weakened and began to collapse. Sensing this weakness, the two great empires that loomed on Iran's borders – the Ottomans to the west and the Russians to the north – moved to seize sizeable tracts of Safavid land. After the murder of Shah Soltan Hossein at the hand of Afghan invaders in 1722, Tahmasp II (1722–32) claimed the Safavid throne. In the meantime, a young man of Turkic origin from the north-east of Iran was rising through the ranks of the army, coming to the attention of Tahmasp, who swiftly made him his military commander. This young man, named Nader, led the Shah's armies to a series of victories that, by late 1729, had driven the Afghans out of the country.

Nader then turned his attentions to the north-west, successfully recapturing much of the land seized by the Ottomans. But again the Afghans resurfaced and drew Nader and his armies back east. In the meantime, with Nader again busy subduing the Afghans, Shah Tahmasp decided to lead an attack against the Ottoman forces himself. This campaign proved to be a spectacular failure and resulted in the king losing much of the land newly recaptured by Nader. A series of negotiations ensued between Shah Tahmasp and first the Ottomans and then the Russians, with whom he eventually signed a peace treaty. When Nader got wind of what had happened he rushed back to Esfahan in 1732 and promptly deposed Tahmasp, replacing him with the Shah's eight-month-old son, proclaiming him Abbas III.

Over the next few years, Nader successfully fended off the Ottomans and kept the Russians at bay by renegotiating the terms of the peace treaty with them. Very soon these two great empires were embroiled in war themselves. At this point, Nader claimed the throne for himself (famously throttling a chief mullah who spoke out in opposition) and was officially crowned shah on 8 March 1736. Internally, Nader Shah set about instigating fundamental changes to Iranian society and religion, moving away from the Twelver Shi'ism imposed by the Safavids and towards a Ja'fari (Ja'far Sadegh was the sixth Shi'i Imam, who died in 765 CE) interpretation of Islam more in line with Sunni beliefs. Outside of Iran, Nader destroyed Kandahar in 1738. With the Afghans seemingly dealt a decisive blow, Nader Shah launched an invasion of Mughal India, whose successful conquest brought him vast wealth – including prized riches such as the Darya-I-Nur and Kuh-I-Nur diamonds, the latter now the centre-piece of the crown made for Queen Elizabeth the Queen Mother's coronation. The Ottomans meanwhile, under Mahmud I (1730–54), had also been busy, defeating the Austrians and the Russians and establishing themselves as the pre-eminent global empire. Their position thus strengthened, the Ottomans denied Nader Shah's claims to Iraq. Predictably, fighting ensued.

During this period, the situation within Iran was growing ever more fractious. Certain factions had long opposed the social and religious changes imposed by the Shah and others were growing weary of his constant warmongering. Even those close to him were becoming steadily more alarmed by Nader Shah's deteriorating mental state – triggered by the remorse for blinding his son, Reza Qoli, for a rumoured assassination attempt that the heir to the throne vehemently denied having a hand in. While he was fighting the Ottomans in Iraq, rebellion broke out back in Iran, forcing him to return and quash the uprising. This he did and promptly returned to his war with the Ottomans, whom, to the surprise of many, he defeated in 1745, reclaiming Iraq. Internal unrest, though, was still rife, and when, in June 1747, Nader Shah was murdered by his own officers, the civil war that had long been looming eventually broke out.

Nader Shah's constant and largely successful warmongering had swelled Iran's armies and expanded its boundaries but the Shah had taxed much of his own country to the point of collapse in order to fund the endless campaigning. Although Nader's reign had seemed relatively successful and stable, it had also been a short-sighted one that left the country wholly unprepared for the deeply unsettling and blood-soaked period of Iranian history that directly followed it – a period that only hastened to confirm Iran's hostility to Europeans determined to colonise and civilise the unruly Orient.

After Nader's assassination, his nephew took the Afshar crown and proclaimed himself Adel Shah. This 'just' king promptly murdered all but one of Nader's family, even going as far as to cut the unborn children out of the pregnant women of the late Shah's harem. Nader's vast army, held together only by the monarch's iron rule, fell apart, splitting into the ethnic groups and factions it had been formed from. The Azeri factions returned to the north-west and the Afghans to the east, each establishing their own independent states. Adel Shah's swift demise was followed by a series of depositions, eye-gougings and general bloodletting as pretenders to the Afshar throne killed one another off.

This dark period of history saw the country's population fall by a quarter, from roughly 9 million to 6 million in just fifty-odd years, as war and pestilence ravaged Iran and drove many to flee to greener pastures. Esfahan, the country's celebrated capital and one of the biggest and busiest cities of the world only a few decades earlier, was practically deserted as the struggle for the throne saw siege and civil war decimate its population from roughly 550,000 at the peak of the Safavid era to just 50,000 by 1736.[5]

Meanwhile, the chief of the Bakhtiari tribe and that of the Zand tribe, Karim Khan (a general under Nader), placed a young Safavid heir on the empty throne, declaring him Ismail III. Having pacified the Lors and the Kurds in the west, Karim Khan returned to Esfahan in 1751. The ensuing twelve years saw an internecine struggle for power between a Turkic Qajar faction on Iran's north-western borders, an Afghan faction from the east and Karim Khan. Eventually Karim Khan came out on top and returned to Shiraz in July 1765. To everybody's astonishment he refused the title of shah, leaving Ismail III as nominal king (albeit in confinement) whilst he ruled as *Vakil* – 'Regent', or more literally 'Representative'. The uprisings continued, with the Afghans recapturing Khorasan, the Qajars controlling much of the Caspian basin and Arab tribes dominant in Khuzestan, but Karim Khan was happy to swallow these losses and rule the greater part of the country. This he did into his seventies, overseeing a period of relative calm within the surrounding savagery and civil war.

When Karim Khan died in 1779, the battle for the Persian throne resumed, this time between the Zand princes and the Qajars, led by Agha Mohammad Khan, for whom it was personal. He had been castrated by Adel Shah Afshar at the tender age of five and was then held in captivity for a number of years (although apparently treated well) by Karim Khan. By 1786 Agha Mohammad Khan had conquered Shiraz and established Tehran as the country's new capital. But the fighting still rumbled on, with Lotf Ali Khan Zand refusing to accept Qajar rule. He was pursued by Agha Mohammad's armies to Kerman, where the locals foolishly took him in – a decision Agha Mohammad made them regret. When Kerman fell, Agha Mohammad ordered the eyeballs of every surviving male of the city to be cut out. All 20,000 of these were carried to him and poured at his feet back in Tehran – grisly proof that his sentence had been meted out. This was just one of many examples of the brutality for which Agha Mohammad Khan was to become renowned. Lotf Ali Khan somehow managed to get away, but only briefly. He was soon captured and put to death, Zand ambitions to the throne being laid to rest with him. The Qajar dynasty went on to rule for over 130 years until deposed by Reza Shah Pahlavi in 1925.

★ ★ ★

Having left Mr Lashgari to go home and rest, I set out to explore Shiraz. Under the mild afternoon sun shining down from a perfectly blue sky, I strolled through palm-lined streets until I arrived at the citadel built by Karim Khan, the man responsible for the construction of much of what now makes up modern Shiraz, including the solid 12-metre-high and 3-metre-thick walls of the imposing fort-like edifice before me. On the four corners of the outer walls, brawny turrets, each 14 metres in circumference, rose up into the cloudless sky. These turrets are adorned with simple but attractive brickwork patterns – not even defensive fortifications were exempt from the gaudy aesthetics of the late eighteenth century, trying, without great success, to preserve the delicacies of the Safavid style before plunging into the full gaudy pink, yellow and blue floral tile-work of the Qajar era.

Inside the sinister-looking walls of the building was a shady court-yard complete with four pools and fragrant citrus trees. This surprising contrast with the earnest brooding of the building's external elevation is explained by the fact that it was built, in 1767, as the residence and military headquarters of Karim Khan. In the Qajar era (1794–1925) the building was adopted as the seat of the governor of Fars before later being converted to a prison. It has now been reclaimed as a museum and exhibition centre and displayed fascinating black and white photographs of Shiraz in the late Qajar and early Pahlavi eras. Some of these images depicted eerily empty streets, still recognisable despite the urban expansion that has engulfed them. The picture that most caught the eye and that I recognised as the work of the celebrated Russian photographer Sevruguin captured a particularly gruesome form of execution favoured by the Qajar kings. A scruffy-looking, long-haired young man with doleful eyes waited, shoulder blades strapped to the barrel of a cannon, for the grinning executioner to light the fateful fuse that would tear his body asunder.

Making my way back to Mr Lashgari's house, I passed the iconic Darvaze-ye Qur'an, a large archway that straddles the old road leading north to Esfahan and Tehran. This archway once housed an enormous Qur'an weighing 51 kilograms. An old Muslim custom has any traveller about to set out on a journey pass under the Islamic holy book. The Qur'an is waved over the traveller, who kisses it before setting off, now fully blessed. The archway and its massive Qur'an provided group blessings for all travellers, leaving the last word to God before the open road. Today's motorway runs just beside the city's gateway, depriving travellers of automatic access to a blessing.

When I returned to Mr Lashgari's ample abode I discovered that the citadel walls I had just come from held powerful memories for my aged host. When he had been roughly my age and was on military service, an epidemic broke out in the then prison. As a young officer in an administrative position, Mr Lashgari was sent to the now quarantined prison to review the inmates' individual cases and deem whether any could be granted early release and escape the fatal epidemic. The exercise proved to be in vain as the fastidious Mr Lashgari, at a tender twenty-three years of age, decreed that none were deserving of early release. But as fate would have it, he had himself contracted the virus and only escaped death with the aid of a renowned military physician, his own youthful vigour and what he simply described as a determination to live.

'Shiraz was a very different place back then,' Mr Lashgari said, before correcting himself: 'The world was a very different place.' Moving to the window, he pushed the net curtain aside and stared wistfully out at his beloved city. 'I remember the day the first car turned up here,' he said as his eyes drifted with reminiscence. 'One car, that was all there was. People waited in the streets for hours just to get a glimpse of it. We were all in such awe of the thing. Now there's one every metre.'

'It seems like you may have preferred things the way they were?' I asked.

'Bah, I don't know about that. Things were ...' – a long pause – 'less complicated then. But life was much harder. Problems back then were real problems. Nowadays so many of our gripes seem so trivial.' I asked him about his work as a pioneer of agricultural engineering in the region. 'Yes, we encouraged technological advancement in agriculture. We saw it as a necessity to combat drought and the frequent food shortages the country suffered. Others saw it more as a means to make money. But Iranians can be pig-headed, set in their ways. If it was not for the commercial benefits, it would have been much harder to instigate change. Now look at what's happening. Things change so fast. It's hard, exhausting for older people like me to keep up.' He walked away from the window and grabbed a handful of pistachios from a bowl on a nearby table, shelled one and popped it in his mouth. 'Maybe things are moving too fast, people are becoming too reliant on technology? I don't know. It's all about balance, about finding the right path between the old,' he tapped a palm to his chest, 'and the new,' he gestured towards me.

★ ★ ★

Accompanied by Mr Zeydabadi, my host's fast-talking driver, who, with his hoary mop-top and flared trousers, resembled an ageing Beatle, I set out to visit the *Shah Cheragh* mausoleum, the resting place of two brothers of Imam Reza – the eighth Shi'i Imam and the only one to be buried on Iranian soil, whose mausoleum dominates the city of Mash'had[6] – who lived and died in the ninth century CE. From the outside this *Shah Cheragh* mausoleum seemed undistinguished, but inside the scene was breathtaking. An explosion of light created by a dazzling chandelier brought to life the ornate, mirrored mosaic, twinkling on every surface of the vaulted rooms except the carpet-covered floor, which glowed with its own array of colours. The overall effect was of a lambent, crystalline realm. The convex central dome of the mirrored ceiling from which the huge chandelier was hanging demonstrated the ingenuity of the fourteenth-century architects and their mastery of domed ceilings – supported by the ever-present squinch – even in this seemingly modest building.

All around tearful pilgrims jostled to reach the silver bars that encased the tomb. Hands devoutly caressed the lattice-work as lips moved silently in prayer before straining to kiss the bars. In separate chambers men busily genuflected and rose as they earnestly pressed their supplications on God.

Beyond the mausoleum's holy walls lay the city's bazaar, the Bazaar-e Vakil. Much like the rest of the city, order and aesthetics reigned under the high vaulted-brick ceilings spilling luminous shafts of light into the spacious merchants' warren thought originally to have been established in the eleventh century. Like much of the city, the Vakil Bazaar owes its existence in its current incarnation to Karim Khan, who ordered a bazaar to be built that surpassed that of Esfahan, the country's previous capital. The wide, airy brick alleyways filled with rugs, spices and the clatter of metalworkers seem not to have changed since the French arch-aeological husband-and-wife team who excavated much of Shush, the Dieulafoys, sketched it in 1881. Two main intersecting alleyways house rows of raised shops. Off these main thoroughfares are a series of leafy courtyards, caravanserais, mosques and teahouses. Many of the bazaars I had visited owed much of their charm to the chaos, confusion and conflict of senses from the seemingly endless jumble of sights, sounds and smells emanating from their every corner, but this was a bazaar of impeccable order. Ibn Battutah, the Islamic traveller of the fourteenth century, a contemporary of Hafez, remarked that, 'In the whole of the east there is no city except Shiraz which approaches Damascus in the beauty of its bazaars, fruit gardens and rivers, and in the handsome figures of its inhabitants.'[7]

★ ★ ★

Some 130 kilometres north-east of Shiraz lies a vast, mountain-encircled tract of land known as the Morghab plain – a small farming village surrounded by plane trees and fields of wheat swaying in the breeze its only inhabitants. In the middle of this windswept plain sits a tomb. Stately in its solitude, sublime in its simplicity, this is the white stone tomb of Cyrus the Great (*c.* 580–530 BCE), founder of the Achaemenian dynasty, king of Anshan, who united the Medes and Persians under one banner, and who went on to conquer and rule an empire bigger than the world had ever seen, proclaiming justice for all and magnanimity to its defeated foes. When he conquered Babylon in 539 BCE, Cyrus decreed that all enslaved peoples were free to return to their homes. This included the Jews who had been in captivity in Babylon for some sixty years. The rule of Cyrus set a precedent for the Great Kings of Persia and empire builders throughout history. 'One characteristic of Cyrus' rule seems to have been a desire to learn from subject peoples, a respect for their religions and customs, and a desire to create a flexible empire,'[8] writes Richard Frye.

'We drove all of this way just for this?' Mr Zeydabadi, my borrowed driver for the day blurted out in the coarse, rustic manner that lent him his charm. 'Why didn't they just build this tomb closer to the others?' He was referring to the royal burial sites at Persepolis and Naqsh-e Rostam that we were heading for next; thirty kilometres away, back towards Shiraz. Although Mr Zeydabadi may have lacked a sense of history and an appreciation of his country's great past, he did have a valid point in that Cyrus's tomb was, unlike the tombs of the other Achaemenian kings, not built to impress. Its allure comes from the panorama heavy with historical significance. As Sir Roger Stevens puts it:

> The majestic calm of this pastoral scene is enhanced by a sense of its history. Here Persia was born, here its founder lived and was buried, here Alexander came to avenge the desecration of Cyrus's tomb; here silence, broken only by the bleating of sheep, the flapping of eagles, and the occasional laughter of children, has reigned for over two thousand years.[9]

Pasargadae was founded by Cyrus on his tribal land after his conquest of Lydia around 547 BCE and comprised two palaces, a royal garden and the mysterious Zendan-e Soleiman, a stone tower thought to be either a tomb or some kind of ceremonial temple – presumably referred to as a *zendan*, or prison, because it had no visible entry or exit point. Very little remains of the ancient site that lies on the ancient caravan route between Esfahan and Shiraz. For centuries the tomb was thought to have belonged to the mother of King Solomon. It was only towards the end of the nineteenth century that archaeologists began to suspect it of being the resting place of Cyrus the Great. This was confirmed by the excavations started by Ernest Herzfeld in 1928 and continued by Marc Aurel Stein.

The unadorned white stone of the tomb, with its gabled roof that reaches 10 metres above the plain, was roped off. A young soldier watched as I hesitated at the barrier. He smiled and gave me a nod, clearly reading my intentions. I ducked under the rope and reverently laid a hand on the smooth stone of the tomb of my namesake, imagining Alexander the Great doing the very same thing over two millennia before me. The understated elegance of Cyrus's tomb was in stark contrast with the scale and grandeur of the tombs of the later Achaemenian kings to be found at Persepolis and Naqsh-e Rostam. Underneath the simple stone, though, it is said that Cyrus – ruler of the first world empire, famed for his humility and fairness – was interred in a coffin of solid gold. Even in death, it seems that Cyrus was shrewdly aware of preserving the image he had so successfully crafted.

* * *

On the road back towards Shiraz, just visible at the far end of a suitably grand, tree-lined boulevard, the mighty stone columns of Persepolis rose up proudly from the Marvdasht plain. Takht-e Jamshid as it is known in Persian (literally 'The Throne of Jamshid', the legendary king of the mythical Kayanian dynasty that brought civilisation to the earth in a thousand-year reign during which man was immortal) was founded by Darius the Great in 518 BCE and expanded by his son Xerxes and successive Achaemenian kings into the fourth century BCE until destroyed by Alexander the Great in 330 BCE before completion. The ancient city of Parsa – known to Greek historians as Persepolis, the City of Persians – was built as the seat of governance of the Achaemenian Empire but

Darius had much loftier intentions for it than even the palaces at Susa and Ecbatana (modern Hamedan). Persepolis was 'developed as a national shrine, as the spiritual focus of the nation rather than its administrative center,' declares Dr Arthur Upham Pope. 'In a long history of symbolic ritual palace-complexes in the ancient Near East, Persepolis was the final and supreme example.'[10]

It was from this throne that the Great King received his annual tribute from his myriad subjects. To this end, the complex was designed to inspire awe. After weeks, sometimes months of travel from the farthest reaches of the empire, envoys would wind through the mountains to reach this plain, at the far end of which was the awesome spectacle of Parsa, aptly raised above the tawny earth. 'Persepolis itself exhibits magnitude. Power and wealth,' writes Pope, 'with a commanding force sufficient to evoke those powers.'[11]

This remarkable site boasted colossal stone columns topped with representations of winged bulls and two-headed kneeling horses perched at their height. An enormous limestone staircase, described by Ernest Herzfeld, the German archaeologist who began excavating the site in 1931, as 'Perhaps the most perfect flight of steps ever built', led up to the 125,000m^2 plateau upon which the palace complex was built.[12] Many of the ancient doorways still stand, images of courtly scenes and religious icons carved into their sides. Amongst these images are depictions of a steady stream of people, each bearing specific items and wearing specific dress. These were the envoys of the various subject-peoples of the Persian Empire paying their annual tribute to the Great King. These depictions are so accurate that individual peoples can be identified by the detail of their dress, their offerings, their hairstyles and facial features:

Medes bearing vases, Elamites with bows, daggers, a lioness and two lion cubs, Aryans with cups and skins, Parthians and Sogdians with camels, Egyptians with a bull, and Bactrians, distinguishable by their boots, with a two-humped camel ... Armenians with a horse, Babylonians with tasselled nightcaps bearing vessels, cloth and a bison, Cilicians with their tight-fitting caps bringing ornaments and a stallion, and Assyrians with a bison ... Lydians with gold flower vases and a chariot drawn by two horses, Cappadocians with a horse, Ionians with cups and two rams, Afghans or Bactrians with a two-humped camel, and Indians from Sind clad in a simple one-piece garment and bearing gold, axes, and a wild ass ... Arabs with a dromedary, Punjabis with a humped bull, Somalis with a mountain goat, and Abyssinians with ivory tusks and a giraffe.[13]

The Great King is also depicted, often waited on by attendants or protected by his Imperial guards, the renowned 10,000 Immortals (known as 'immortals' because whenever one was slain in battle, another was waiting to take his place so their number never changed). Amidst these bas-reliefs is the image of a lion wrestling a bull, an iconic representation of the 'two essentials of agriculture, sun and rain' and the astrological symbols representing the spring equinox: 'the moment when the constellations Leo and Taurus are at their zenith'.[14] Persepolis was the chief site of the annual celebrations of the *Nowrouz* festival so fundamental to Zoroastrianism, the religion of the ancient Persians.

Beyond the towering remains of the Apadana – or vast audience hall – a series of chambers and palaces was built as Darius's successors expanded his grandiose project. All that now remains of this once magnificent palace complex are knee-high outlines that give the impression of a life-size architectural plan. With a little imagination, though, one can reconstruct the lofty stone pillars, add the roof of Lebanese pine resting on the two-headed kneeling-horse capitals, picture the splendour of silks hanging from walls bursting with colour from the precious metals and stones inlaid in them, a pair of royal guardsmen stationed at every doorway.

Historians theorise that the approach up the immense staircase, through the vast doorways into the Apadana and on to the foot of the royal throne, was deliberately designed to be long and winding in order to create anticipation and reverence for the eventual encounter with the King of Kings. An empire as large as that of Achaemenian Iran was no easy place to keep subdued and the kings realised that two powerful tools at their disposal were tolerance and ostentatious displays of power. The mightiest man in the world had to appear to be just that in order to anticipate even the earliest murmurings of rebellion, for who dared to rise up against a demigod with infinite resources?

Thus, rather than opting for the more obvious route to power preservation – the promotion of fear – the Achaemenians chose to display grandeur and an aura of stability. In an interview with BBC Persia, Kourosh Afhami, an Iranian architect who has dedicated years to the study of Persepolis, said that 'the architecture does not instil fear but instead shows splendour and grandeur; it is inviting … If you compare the faces and reliefs of Persepolis to the Babylonian and the Assyrian engravings, you will see that [those found at Persepolis are] very calm and gentle and spiritual.'[15] Pope concurs. 'There is nothing of the violence and agony of Assyrian sculpture,' he writes. 'Instead there is a lucid and suave simplicity, reserve and tranquillity appropriate to a great, vital moment and to an awareness of a transcendent presence.'[16]

The work, innovative and carefully executed, was carried out by the most skilled craftsmen and artisans the empire had to offer, the materials used the finest in existence. The scale of the project and the near-century it took for completion testify to the vision of the Achaemenian kings. But vision seems to have been laced with a brand of wisdom not usually found in autocracies, ancient or modern. Darius, like his great predecessor Cyrus, was famed for his tolerance and just governance. Persepolis has, in many ways, become the icon of this Great King's magnanimous rule. The *kurtash*, or labourers on the site, were made up of the many different ethnic groups under the Great King's rule. As slavery was forbidden by the Zoroastrian religion and prohibited under Cyrus the Great's Charter of Freedom recorded on his famous Cylinder, all of these labourers, although forcibly relocated and put to work, were believed to have been well recompensed for their work.[17] Historians believe that this fact makes the site unique. At a time when entire nations were being enslaved and transported immense distances to be worked to death as unpaid labourers, Darius, and his son Xerxes after him, guaranteed that every worker was duly rewarded for their efforts – perhaps another ingenious piece of image-building by the canny Achaemenian monarchs. This idea of using the architecture of the site to project a picture of tolerance and humanity alongside a sense of unshakeable power is noted by Pope. 'Humane sentiments found expression in the nobility and sheer beauty of the building: more rational than the work of the Assyrians or Hittites, more lucid and humane than that of the Egyptians,' he writes. 'The beauty of Persepolis is not in the accidental counterpart of mere size and costly display; it is the result of beauty being specifically recognized as sovereign value.'[18]

Looking down on the site are two immense tombs, those of Artaxerxes II and III respectively, carved out of the barren cliff-face behind the terrace. Under the baking midday sun I scrabbled up the hillside towards one of these tombs and was immediately taken aback by its scale and the intricacy of the carvings hewn so high on the rock nearly two and a half millennia ago. The height of the tomb afforded a stunning panorama of the entire Marvdasht plain. Beyond the terrace itself, whose vastness one only begins to appreciate from this raised vantage point, fields of brown and green stretched away to the distant mountains that encircled the vast plain.

Persepolis was the very symbol of Achaemenian power and grandeur. As such, it was much coveted by the Macedonian prince Alexander, son of Philip, whose ingenuity and self-belief carried him on a charge through the western reaches of the Achaemenian Empire and right to its very heart. Young, ambitious and a ruthless general, Alexander was also a pupil of Aristotle and had developed a philosophical bent. He was obsessed with the Iranian concept of the divinely ordained just monarch. He was said to always carry a copy of Xenophon's *Cyropaedia* when on campaign and famously paid his respects at the tomb of Cyrus in Pasargadae. It is for these reasons that the destruction of Persepolis in 330 BCE is much debated by scholars. Whether as an act of symbolic vandalism, drunken envy or simple mistake, the palace of the Achaemenian kings was burnt to the ground shortly after its capture by Alexander, who, according to Plutarch, needed 20,000 mules and 5,000 camels to carry away the ancient city's plunder.

★ ★ ★

Leaving Persepolis behind, we drove to the nearby burial site of some of the earlier Great Kings of ancient Persia. Naqsh-e Rostam is the name (again a misnomer, attributing the celebrated deeds of the Great Kings of old to the mythical Rostam of the *Shahnameh*) given to the area made up of four Achaemenian tombs, immense in their scale, hewn out of the sheer rock-face as high as 30 metres overhead. The only one of these tombs with an inscription identifies it as that of Darius the Great (522–486 BCE). The others are thought to belong to Xerxes I (486–465 BCE), Artaxerxes I (465–425 BCE) and Darius II (424–405 BCE).

Dispersed between the tombs are bas-reliefs depicting various coronations and victories of Sasanian kings, whose Persian rule began more than 500 years after the end of the Achaemenian era. The most renowned of these bas-reliefs depicts Shapur I (239–70 CE) victorious in battle with the defeated Roman emperor Valerian crouched in submission at the feet of his steed. Despite this sizeable tranche of history – and the entire Parthian dynasty – separating these two eras, the much later Sasanian carvings seem quite at home next to the Achaemenian tombs. This juxtaposition is deliberate, designed to strengthen Sasanian imperial credentials by linking their glories to those of their illustrious predecessors. The Sasanians are far from the only dynasty to do so. One of their images depicting Bahram

II (276–93 CE) is carved over a much older Elamite bas-relief thought to date to around 1000 BCE. Just as the Sasanians had wanted to associate their glories with those of Darius and his lineage, the Great Achaemenian king had also linked himself to the glories of Elam by choosing to be entombed at a location revered by this ancient civilisation.

Opposite the cliff-face adorned with displays of Persian regal power that span 1,300 years is a rectangular building known as Zoroaster's Enclosure, very similar in appearance to the structure known as Solomon's Prison at Pasargadae. Although the exact function of these buildings is uncertain, the general consensus amongst historians and archaeologists is that they were used for ceremonial religious purposes or to store sacred items.

★   ★   ★

Whilst I marvelled at the detail of these ancient bas-reliefs, Mr Zeydabadi paced agitatedly to and fro. He had insisted on taking me on this day trip: 'You don't want to go with a tour. You are rushed about by impatient tour guides. It's so impersonal and you can't take your time. Come with me, I will wait eight hours, more if you want.' I warned him that I would do just that, making notes and taking pictures. 'Sir, I will stand as long as the stones themselves have stood if you want me to.' Two hours into my wanderings at Persepolis he had begun to make impatient noises. Now, at Naqsh-e Rostam, the tombs had engaged him for a whole five minutes before he retreated to squat in the shade of a nearby tree. Catching my eye, he pointed impatiently towards his watch. I told him I had a couple more bas-reliefs to look at and disappeared around the corner before he had a chance to protest. When I reappeared half an hour later, he was pacing around the car like a vulture tapping its talons waiting for a wounded animal to perish.

As part of his exclusive bespoke tour, Mr Zeydabadi broke up our journey back to Shiraz by pulling over in the shade of an idyllic orchard bordered by flowing streams. 'A Persian', observed E.G. Browne in his *A Year amongst the Persians*, 'will never be happier than when seated under the shade of a poplar tree by the side of the stream, sipping his tea and smoking his kalyan.'[19] Sitting under the cool canopy of mulberry and pomegranate trees, I reclined against a trunk and swiftly dozed off as my by-now-pacified driver was firing up the *manghal* brazier and readying skewers of marinated chicken for the lunchtime feast that, I now realised, had been the principal source of his impatience.

'*Befarma* ...' Mr Zeydabadi's husky voice jolted me from my sleep to find him motioning to the farmer on whose land we had spread ourselves to come join us. The farmer refused the food but accepted a glass of tea, which he sipped silently, a sugar cube clamped between his teeth. Thanking us with a palm to the heart and a slight bow, he disappeared. Ten minutes later, just as the last of the chicken wrapped in flatbread had been eaten, his young daughter appeared with a basket of freshly picked fruit which she left us with a shy giggle before scuttling back to her mud-walled home.

★　★　★

The following evening I was invited out by Amir, Mr Lashgari's nephew and a professor of English at Shiraz University. He and his friends took me to a trendy coffee shop full of peacocked boys and powdered, pouting girls flitting and flirting. The scenes were much the same as those in Tehran but generally more relaxed. I put this down partly to the more laid-back nature of the Shirazis but predominantly to the less conspicuous presence of authority on the streets. Despite a worldly air, Shiraz still retained a tinge of quaint provinciality that added to its charms, its wide boulevards and peaceful gardens complementing the grandeur and beauty of the surviving Zand-era buildings.

Shiraz, situated in the original heartland of Persia, has been famed for beauty, wine, poetry, fragrant gardens and cypress trees that John Fryer, an eighteenth-century English traveller to Iran and India, giddily declared to be 'the loftiest in the universe'. The city certainly stands out on the otherwise parched plateau of central Iran. Sir Roger Stevens writes of Shiraz that 'A kind of cosmopolitan breeze seems to have blown over this city, bringing it into touch with distant lands, like Spain or India, and exotic plants and thoughts; it has a gentle glow, an inner calm, a sort of lush contentment quite alien to life on the rest of the plateau.'[20] Stevens was writing in the sleepy years of the 1950s and much has changed since then. Yet the gentle glow, the inner calm and the lush contentment he describes are still very much part of the character of this city.

Chapter Fifteen

A map of Iran shows Shiraz to be a mere stone's throw north of the Persian Gulf, so it did not seem such an outrageous idea to make a detour south to get a taste of a corner of the country which had not been on my original itinerary when I was offered a lift to Bandar Abbas by Reza, a friend of Mr Zeydabadi's who was going to visit his family. Reza must have been at least 2 metres tall and it was quite a sight watching him fold himself, one gangly limb at a time, behind the wheel of his small car. The 600-odd-kilometre drive south-south-east took us through Jahrom and Lar, winding through the mountainous coastal region before depositing us at the bustling port of Bandar Abbas. Not much of a conversationalist, Reza spent the journey working his way through an enormous bag of sunflower seeds which he would gnaw incessantly before noisily spitting the husks out between his feet. By the time we reached the south coast the driver's already cramped footwell was so full of discarded husks that I worried they would jam the car's pedals and prevent him from braking.

As we drove further south, the fields of wheat and corn were slowly replaced by date-palm groves heavy with the final fruit of the season. The palms were in turn slowly replaced by rugged, barren hillsides that were notorious for brigandry, again on the rise in the region. The glorious desolation of the southern plain was interrupted only by the odd lonely dome reaching up for a breeze to cool the water stored in these *ab anbar*, underground cisterns filled by *qanat* water channels carrying meltwater from the mountains stored for use in the dry season. The Zardkuh mountain range splits from the southerly stretching Zagros Mountains, the traditional land of the Bakhtiari tribes.

★ ★ ★

The Bakhtiari, along with the Qashqai, are the two biggest and most famous of Iran's ethnic tribes. The Bakhtiari speak a Lori dialect but are thought to be of Kurdish origin. Their tribal lands are spread through these mountainous regions of the south-west – around Fars, Khuzestan and Lorestan. The Qashqai, who speak a Turkic dialect, believe that their ancestors came from Turkestan as part of the Mongol armies that invaded Iran in the thirteenth century, although some historians theorise that they may have arrived as part of the great tribal migrations of the eleventh century. The Qashqai are thought to have originally settled in the area around Ardebil in the north-west of Iran but were ordered to move to their current tribal lands in the southern province of Fars by Shah Ismail, in the early sixteenth century, to defend the south from Portuguese colonisers.

From the late eighteenth century onwards, with the establishment of the Qajar dynasty by Agha Mohammad Khan in 1794, the history of the Qashqai has been dominated by struggles with authorities determined to curb tribal influence and autonomy in an effort to centralise the country's power-base. Agha Mohammad Khan Qajar led a series of campaigns against the tribes with mixed success, but it was in the reign of Naser al-Din Shah in the latter half of the nineteenth century that the centralised government came closest to quashing the tribal unrest and banditry that has been such an age-old thorn in the side of the authorities. Coupled with a brutal famine that coincided with his reign in the early 1870s, this brought the survival of the Qashqai tribe under real threat. But the corruption that blighted the reign of Mozaffar al-Din Shah (1896–1907), the successor to the Qajar throne, weakened the government's grip on power and afforded the Qashqai the chance to recover much of their provincial influence.

The twentieth century was the most unforgiving to tribal life. Determined to end tribal influence once and for all, Reza Shah arrested the tribal leaders and forcibly settled the Qashqai, using the army to block their migration routes in the hope that they would exchange their traditional nomadic, pastoral way of life for a sedentary, agricultural one. As they knew little of arable techniques, this merely resulted in them losing large numbers of livestock. Once again they struggled and were faced with poverty, famine and the very real possibility of extinction. After Reza Shah's enforced abdication in September 1941 – engineered by Britain, anxious to see a pliant Iran during the existential British–German struggle in World War II – the tribal leaders imprisoned in Tehran escaped back to Fars and repossessed their tribal territories, ordering the resumption of the annual migrations between summer and winter pasturelands that have defined nomadic life for millennia.

In 1963 the government of Mohammad Reza Shah officially declared tribes to be non-existent and the tribal leaders were stripped of any vestiges of provincial power that remained. Since this time the modern era has seen the growing sedentarisation of nomadic tribes. Nowadays there are between 1 and 1.5 million Qashqai in existence, and though the annual migrations (which can reach over 480 kilometres in distance) still take place between summer and winter pasturelands, more and more of their number have turned their backs on the traditional way of life in favour of a more stable, modern one.

* * *

We reached Bandar Abbas just in time for the *eftar* breaking of the Ramadan fast. A viscid heat and the powerful smell of prawns piping out of every kitchen window engulfed us as we clambered out of the car. Lights from trawlers netting prawns by the thousand bobbed in the darkness of the sea. Stalls along the seafront sold their fresh yield by the bag to eager customers, whilst waiting pickups whisked boxes of the carnation-coloured crustaceans to bazaars and restaurants the length and breadth of the country and even further afield.

'Mmmm, prawn season,' said Reza, taking in a big lungful of the heady scent that, combined with the overpowering humidity, was making me feel quite light-headed. He insisted I accompany him to his parents' house for a dinner of what else but prawns, expertly cooked by his mother, who, despite not expecting her son let alone a strange guest, managed to throw together a veritable feast in no time at all. After the customary few cups of tea that revive the weary traveller on arrival at an Iranian homestead, we were ushered into a breezeblock outhouse with cushions laid out around a *sofreh* (spread) on the floor.

Fresh prawns – whose shells my host sucked on gleefully before dis-
carding in the same manner as the sunflower husks, straight onto the
floor I would later be sleeping on – were accompanied by Bandari bread
(a savoury pancake) sprinkled with a sauce made from fish powder, oil
and, rather bizarrely, red-hued earth from the island of Hormoz, apparently a local delicacy and quite tasty. When we had finished eating,
two young girls wearing headscarves scuttled in to clear the meal and,
much to my relief, sweep the floor. Soon all trace of the lavish spread
had disappeared, the cushions had been arranged into a makeshift bed
and a rug left neatly out on top of them. I thanked the girls, who smiled
embarrassedly, eyes glued to the ground, as they disappeared back into
the part of the dwelling that was off-limits to male guests. They were
soon followed by Reza, who left me to get some much-needed sleep.

★   ★   ★

It is only in the last thirty-odd years, a period that has seen widespread
urbanisation, that Bandar Abbas has transformed itself from a sleepy
fishing port into Iran's main maritime hub and a bustling city. Its population of roughly 34,000 in 1966 had grown more than ten times by the
beginning of the twenty-first century. Nowadays, it is inhabited by the
more well-to-do urbanised provincials from the region's villages and
towns. Ethnically, Bandar is a curious hotchpotch of provincials, Arabic-
speaking Arabs (many of whom are Iraqi refugees from the recent wars),
Persian-dialect-speaking Bandaris and it even has a black community –
a result of the port being the principal entry point for East African slaves
before the slave trade was officially banned in 1929.

Previously known as Gameron, Bandar Abbas is the capital of
Hormozgan province and lies 85 kilometres away from the coast of
Oman on the opposite side of the Persian Gulf. Originally on the island
of Hormoz, the port was moved to the mainland by the Safavid shah
Abbas I (1588–1629) when he defeated the Portuguese, who had controlled it since 1507. Like much of Iran, the town suffered from the
instability that followed the collapse of the Safavid Empire and the
Afghan invasion. From the late eighteenth to the mid-nineteenth centuries, the port was leased to the Sultan of Muscat, who re-established it
as a trading post for the East India Company, and it remained under his
control until reclaimed by the Qajars in 1868. It was only in 1967, with
the completion of a new deep-water port, that the town's fortunes began

to pick up once more. In 1973 the Iranian Navy moved their headquarters to Bandar Abbas from Khorramshahr on the Iranian banks of the Shatt al-Arab waterway, and it soon usurped the unstable westerly port as Iran's main maritime hub when Khorramshahr was captured by Iraqi troops during the Iran–Iraq War.

Plenty of long, white Arab *deshdashes* were worn by the men, whilst the women wore tapered, colourfully braided trousers of a distinctly Indian hue under thin, sequined chadors and some wore the *burkhe* face mask. Unlike the Sunni-dominated island of Qeshm, the population of Bandar Abbas is predominantly Shi'i. The old town is still a warren of mud-walled bungalows, but modern apartment blocks, hotels and shopping malls have started to spring up along the shoreline.

★ ★ ★

Having expressed my gratitude and said my goodbyes to Reza and the rest of my impromptu hosts, I was now standing at the kiosk in the Bandar Abbas bus terminal, scratching my head and trying to make sense of the chaos around me. 'I am sorry sir, our timetable changed yesterday; it was New Year. We haven't been sent the new timetables yet so it's all a bit of a mess. God willing, it should all be sorted out by tomorrow.' It was *Eid-e-Fetr*, the end of Ramadan and the conclusion of the month-long fast.

★ ★ ★

Although it is said that Mohammad received his first revelation in the month of Ramadan, the tradition of fasting long predates Islam. The fast requires abstinence from more than just food. During daylight hours one must refrain from eating and drinking, sexual intercourse and even smoking. Travellers, menstruating women, the elderly and infirm are exempt from the fast but are traditionally expected to make up for the number of days missed before Ramadan comes around again. Fasting is meant to instil humility and compassion for the poor and needy, as well as being a healthy exercise in self-restraint. It also brings people together to celebrate *eftar*, the fast's end after the evening call to prayer, thus creating the sense of community so important to the Muslim faith.

The month of Ramadan has particular significance for the Shi'a, as the anniversary of Imam Ali's death falls on the twenty-first day of the month. Ali was the sword-wielding right hand of the Prophet Mohammad and a central figure in Shi'ism. He was dealt a blow to the head with a poisoned sword, whilst performing his prayers, by an assassin in revenge for the slaying of his brethren in the conflicts that bedevilled the Muslim world in the years after the Prophet's death. The assassination was part of a larger plot to eradicate the three leaders of the Islamic community and irreparably damage the caliphate. Ali's martyrdom had the opposite effect, increasing the clamour for the succession to be based on bloodlines, which would see his sons Hassan and Hossein as the rightful leaders of the Muslim community. Ali clung on to life on the floor of the mosque for two days. As word spread through the streets of Kufa, a growing crowd gathered around the son-in-law of the Prophet Mohammad, wailing and mourning as the life drained out of him. To this day, Shi'i Muslims hold a three-day vigil mourning the martyrdom of their first rightful Imam.

Travelling throughout the whole month of Ramadan had been an enlightening experience. Although as a traveller I was exempt from fasting I had, on the whole, obeyed its principles. When no restaurants or shops are open and when every hungry eye is on the stranger who has just strolled into town with his cumbersome rucksack and rudimentary grasp of Persian, it is hard not to. It was fascinating to see how provincial towns were deserted during the day and touching to see the festive atmosphere and sense of communality that came with the setting of the sun, with people stopping strangers to wish them well and give them a bowl of soup or some dates. It was also intriguing to witness the varying attitudes towards the fast. Many adhere to its strictures with pious precision. But in Iran, more so than in many other Islamic countries, there are a significant number of people who will adhere to the fast in public whilst being less exacting with their adherence behind closed doors.

★ ★ ★

I was eager to carry on my journey. My confusion in the maelstrom of the bus terminal was not helped by overbearing salesmen yelling destinations in my ear. One particularly pushy vendor picked up my backpack and led me by the arm out of the terminal building and towards a waiting bus. Confused, I asked the man where the bus was going. 'It's this way. Hurry, you'll miss it.'

'But where is it going? I might not want to get it.'

'Of course you want to get the bus. Why else would you be in the terminal?'

'I'm getting a bus alright. I just prefer knowing where it's going. I'm trying to get to Kerman.'

'The Kerman bus left an hour ago. This one is just as good, better even. The seats are more comfortable, better driver.'

By this stage we were standing in front of a bright pink bus. *GODSPEED* cried peeling red letters on the windscreen above the doleful expression of Imam Hossein. The rest of the windscreen was obstructed by swirling Qur'anic quotations and an image of a young girl with heavily made-up eyes and bawdy, pouting lips. Barely detectable in the middle of this extraordinary display was a wisp of paper stuck to the inside of the windscreen. It read 'Ahvaz'.

After a prolonged verbal tussle, I managed to convince the brash vendor that I had just come from that direction and that I was very certain that I wanted to head up into central Iran and not back west. 'Good bus, your loss,' was his parting shot. Back in the terminal, having almost been shanghaied, I weighed up my options. Spending more time in Bandar was not an option. My detour south had put me well behind schedule.

That instant, a vendor strutted past announcing a solitary remaining ticket for Yazd. Impulsively I lunged at him and, before I had thought anything through, I was on a ten-hour bus to central Iran. Behind me was a tribal woman muttering to herself and chiding her two unruly little boys: 'I swear by Almighty God and all the Imams that I shall feed you to the wolves when we arrive.' That prospect seemed to attract the boys, whose shouting and fighting only intensified with every threat from their mother. As I tried to sleep, or at least doze my way through the family din, I dipped in and out of dramatic half-dreams of the two brats being pursued by a pack of she-wolves.

★ ★ ★

I stepped into a leafy courtyard with a fountain cascading softly into a large pool. Around the pool was arranged a series of *takhts*, wooden platforms covered in rugs and cushions. Sprawled on these *takhts* were the unexpected yet hugely welcome blonde beards, dreadlocks, bare feet, beer guts, piercings and bikers' leathers that could only mean one thing: overland travellers. In the 1960s and 70s, streams of travellers

made their way from Europe to Turkey, through a much more accom-
modating pre-revolutionary Iran, and on to India and Nepal on what
came to be known as the Hippie Trail. I was surprised to discover so
many people still taking on a now much more challenging and dangerous route, through some of the world's most turbulent regions and over
many of its least welcoming borders.

I had made a beeline for a hotel beside Yazd's Old Quarter that had
come highly recommended by a number of people; a renovated house
in the traditional Iranian design, built around a large open-air courtyard. Having barely seen any Westerners after six weeks of travelling,
and none outside of Shiraz and Persepolis, I was taken aback by the sight
of all these Europeans lounging about the place. Snippets of conversations in French and Spanish wafted through the cool night air, sun-
burnt Scandinavian features peered out from behind dog-eared guide
books and the unmistakeable lilt of an Irish accent chirped excitedly
beside me.

A floppy-haired Dutchman with a big smile and an appalling grasp
of Persian had greeted me, instructing me to sit and have a coffee while
he found me a room, not once asking for the usual identification and
payment upfront that every other hostel demands the moment its thresh-
old is crossed. A tranquil oasis nestling against a desert wilderness, Yazd
has always attracted cosmopolitan crowds. I soon found myself thrilled
by the mere fact of speaking English with a Brit for the first time in
what felt like an aeon. Most of the travellers turned out to be over-
landers hurrying through Iran to what they considered a more welcoming Pakistan and beyond. In the evenings, like Ibn Battutah in the
fourteenth century, I bunked down on the roof of the hospice and marvelled at the clarity of the night sky alive with stars and the majestic pink
sprawl of the Milky Way.

*   *   *

Badgirs in an array of shapes and sizes stretched up to the cloudless blue
sky, desperately trying to catch any gust of wind that could be drawn in
to cool the mud-walled abodes of this desiccated desert town. Crumbling
arches straddled the narrow, labyrinthine alleyways of Yazd's old quarter, empty bar the odd scurrying *chadori* weighed down with provisions
or the cacophonous charge of a motorcycle. I wandered down alley after
alley, each identical to the last and often leading nowhere – a veritable
medieval maze in which it was a pleasure to wander lost. Above all

towered the twin, spindly, mosaic-clad minarets of the Jameh mosque; my North Star as I attempted to navigate the turbid streets.

These minarets are the tallest in Iran. Behind them a long court-yard leads the eye to the imposing *iwan*, a large portal adorned with calligraphic mosaic-work, rather like a gateway to God, with a *mihrab* that dates back to 1365 indicating the direction of the Ka'aba in Mecca. Behind this sits a squat tiled dome with faience mosaic. The mosque was originally built in the twelfth century but was largely rebuilt 200 years later in the mid-fourteenth century. Despite its discordant propor-tions – the minarets, the dome and the *iwan* seem to be devoid of any relationship with one another – the mosque somehow holds together magnificently and is considered one of the finest buildings of its type in the Islamic world.

From the old city, I wandered past the mesmerising minarets of the mosque and on to the partially open bazaar. Despite many stalls being shut because of a religious holiday, it was awash with shoppers. Out of a side entrance I came across the impressive Amir Chaqhmakh complex at the end of a crowded square. With its three tiers of arched balconies topped by a pair of minarets, it resembled a sort of Islamic wedding cake. I entered the building to find that the 'bride and groom' could be climbed. From the lofty heights of the minaret I was treated to a breathtaking panorama of the mud-coloured city and its bustle of domes, minarets and *badgirs*.

I headed back to the cooler confines of the hotel to avoid the mid-day sun with a glass of tea and a nap, after which I decided to stoke the flames of my Zoroastrian passions by visiting the city's fire temple. Yazd is the nerve centre of Zoroastrianism in modern Iran, although there are only 5,000 registered practitioners of the faith out of a population of over 500,000. I was asking one of the hotel staff directions to the tem-ple when I was informed that I could get a lift to a brace of Zoroastrian sites if I did not mind waiting half an hour for another two people to join me.

These two men turned out to be exchange students attending Tehran University. As if this was not unusual enough in itself, they told me they were from Havana, Cuba of all places. I was surprised by their grasp of Persian even after I learned that they had been in Iran for almost six years. *El Comandante* Castro was shown around Tehran University during a state visit six years earlier and was so impressed by the campus that he decided to implement an exchange system there and then. This decision resulted in my two new acquaintances arriving in the Islamic Republic shortly after.

Communist groups had certainly had an influence in Iran, with the *Tudeh* Party active since the 1940s, and the 1979 Revolution had been helped along by Marxists and Marxist-Leninists, but I was nevertheless surprised to learn that Iran, now an international pariah, had good relations with the Communist island-stronghold. '*El enemigo de mi enemigo es mi amigo*,' said one of the Cubans when I voiced this surprise. Together with my newfound comrades, I set out to explore the city's Zoroastrian heritage.

★ ★ ★

Though the Mongol invasions of the thirteenth century may have had the most immediate and direct impact on Iran, decimating the population and reducing many of the great cities of the ancient world to rubble, the Arab Muslim invasion of the seventh century must surely go down as the most influential event in the long and turbulent history of the country. The success of this grand venture seems by any objective criteria a most unlikely outcome. The Arabs, riven by tribal conflict, presented a rag-tag army, ill-equipped and inexperienced in major warfare. They faced the might of the Sasanian Empire. In one of the truly seismic global events of history, the passion-driven chaotic forces from Arabia changed the face of the world for ever. The Arabs were helped by what, with hindsight, seems like a string of misfortunes facing the Sasanians.

A series of long and unsuccessful campaigns against the Byzantine Empire in the west and the emergence of the Huns from the east, the proto-communist Mazdakite revolt in Iran itself and the sudden emergence and spread of Christianity through the region all conspired to weaken the foundations of a once indomitable empire. Internally, unrest was creeping in thanks to the increasing corruption of the Magi priesthood and the resultant growing disparity in wealth, as people were taxed to within an inch of their lives to support both the constant warring of the empire and the ever-more-opulent Magian temples.

Were it not for the successful campaign against Iran, it is no exaggeration to say that the history of Islam would be vastly different. For a start, the spread east would have been halted by a failure in Iran and the Sasanian Empire would have remained an insurmountable barrier isolating the nascent religion in the Arabian Peninsula. Moreover, without the riches of the Sasanian treasury the Arab armies would not have had the finances to carry on their campaigns east and, in all likelihood, would not have reached the Mediterranean, either. Many of the wiles of governance that created the infrastructure that maintained the vast Islamic Empire were also taken directly from the Sasanian model.

The events leading up to the Arab invasion of Iran bear retelling. An Arab envoy was sent to the court of Yazdegerd III granting the king an opportunity to avert war by embracing the new religion of Islam. But the cocksure monarch dismissed the envoy out of hand. 'Like a true son of Iran,' writes Sir Percy Sykes in his *History of Iran*, 'in his reply he referred with contempt to their misery, their eating of lizards and their infanticide.' He raged 'at the lack of respect shown to him and at the tenor of the message' and intimated that 'were it not for their being ambassadors, he would have put them to death.'[1] In the same hubristic way that Darius III dismissed a young Macedonian general a thousand years earlier and that the Iranian ruler of Khwarezm dismissed the envoys of a little-known Mongolian warlord six centuries later, or indeed the way that the last of Iran's monarchs, in the late 1970s, ignored the threat of seemingly lowly priests at the expense of the entire institution of monarchy, so too did Yazdegerd's contempt for the Arab Muslim armies spell the end of the Sasanian dynasty.

The Sasanian Empire fell to the Arabs in stages. First, in 637 CE, came the loss of their capital in Ctesiphon, and with it control of the financially and strategically key area that comprises the eastern bulk of what is now Iraq. It was at Nihavand in 641–2 CE, though, that the Sasanian Army suffered its greatest defeat, despite significantly outnumbering an Arab Muslim army spurred on by their faith in the revelations of the Prophet Mohammad. With discontent rife within the moribund Sasanian Empire, many Persians submitted to the new order without much resistance, particularly as the Arab Muslims showed mercy to those who did. A host of incentives, both social and economic, were offered to those willing to embrace the Muslim faith. The victorious Arabs had declared that persecution of the pre-existing Zoroastrian faith would not take place. But, in line with the mercantile foundations of their faith, they tightened economic screws, implementing a *Jazia* tax for all non-Muslims and declaring that only converts were allowed to do business with Muslims. This forced many to change faith for practical and financial reasons rather than any spiritual inclination. Even so, it was not until the ninth century that the majority of Iranians had turned to Islam.

Uprisings continued to break out in various parts of Iran, recapturing pockets of the country from the Muslim Arabs. Although most were suppressed, some areas deemed less strategically valuable were never fully under the control of the caliphate. A number of the uprisings started up in opposition to the stringent taxes rather than for any more nationalistic reasons. This instability resulted in many Muslim Arabs being settled in Iran specifically to keep the peace and ensure tax revenues kept streaming into the coffers of the caliphate. Over time, Islam slowly spread through the Iranian population. Arabic was adopted as the official language of the court in 696 CE and subsequently became the language of scientific discourse and, to a large extent, literature as well.

The adoption of Islam – and concurrently Arabic as the *lingua franca* – would prove to be of vital significance to Iran. With creative ideas and scientific innovations pouring in from all corners of the vast Abbasid Empire (750–1258 CE), both Islam and Iran flourished in a Golden Age that was only brought to a violent end by the Mongol invasions in the mid-thirteenth century. This period saw the emergence of many of the most celebrated intellectuals in Persian history, names such as Ferdowsi, Omar Khayyam and Rumi in the arts and Abu Ali Sina (Avicenna), Khwarazmi, Razi and Biruni in the sciences.

★ ★ ★

The *Atashband*, Keepers of the Holy Fire at the Zoroastrian temple, nurture a flame claiming to originate from one of the pre-Islamic sacred fires, the same fire whose holy embers were taken by a group of believers fleeing the persecution of the invading Arab Muslim armies 1,400 years ago. These refugees made their way by a perilous land and sea voyage to India, where they settled and have since thrived, both spiritually and economically, as the Parsee community based predominantly in Bombay. Back in Iran, the fire had to be hidden from the zealous Arabs, who viewed the Zoroastrian devotion to the symbolic flames as anathema.

Leaving the fire temple swarming with curious visitors, the Cubans and I piled back into the car and drove to the outskirts of Yazd. Dramatic jagged peaks surged heavenward from a dusty plain, silhouetted against the horizon by the setting sun. Vaulted roofs of *ab anbar*, ancient underground water stores, were dotted around the foot of two dessert-bowl-shaped hills with a circular protrusion atop one like an erect nipple.

These millennia-old mounds were being used for the disposal of the dead until as recently as forty years ago. Originally located some distance from the settlement that became Yazd, the country's alarming urbanisation meant that the sprawl of the suburbs had reached too close to these Towers of Silence in the opinion of Mohammad Reza Shah's health inspectors. Zoroastrianism is considered by many to be the first religion with an actual doctrine, a set of principles by which Zoroaster, the first prophet, declared one should lead one's life. The central tenet of Zoroastrianism is the tripartite decree of 'good thoughts, good words and good deeds', but many of the beliefs and practices incorporated in the religion can be traced back to more ancient pagan ideas of veneration for the things which sustain life: the elements.

Zoroastrians consider the earth to be sacred, so the burial of bodies – of tainted human flesh – is seen to contaminate its purity. Thus cadavers were taken to these Towers of Silence, where they were left exposed to the elements and to the vultures and insects. Zoroastrians have a deep affinity with nature and believe that in this way their dead are being of service to the natural world. A priest would return weeks later to sweep the bones into a pit in the middle of the tower and dissolve them using strong vinegar as a corrosive. In more recent times Zoroastrians have switched to the far more effective nitric acid.

My Cuban friends and I sat in silence, our legs dangling into this ancient bone-pit, as we watched the sun slowly set behind a distant mountain range, leaving a diaphanous mess of colours long after it had been lost from sight.

Back at the hostel that evening, I ate a local delicacy of camel stew. Yazd's geographical location on the cusp of the Kavir Desert means that a plentiful supply of camels are always to hand and much easier to keep in this barren region than other livestock. Now largely redundant as a means of transport thanks to the increasing prevalence of the pickup truck, camels are these days predominantly used for nourishment and drug smuggling, opium reportedly being stitched into their capacious humps.

★ ★ ★

The next day, an early start was necessary to fit in a trip to Chak Chak, one of the most sacred and important Zoroastrian sites still in existence. The hotel had provided a guide for this excursion, a young, knowledge-able Zoroastrian whom I probed mercilessly for information regarding contemporary religious practices. Accompanying us was a Swiss couple, retired journalists in the process of an arduous journey through the

Middle East and central Asia. Our guide decided to break up the long journey to Chak Chak by stopping at an old caravanserai in the desert village of Kharannakh.

The village was still partially inhabited despite the state of steady decline of the majority of its mud-walled dwellings. Traditional mud walls are restored once every few years so as to withstand the elements, but since this old part of the village had long been abandoned, the walls had been left to crumble away. The small agricultural settlement was encircled by fragrant apple, pomegranate and mulberry trees. In the valley below lay a dwindling river above whose banks tiered fields yielded plentiful crops. In this idyllic setting our guide unfurled a plastic mat and laid out an impressive spread of *kashk-e-bademjan* (aubergine and whey), freshly baked *sangak* bread, a mint-flavoured yoghurt drink called *dough* and tea.

Chak Chak, or Pir-e Sabz as it is also known, is nestled into the steep face of an isolated mountainside. It is the most important of five Zoroastrian holy sites known as the Five Pirs. Yazdegerd III, the last Sasanian king, fearing the increasingly unstoppable advance of the Arab Muslim army, sent his wife and daughters to take refuge in this vast and barren plain. Legend has it that the fleeing queen and her daughters were separated from one another in the confusion of flight. The subsequent demise of each of these females has been ingrained into Zoroastrian folklore; each of their resting places has become a sacred site much revered by worshippers.

Shahbanou Hastbadan, Yazdegerd III's queen, threw herself into a deep well in order to protect her honour from the pursuing Arab Muslim army. Many years later, a shrine was built on the supposed location of the well. The story – or rather the myth – of how this came about is a colourful one. A Zoroastrian from Yazd had been imprisoned for entering the city of Mash'had and sentenced to death, the penalty for any non-Muslim entering the holy city. Awaiting execution in his cell, one night the man had a dream that recounted the forgotten story of Seti Pir, the mythical name of Queen Hastbadan. He received instructions to spread the story of his dream and to build a shrine at the location at which he would find himself the following morning when he awoke. Sure enough, the prisoner woke up to find himself out of his cell, out of Mash'had and back somewhere on the outskirts of Yazd. As instructed in his dream, he built the shrine at the precise spot where he came to. This site is the sacred well of Seti Pir, the oldest of the Five Pirs and still a site of pilgrimage for Zoroastrians.

Princess Nek Banu had been split from the queen and her sisters. Her father had been slain and his empire lost. Now her own life was in peril. Dehydrated by the searing heat of the arid plain and with nowhere to take shelter, she turned to Ahura Mazda, the Wise Lord of the Zoroastrians, for salvation. As she knelt in desperate prayer, the very mountainside on which she was crouched suddenly gave a mighty rumble as tons of bare rock parted to reveal a cool, dark grotto. Thanking the Wise Lord, she clambered into the opening and away from the fast-approaching Arab Muslim hordes as the mountainside closed behind her. Inside, she heard an unmistakeable noise: *chak ... chak ... chak* came the sound of a steady trickle of precious water as it dripped from the cave's ceiling. This, so the myth goes, is how the site got its name.

Chak Chak itself is much less remarkable than its legend and the breathtaking scenery that surrounds it. Two brass doors embossed with the image of Sasanian royal guards protect the entrance of a damp cave with a small central fire burning under an incongruous chandelier. Another three-pronged candle-holder sits in an alcove on the opposite wall. Outside, a series of buildings have been added to accommodate the thousands of pilgrims that visit the site. Once a year, between 14 and 19 June, Zoroastrians from all over the globe flock to this remote mountainside to give thanks to Ahura Mazda and celebrate their faith. This pilgrimage, as well as that to any of the Five Pirs, is considered an act of great merit in the Zoroastrian faith.

The day of our visit was a public holiday so every nook and cranny of the tiered concrete stairway leading up to the sacred cave and its bronze doors was filled with large families noisily grilling kebabs, drinking tea and smoking *ghalyan* water pipes.

* * *

I had opted for an overnight train back from Yazd to Tehran. So, I discovered upon arriving at the station, had a lot of others besides me. People milled around, impatiently pushing cardboard boxes bound with twine or strolling in circles with cloth bundles over their shoulders. *Chadoris* huddled together conspiring like a murder of crows, students laughed and aped around, old men muttered to themselves, but all conversation revolved around one thing: how busy it was. Iranians of all shapes and sizes were making their way back to the capital they systematically desert every public holiday to see sights and visit relatives whilst littering indiscriminately.

Near the entrance to the platform there was a triple barricade of ticket inspectors, policemen and soldiers directing passengers this way and that before they could queue for the security checks. They only opened the way towards the security searches fifteen minutes before the scheduled departure time, causing a chaotic stampede. Having long since cast off my British reticence and emerged as a bull-minded Iranian, I dropped my shoulder and took on the seething crowd as though my life depended on it. Using my weighty backpack as a makeshift battering-ram to barge *hajjis* and *chadoris* aside, I emerged unscathed into the cool night air of the platform.

The train was in good shape – clean and tidy – and the 'luxury' ticket I had purchased for an extra 70 pence buoyed my hopes of a much-needed night's rest. I grunted and groaned my way down the narrow corridor, the aluminium kettle hanging from my backpack clanging with every step, announcing my imminent return to the capital like a town crier.

Inside my compartment were six seats that folded out to become bunks, a bottle of water and a few plastic cups. Next to the cups and fused into the miniature table was a plastic vase complete with plastic flower. A hunched old man waddled in, his wrinkled cheeks given a silver sheen by a thick layer of stubble. He slid a tatty bag under the seat whilst mumbling a barely audible greeting to nobody in particular. He was soon followed by two students, whose greeting was probably heard at the other end of the train. They instantly quizzed me about my status and were puzzled by the fact that I was neither student nor soldier – the usual status of an Iranian male of my age. On discovering my foreign upbringing all three beamed at me as I shrank behind my bag in anticipation of the barrage of questions that was to follow. But the interrogation was cut short by a ticket inspector who relocated the students to the non-luxury carriage stipulated on their tickets, leaving me with the still grinning *hajji* eyeing me as though I were a museum piece.

'What's the difference between this luxury cabin and the others?' I asked as the students were gathering their belongings.

'You get beds … and a flower,' said one with a nod to the vase, winking at me as he was ushered out of the compartment. The train juddered into life, crept out of the station and through sleepy suburbs before picking up speed and rattling its way to Tehran. The steady, rocking motion and my state of exhaustion soon had my eyelids weighing down and I drifted off to sleep.

I awoke some time later to find that two rough-looking, beady-eyed men in stained black shirts had replaced the students – the sort of people my instincts told me it was best to avoid conversation with. I quickly closed my eyes hoping that my stirrings had gone unnoticed. 'Ah, our *farangi* friend is awake. He went to university in Scotland!' came the hoarse voice of the *hajji*. I opened my eyes to find both newcomers staring at me quizzically.

'Where is Scotland?' one of them asked the old man.

'Scotland is in England,' replied the *hajji* with assurance.

I nodded and gave a wan smile.

★ ★ ★

When I next awoke, this time in semi-obscurity, it was to find the compartment now full, with a young boy and his father busily unfolding their bunks. The father looked at me sheepishly and asked with some awkwardness whether I could sleep in the top bunk so that he could be next to his son. The meddling *hajji* informed him that I was a foreigner and that I was worried about my bag. The two ruffians instantly looked at my backpack and then at each other. I assured the father and the ruffians that I did not have any concerns about my bag and that I was perfectly happy sleeping up top. With that, I clambered into the coffin-like berth, pulled a musty-smelling sheet over me and drifted off again.

An announcement over the PA system jolted me out of my slumber after what seemed like no more than a few minutes. But first light was now pouring through the window so I must have been asleep for a good five hours. 'It's six thirty. The train has stopped for prayer,' the *hajji* pronounced. I did not stir. The rest of the compartment – the rest of the train – was busy with their ritual ablutions and genuflections, some on the ground beside the train, others in compartments designated for this particular purpose.

After twenty minutes of prayer, the passengers shuffled back along the corridors and into their seats as the train's engine slowly stirred back into life. The father and son had alighted in Qom but the two men returned, as did the *hajji*, whose friendly smiles and obsequious tone had given way to a suspicious scowl. I shifted uncomfortably and stared through the window at the steady flow of desert scenery bathed in the soft dawn light, trying to avoid the old man's stares. It seemed a stranger was a curiosity, a stranger to God a canker.

Chapter Sixteen

I had spent the last few months waiting out the worst of the winter weather in Tehran. As the meltwater that started rushing through the city's system of *joub* canals heralded the welcome arrival of spring, I knew it was time to set out on another journey. I was once again on board a train, but this time I was heading north-east out of the capital.

The train rattled through dusty tracts of wasteland occasionally stained with the musty colours of mineral deposits. A hunched old woman sitting opposite me, now the only other passenger in the compartment, clutched a metal pot of rice wrapped in a plastic bag on her lap. Her maroon headscarf framed a bespectacled, wrinkled face. The furrows of her brow and cheeks ran deep and her calloused fingers and palms held on firmly to the pot as though this was her treasure and hers alone. A ticket inspector arrived, greeted us cheerfully, enquired after our health and apologetically asked to see our tickets. The woman hoisted her flowery skirt to reveal a varicose-vein-riddled leg clad in a laddered stocking. From somewhere in this confusion of clothing she fished out two brown, tattered notes held together by yellowing Sellotape and handed them to the ticket inspector.

The train that scaled the mighty Alborz Mountains, linking Tehran and the central plateau beyond it to the fertile and prosperous Caspian basin, arced out around the barren rim of the Kavir Desert before winding up through a brown and grey mass of sedimentary rock thrust heavenward and broken into jagged triangles by millions of years of tectonic pressure – the different shades and sizes of the layers of rock reading like lines from nature's narrative.

A drop in temperature was the first indication of the steadily increasing altitude, shortly followed by flashes of white as the train chuntered past pockets of snow. Soon it was clinging to the base of snow-capped mountains as if to avoid the perilous drops that plunged directly below my window. Mountain villages with blue rooftops were embedded into the rocky hillsides. As the train snaked its way up the mountain range, slowly, meticulously twisting up the treacherous sides, it disappeared into tunnel after tunnel, burrowing its way through the mountains. Sir Roger Stevens writes of the Trans-Caspian Railway that 'There are some sixty tunnels within fourteen miles, which must represent one of the most remarkable engineering feats in the world.'[1]

The young men who now dominated the passenger list whooped and cried Apache-like whenever the train entered the obscurity of the tunnels; a bizarre combination of *joie de vivre* and the opportunity for a burst of freedom from a dreary society in which religion ruled. I later learned that this practice occurs throughout the country whenever trains or cars enter tunnels, as if the darkness wipes away all the inhibitions the young feel towards their world.

Beyond the snowy peaks, thick clouds of mist enshrouded the bare rock and engulfed the valley below. This mist, a sign of increasing moisture, heralded a gradual descent towards the Caspian Sea and with it a dramatic change in scenery. As the train cut through the mist, the rock now became covered with verdant moss, and by the time we had descended through it, the whites and browns of the snow-spattered peaks had given way to a landscape of lush green. Little streams cascaded down the mountain-face, flowing around trees clustered together in open spaces among the rocks. As we descended the mountain, mud-walled houses began to appear signalling the rural world of the northern face of the Alborz Mountains.

The old woman and her pot of rice had by now been replaced by a family of local *chadori* women and their farmer patriarch. They talked loudly on their mobile phones, discussing the purchase of the daughter's laptop computer. The father spelled out the sacrifices he had made to acquire this costly item. 'But the young these days, they are grateful for nothing,' he intoned. She was to attend university next year, her proud mother told me. Hers was a common story: the poor, rural family financially destroys itself to educate their children in the hope that they will see ample returns on their investment from degrees and well-paid jobs. Sadly, though the family did not know this, the daughter was more than likely to be one of the many unemployed graduates that the disproportionately youthful population and sudden explosion of universities have begun to churn out each year and that the labour market cannot sustain.

This pockmarked, po-faced village-girl was discussing a blog with her aunt – yet another occasion where the discussions I witnessed gravitated around the internet as the key platform for change in the country. My travels had taken me to countless internet cafés in countless small towns across the country. In each, I had been surprised by the level of technology on offer and the level of computer proficiency on display. Every evening groups of young men huddle around a monitor to watch streams of alien culture or to flirt with girls hundreds, often thousands, of miles away on the only forum available to them in their far-flung towns. The pervasive presence of technology in a country as unplugged in every other way from the rest of the world is one of the truly portentous contradictions which any traveller to Iran will repeatedly witness.

★ ★ ★

Sari is an unremarkable, overdeveloped Caspian town. The coast lies 30 kilometres to the north, a fact that had partially saved it from the neon nightmare, fast food and *veela* disaster of other seaside towns. For a provincial town, Sari boasted a surprising degree of trendy modernity – or aspirations to trendy modernity: chic young women tottering about on high heels with faces caked in make-up; colourful faux-Dior headscarves; 'tight in all the right places' *manteaux*; shop after shop of electrical goods hawking expensive mobile phones, DVD players, plasma-screen televisions and laptop computers. Everything shouted newfound wealth. Mazandaran has always been an affluent province of Iran, benefiting from the fecundity of its soil, its geographical position and its plentiful natural resources.

The town of Sari itself has a long, if unremarkable history. Records of it can be found as early as the sixth century BCE in Greek histories that refer to it as Zadrakarta. In Iranian folk mythology, the town was founded after a local blacksmith named Kaveh[2] defeated the evil Zahhak. Back in the realms of reality, Sari did not make its mark on Iranian history until 1782, when Agha Mohammad Shah Qajar briefly proclaimed it his capital before moving his seat of power south of the

Alborz to Tehran in order to avoid the constant raids of Turkoman and Afghan tribes.

Sari offered little of interest, so after a brief exploratory wander and a quick kebab, I prepared for my onward journey by arranging a lift with a local taxi driver named Mr Ghasemi and grabbed an early night.

The next morning Mr Ghasemi was right where he was supposed to be, busily polishing his decrepit Paykan. He greeted me with a big smile, two raised arms and a loud '*Ya'llah*'. My handicapped cab driver had agreed to take me to Gorgan via Bandar-e Torkaman, something he vehemently insisted that he did not usually do. 'But I like your attitude,' he informed me. The feeling was mutual. I was particularly fascinated by his personally modified hand-operated clutch that compensated for his clubbed left foot.

'Are you going to chase the ladies?' he asked with a lascivious wink. 'Turkoman girls are exceptional,' he beamed, and so I had heard. 'Just watch it though, they're Sunni. If you get into a fight there, you're finished,' he said trailing an index finger across his stubbly neck.

From the glove compartment he produced two oranges that he proudly told me were from his own garden. We drove past fields of newly planted wheat and barley as the oppressive grey clouds, a near-perennial presence along the shores of the Caspian, loomed broodingly overhead. The lush greenery of the rolling hills was frequently invaded by large squares of brilliant yellow rapeseed.

★ ★ ★

'The bazaar is on Thursdays,' Mr Ghasemi informed me as we approached Bandar-e Torkaman, a small market town and fishing port on the south-eastern rim of the Caspian. 'You can buy anything you want. TVs, DVDs, cameras, stereos, washing-machines. Anything!'

'What about traditional Turkoman clothes?'

'What do you want with them? Sari has some good clothes shops. You like these jeans? Ten thousand *toman*,' he said, slapping his denim-clad thigh.

We drove past a horse, then another couple. Turkomans are, like any nomadic steppe-dwellers worth their salt, renowned for their equestrianism. I had heard about an annual gathering in this region in which riders performed traditional equine feats and indulged in a physical game resembling a primitive type of polo in which the dismembered carcass of a goat is used as a ball. The origins of polo can purportedly be traced back to ancient Iran. The sport is frequently mentioned in Ferdowsi's *Shahnameh* as a courtly activity used to single out the bravery and athleticism of young heroes and princes. I had also read of the epic matches put on by Shah Abbas in the great royal *Maydan* of Esfahan. I wondered whether the regal sport could be traced back further still to the Turkoman steppe-lands and the tradition of the *bozkeshi*. Mr Ghasemi pointed out a racetrack, the centre of which was thickly carpeted with the region's pervasive rapeseed flowers.

'Racing is a big deal here,' he said nodding vigorously. Despite gambling being strictly forbidden by Islam (even cards are illegal in Iran), betting on horses is curiously tolerated, even encouraged, and people flock to this area for the races. The season opener was scheduled to start on the upcoming weekend, but the rains had come late this year and the track was still a quagmire.

As we drove into the town itself, Mr Ghasemi explained the significance of the earth-coloured dress of the women. A long headscarf meant they were betrothed or married, a shorter one that they were single and available. The younger women were tall and slender, with exquisitely proportioned limbs and hard yet attractive rural faces. The older women, though they retained their height, seemed to lose their slender figures in the way common to rural women. They padded along with burly strides, their eyes still holding a certain youthful charm. The men had patterned cloths tied around their heads similar to the Kurds and the Arab *chafieh*, but the crown of the head was covered by a skullcap – some with embroidery, others simply patterned – which leant a delicacy to their hard physiognomies. Eyes were slightly more drawn and cheekbones more prominent, similar to Hizara Afghans. These were Asiatic faces that spoke of their descent from the Turkoman warriors who came to Iran with their ruler Timur when he conquered the country in 1385. The Turkoman onslaught on Iran became a kind of migration, with many of the new arrivals assimilating with the local population. Some chose to stay separate, maintaining their own communities and cultures in the plains of north-eastern Iran. Their appearances and physiognomies suggest a continuum that has survived undisturbed for over 600 years.

The streets were lined with crumbling brick bungalows more like shacks. The affluence of the north seemed not to have reached this particular spot where the Turkomans lived, despite it being a trade port. At Mr Ghasemi's insistence we visited the fish market: a small, square

courtyard where pavement stalls spewed still-gawping fish. I then per-
suaded Mr Ghasemi to drive me to the sea. We followed signs for the
'Swimming Port' which led north out of town. A rusting sign read
'Welcome to the beautiful beach of Bandar Torkaman'; there was no
beauty and certainly no beach, but the dull-green stormy waters of the
Caspian were a welcome sight nonetheless.

'You speak English? Full? Full?' Mr Ghasemi asked, bewildered, as
we drove away from the port. I explained that I was born, grew up and
studied in England.

'Are there Iranians there, in Engelestan?'
'Yes. Not as many as in some places.'
'Do they speak Persian there?'
'The Iranians? The older ones do but most of my generation sadly
never learnt to.'
'Do the Engilisi speak Persian?'

★ ★ ★

Gorgan is a large, flourishing town; a melting pot of Turkoman and
Mazandarani bloodlines which proves an attractive combination, especially amongst the women. The chador far outnumbers the sombre but
attractive colours of Turkoman dress and the headgear so common on
the men in Bandar-e Torkaman is a rare sight here. Accents are more
comprehensible than the usual mumbled drawl of Mazandaran. The
people are friendly, with a playful air, especially the women, who are
noticeably less downcast than in the majority of towns of similar size.

Historically the region was known as Hyrcania, or Varkhana in
Pahlavi – the language of ancient Persia in its immediate pre-Islamic
period when the country was ruled by the Sasanians (224–651 CE).
Varkhana means 'Land of the Wolves' and these predators still roam
the foothills and fields of the area in considerable numbers. Thanks
to its production of fruit and raw silk, Gorgan thrived for centuries
before being ravaged by the Mongols in the thirteenth century.

To get my bearings, I sat on a bench in the municipal park. Around
me a group of young boys played energetically amid the soft pink and
white clusters of blossoming trees. Despite a substantial area of the centre
of town being a military zone, the usually ubiquitous authoritarian presence was noticeably lacking. The street on which I had chosen my lodgings was by day lined from one end to the other with shoe shiners. At

least forty scruffy, stubbly old men in woollen caps and stained trousers squatted on the sidewalk waving brushes in their polish-streaked hands, each no more than a metre away from the other. Given the Iranian propensity for *dampayi*, sandals usually worn with socks, this was not a little curious.

My theory that Iranian towns only revealed their true character in the evenings again proved correct, as Gorgan exploded with vitality as soon as the sun had set. Young and old thronged the streets: families and friends all holding hands, smiling, chatting, occasionally arguing. As with other provincial Iranian towns, the atmosphere was warm, almost carnival-like. Families comprising different generations queued for kebabs and fruit juice while kids ran around and the occasional flirtatious glance was exchanged amongst teenagers. The mischievous smiles of the young teenage girls seemed to be emphasised by their tightly clasped chadors. Despite its limited provincial offerings, Gorgan had an endearing charm. My one disappointment was that a trawl through the bazaar in search of Turkoman wares again left me empty-handed. I was encouragingly told that Gonbad would be more fruitful.

★   ★   ★

Gonbad, or Gonbad-e Kabus to give the place its full title, is much more of a Turkoman stronghold. Smaller in size and not such an economic force as Gorgan, it seems only to have been saved from the monotony of small-town Iran by its extraordinary landmark, which, according to Robert Byron, 'ranks with the great buildings of the world', and which was described by Pope as 'a supreme architectural masterpiece'.[3] The Mil-e Gonbad[4] was built in 1006 CE by the town's benefactor and ruler of Gorgan, the Ziyarid Kabus-ibn-Washmgir (978–1012), as his own mausoleum.

Famed as a patron of the arts and as a poet in both Persian and Arabic, Kabus counted some of the greatest minds in history at his court. Al-Biruni dedicated his *Chronology of Ancient Nations* to him and Avicenna took shelter at his court when ignoring a summons from Mahmud of Ghazna. Despite his renown as a man of letters and his reputation for wisdom and magnanimity, Kabus's reign was blighted by a number of poor political decisions and a constant clamour to remove him from power. He was exiled for offering refuge to the Buyid prince Fakhr al-Dowleh, only to return to the throne over ten years later in 997 CE.

His tyrannous and often heavy-handed approach soon gained him many enemies and he was again hounded out of his domains by high-ranking figures in his own army. Manucher, Kabus's son, was placed on the throne and pressured to hunt down his fugitive father. Trapped by his son's forces, Kabus eventually agreed to abdicate and retire to a castle where he would dedicate his life to his writings and spiritual beliefs. His enemies still considered him too much of a threat and allegedly had him frozen to death in 1012.

The tomb itself has been described both as a skyrocket and a giant brick pencil. Over 50 metres high and with considerable foundations, its phallic image towers over its surroundings, recently developed into a pleasant park. A sign next to it spuriously proclaims it to still be the tallest brick structure in the world at 52 metres. What does make it an extraordinary spectacle is that, over 1,000 years old, it stands almost perfectly preserved despite the elements, earthquakes and even a shelling at the hands of the Russians. The hollow interior once housed the body of the monarch-poet suspended in a glass coffin. A single step inside the hollow brick tube revealed its phenomenal acoustics with a fabulously amplified crunch of earth underfoot.

★ ★ ★

The streets of Gonbad were awash with the distinct darker colours of Turkoman clothes and the equally distinctive Asiatic visages of older men with weathered faces, white billy-goat beards and patterned head-dresses, speaking a dialect of Turkic, a language group that spans a belt of land from eastern Europe and Turkey right through to western China. The tall, slender women I had seen in Bandar-e Torkaman were notably absent. Here, there were plenty more tall men, many of whom wore the typically Afghan *shalwar kameez*. This, I later learned, was due to the considerable presence of Zabolis and Baluchis, whom the locals treated with no little suspicion, branding them all as thieves. A large number of them immigrated in the 1950s and 60s, escaping a drought-ravaged Sistan province and looking for work in the region's booming cotton industry. The ballooning pantaloons of Kurds could also be spotted floating down the street. I wondered whether these were descendants of the Kurds settled in the area by Shah Abbas to defend the border against the frequent incursions of the Turkoman and Uzbek tribes in the late sixteenth and early seventeenth centuries, or whether their arrival in the region was more recent. In the late 1930s Reza Shah had uprooted many Kurds, whom he considered troublemakers, from their tribal lands in western Iran to this area of the north-east. The Turkomans were soft-spoken and jovial, though the men had that same tough air about them as the Kurds.

Chapter Seventeen

'You're no longer in Iran here, you're in central Asia,' said the spirited septuagenarian with vibrant, deep-blue eyes exuding experience. 'If you go up onto that hill over there by Alexander's Wall and look across, you can see a very distinct line. On one side it's all yellow and green and on the other, the nature is completely different. It is as though someone traced a finger along the horizon and said that this side is Iran, the other central Asia.' My early-morning appearance at this secluded farm on the Turkoman plain was followed by a steady stream of visitors to this unique homestead.

From Gonbad I had got a string of *savari* taxis from village to village further and further into Turkoman territory, through the familiar sleepy rural villages of dilapidated brick shacks, walls daubed colourfully with advertisements for everything from paint to pots and pans. The view beyond the villages, though, had been novel and stunning. The perennial grey clouds hung so low as to seem within reach, swallowing the softly rolling hills and their picturesque patchwork of yellows and greens in their misty murk.

A quick change of *savari* in Kalaleh had seen me bouncing along a dirt road towards the small rural settlement of Ghaleh Tappeh Sheikh. There, an American woman by the name of Louise Firouz had dedicated the last thirty years of her life to back-breeding the Caspian horse, thought to be the genetic predecessor of the thoroughbred. I had heard and read much about her farm and my determination to visit it had only been compounded by the curious coincidence that the Firouz she had married many, many moons ago was my grandmother's first cousin.

Through these very lands the nomadic Aryan tribes who later settled the Iranian plateau and evolved into the Medes and Persians, ancestors of the Parthians, first descended into Iran, and it was from this area that the Parthian kings hailed. Originally called the Parni, this nomadic tribe invaded the area of north-eastern Iran known as Parthava or Parthia around 245 BCE. They went on to rule Iran (or at least different parts of it) for close to 500 years, between 247 BCE and 228 CE. Sandwiched between the more celebrated Achaemenian and Sasanian dynasties and with scant records of the era, the Parthians are possibly the most overlooked of Iranian dynasties. Masters of the saddle, they gave their name to the 'Parthian shot', a singularly difficult technique of firing a bow whilst mounted, in which the shoulders are rotated to fire behind, allowing riders to rain down arrows on their pursuing enemies whilst seeming to retreat. Fearless warriors, they wrested control from the Greek Seleucids and staved off the advances of the Roman Empire.

It was under the rule of King Mithridates the Great (171–138 BCE) that the Parthian Empire burgeoned, conquering first Bactria to the east (parts of today's Afghanistan and central Asia) and then Media (western Iran) to the west. By 141 BCE, Mithridates had defeated the Seleucids and taken their capital of Seleucia, just south of modern Baghdad, before turning his attentions to Babylon and Elam. Soon the Parthian Empire had expanded to comprise the vast mass of the Middle East and central Asia. Riches poured into the Parthian coffers, both in the form of tributes from their conquered lands and from the taxing of mercantile traffic along the Silk Road, now largely under their control.

The Parthians allowed many of the existing local administrations to remain in place, governing their captured cities as vassals. That there was no centralised seat of Parthian power allowed their empire to survive the constant incursions it suffered at the hands of the Romans. Whilst the Parthians had been busy conquering the Seleucid lands to the east, the Romans had seized what was left of the waning Alexandrian Empire to the west, with Pompey conquering Syria in 64 BCE. With the two great empires of the era now toe-to-toe, it was only a matter of time before the Romans and Parthians turned their hostilities towards each other.

In 53 BCE the Roman general Crassus disastrously invaded Parthian territory, resulting in the annihilation of more than 40,000 Roman troops. This incursion triggered an ongoing enmity that rumbled on for nearly 300 years, only occasionally interrupted by civil unrest in the Roman Empire and by Parthian expansionist ambitions towards the Indus Valley. Sixty-odd years into the Common Era, fighting broke out anew when the Roman emperor Nero and the Parthian king Vologases I (50–56 CE) squabbled over control of Armenia, but a truce was reached between the two empires. The war resumed in 114 CE under Emperor Trajan. This saw the Parthians suffer major losses and relinquish control of Ctesiphon and areas of Assyria and Babylonia.

Militarily, the Romans and the Parthians had almost diametrically opposed tactics. Where the Romans relied on heavy infantry, the success of the Parthian Army was built on their cavalry. This made the far more mobile Parthians very effective both on the battlefield and in quick, unexpected invasions of hostile territories. These tactics overwhelmed the slower, more solid Roman Army, which was better suited to siege warfare and consolidating invaded lands. This military counterbalance is key to understanding the wars between these two empires: why the Romans were able to seize cities like Ctesiphon so often and why the Parthians were so effective at capturing foreign lands but so much less effective at retaining control of them. It was only a matter of time before the Romans adapted their military tactics to better deal with the Parthian armies.

By the end of the second century CE, the Parthian Empire was beginning to weaken as a result of internal divisions. Despite this, Vologases IV resumed hostilities with Rome by invading Armenia in 190 CE. The Romans were swift to retaliate, recapturing Ctesiphon and with it Mesopotamia. But it was only when Vologases V (*c.* 191–208 CE) attempted to retake Mesopotamia that the Parthian Empire was dealt a fatal blow. In 224 CE a warlord named Ardeshir revolted against Artabanus IV, the last of the Parthian monarchs, and established the Sasanian dynasty.

It was not just on the battlefield that the Parthians forged a legacy as innovators. They pioneered crucial developments in architecture such as the vaulted *iwan* and squinch that would go on to have such a resounding impact on Islamic architecture the world over.

'This,' said Louise Firouz flicking the ash from her white-tipped Kent cigarette nonchalantly into what looked like a candlestick holder, 'is Sasanian. Now it's my ashtray. You walk around up here in the rain and things, bits of broken ceramic like my ashtray, just appear from out of the mud,' she continued, taking another drag of her cigarette. 'Much of the region's history remains neglected, buried under the very earth we walk on, our crops grow on and our animals graze on. It is an exciting prospect that one day, *ensha'llah*, people will come with the tools, the skill and the patience necessary to unravel these long-forgotten mysteries.'

★　★　★

It was to precisely one of these mysteries that my next adventure led. Having rested up in Mrs Firouz's farmhouse, I awoke to find a grey, misty morning. I had heard much about a bizarre local site, the shrine of Sheikh Khaled Nabi, and this would be the only opportunity to see the place for myself despite the weather doing its level best to thwart me. A dawn rainstorm had left the ground a muddy sludge that would prove hard going for the ascent to the hill-top shrine. I consulted with Rajab, the stable manager (if a hierarchy could be said to exist in such a utopian atmosphere) about how best to approach the 40-odd-kilometre drive. He left me to gather my things as he drove off to the village – a small Turkoman settlement of thirty families located at the end of a short muddy track. There he enlisted the services of his cousin, who had a pickup and was apparently my best hope of a successful ascent.

Half an hour later Kheder pulled up in his blue Saipa pickup. As I hopped in, Kheder extended his hand. 'I used to work for Mrs Louise,' he said by means of introduction, 'until she threw me out.' The way he intoned this last delayed statement made me think better than to enquire why.

The drive first took us over a paved road, up through gently rolling hills with every conceivable stretch of flat land cultivated. The patchwork of deep-green wheat blades and bright-yellow fields shimmered in the distance, as if to suggest nature's version of a Turkoman tribal rug.

'In a few months this is all dry, brown and golden,' Kheder said. I remembered the countryside of Kurdistan and Ilam in western Iran that I had passed through in autumn. Then, I had been told the exact opposite – that the soft-brown, gold and tawny hues of the desiccated countryside there would become an explosion of colours with the onset of spring. The road meandered through a hilly gorge, rising almost imperceptibly to reveal a sweeping panorama of fairy-tale countryside before the view was again blocked by the undulations of the terrain.

The final climb to the shrine was up a steep dirt track that had been softened into slippery mud by the earlier rain. Kheder now had serious doubts as to whether his truck would make it up. After some handy driving from him and a lot of clanging and grinding noises from the truck's gears, we emerged onto a small plateau dotted with stalls selling tea and trinkets. The view that stretched before us defies description. A vast plain extended out as far as the eye could see. All of the hills we had driven through lay before us like so many terracotta and green wrinkles on the surface of this ancient land. Within minutes of our arrival, the fog that had earlier enshrouded the morning again closed in on us. I reached for my camera, desperately trying to capture the view before it disappeared behind the gloomy veil.

* * *

Kheder pointed me in the direction of a well-trodden path that wound its way over various ridges, disappearing into the fog that was now rising from all around. 'The stones are along this path,' he said before mumbling various sentences that less than subtly implied he would rather not accompany me. I told him I could find my own way and promptly set off. 'If it starts to rain, run back or we'll be stranded up here,' he shouted after me.

Not far along the path I came across a 2-metre-high stone carving with a bulbous end that was unmistakably phallic in intent. A few hundred metres further on another lay on the ground, overgrown with grass and small-petalled white flowers. By this stage the stunning view had been wholly swallowed by the voracious fog and my vision was restricted to the few metres in front of me. I carefully picked my way along the muddy path, very aware of the occasional sheer drop even though I could not see it. Around the next hill I was confronted by a veritable forest of petrific penises – some waist-high, others towering well over my head. Amongst them was the odd wing-shaped stone described by some as butterflies. Pagan and primitive in their symbolism, these stone sculptures were curious objects long presumed to have been gravestones, with the height of the phallus presumed to represent the age of the deceased. It did not take much imagination to identify the butterfly-shaped stones, thought to represent the gravestones of women, with breasts. I peered at them through the fog, looking for patterns; families possibly being buried side by side. The more I looked, the more the spread seemed unrelated. There were no obvious correlations – between male and female stones or between shorter and taller stones – that might represent families. Another peculiarity was the noticeable predominance of the phallus. To my knowledge, men did not outnumber women to such a degree in any era of human history. Louise Firouz was later to tell me that some of the stones had recently been removed and the earth below excavated but no trace of bone or any other signs of burial were detected.

Similar phallic stones have been found in a surprising number of countries, from Scotland and Ireland through Europe and Scandinavia, central Asia, India, China and even in parts of Africa. These stones are all shrouded in a certain amount of mystery. What is known is that these megaliths are prehistoric, thought to be at least 6,000 years old and very possibly much older. People have speculated as to their function: ancient calendars, altars for human sacrifices, territorial markers or burial sites. The most widely held opinion nowadays is that these phallic stones related to fertility rites.

Whatever the scholarly speculation, it was certain that this place on the Turkoman plain had a special aura about it. The elevated position, the sweeping view, the mist blanketing the plain, then rising and swirling playfully over the hilltops – all this gave the landscape an originality that extended beyond the mysterious stones.

★   ★   ★

Muslims make the pilgrimage here not for the stones but for the mausoleum of Sheikh Khaled Nabi and two other shrines. One, according to the locals, belongs to Sheikh Nabi's father and the smaller one, on a lonely outcrop with giddying views, belongs to an unnamed *choopan*, or shepherd. Sheikh Nabi is thought to have been a Nestorian Christian mystic from Yemen who lived in the fifth century CE. The locals revered him as a prophet despite Islam categorically declaring Jesus the penultimate prophet in the chain that ends with Mohammad. Although historical accounts confirm that many Nestorians relocated to Sasanian Persia after Nestorius (the bishop of Constantinople) and his teachings concerning the human nature of Jesus were deemed heretical at the Council of Ephesus in 431 CE, to date no further historical evidence surrounding the existence of Sheikh Khaled Nabi has been uncovered.

The shrine itself is spectacularly unspectacular – a lop-sided building with a disproportionate and uneven green dome on its roof like a discarded watermelon husk. The doorway is made up of green bars and cracked window panes that give the lonely building a distinctly gaol-like look. The interior is just as stark: a stone tomb in the middle of a room decorated with peeling green paint and a couple of Turkoman rugs. The room is illuminated by a naked bulb hanging from the ceiling by the single electrical cable that runs into the structure from a nearby pylon. But what the shrine lacks in beauty and mystique, the panorama and stones more than make up for, and the view of the undulating plain below from the outcrop of the even more ramshackle Shepherd's Shrine is one that is not forgotten in a hurry.

Many sites in Iran that predate the Arab invasion have been incorporated into the narrative of modern Islam. Some, like this one, have continued to be venerated though nobody is quite sure why – and may not even have been during the early Islamic period. Others, especially Zoroastrian sites, had *Imamzadehs* built over them, or biblical names that have links to the Qur'an attached to them, to protect them from destruction by the Arab Muslim army.

Outside the Father's Shrine stood an *Arbre Sec*, or wishing tree, its desiccated branches leaved by countless flapping scraps of fabric tied on as votive offerings, predominantly by women praying for husbands or pregnancies. 'The custom is to make a vow at such a tree,' writes Sir Percy Sykes, 'that, if one's wish be fulfilled, a sheep will be brought and sacrificed beneath it; in token of the vow a strip of clothing is torn off and tied to the tree, which thus presents a curious image.'[1]

Back in Kheder's Saipa, I asked him what he knew of the stones. In an earnest voice he recounted the local legend that surrounds them. 'When Sheikh Nabi left the area, the locals turned their backs on God and started worshipping the sun again, as in pagan times. As punishment for this heresy, they were all turned to stone and still stand there to this day.' There was a lengthy pause as though he was thinking this over before he went on: 'But that's rubbish. Apparently they're graves,' he added with a shrug. After an hour atop the hill, we descended and stopped at a sleepy village to have tea with a relative of Kheder's.

'This fellow,' he said, slapping an arm around the slight frame of a smiling man with intelligent eyes, 'is a mullah. His sort has made all our lives hell.'

'And this fellow is a thief,' came the riposte. 'He has stolen land from me and the son of a dog won't give it up.' Then they both erupted with laughter that was quickly muffled by a hearty embrace. We sat and had tea and freshly baked bread with local cheese as I listened to the two friends chat in their Turkic dialect, one in the measured tones of a sermon, the other in punchy, playful bursts. A cock strutted through the mud outside the window as the mullah's daughter, a shy, rosy-cheeked little girl, tried to steal a clandestine glance at the stranger who had invaded her house.

★ ★ ★

Back at the Firouz farm I was told by Alam to head over to Rajab's house in the village. Rajab seemed to be the accountant, administrator and right-hand man of the place, whilst Alam was the arthritic, loyal left hand who could cook up a mean goat stew. Rajab greeted me with an irresistibly contagious smile, which the naturally drawn eyes and high cheekbones of the Turkoman seem to accentuate. I was plied with cup after cup of steaming tea as we looked through photographs of the farm on a laptop whilst lying on the floor, propped up by a cushion under the armpit 'in true Turkoman fashion' according to my host.

That evening I was treated by Rajab, who, together with his tireless wife, seemed constantly swathed with smiles, to a Turkoman speciality. 'This is *ghotab*. We cook it for honoured guests,' said Rajab placing a tray of what looked like oversized biscuits in front of me. The pastry shells were filled with minced meat and onions and tasted remarkably similar to a Cornish pasty. I tried to explain the history of Cornish miners' fodder to the charming couple and their pretty young daughter, but once I realised that their warm smiles disguised mystification at my ramblings about some unheard-of land, I reverted to dishing out compliments. After dinner I was led to the adjoining room of the cement shack, where a place had been carefully laid out for me on the floor. Rajab, his wife and daughter laid their places next to one another on the floor of the main room next door and bade me a good night.

The day's wanderings and the bracing country air soon had me fast asleep and it was only the loud rumbles of an almighty morning thunderstorm that roused me. From a gap in the roof I could see forks of lightning setting the dawn sky ablaze. Peals of thunder so loud they drowned out the racket of the driving rain reverberating on the corrugated iron roof made me leap out of my makeshift bed.

★ ★ ★

Back in Gonbad, having left Mrs Firouz and her farmstead, my taxi driver and I were in a frenzied search for traditional Turkoman hats, made from lamb's hide, that looked remarkably like a fake Afro you would find in a fancy-dress shop. Our enquiries were met with laughter and joking instructions to go to a museum. 'Nobody has worn those things outside of traditional wedding ceremonies and entertainment for tourists for the past fifty years around here,' explained my taxi driver. As luck would have it, one last desperate attempt ended in success. But every upside has a downside. My determination to find this hat had caused me to miss my bus onwards. The taxi driver had a solution of sorts. He took me to a crossroads at the edge of town, cheerfully dropped me off and said, 'Don't worry; in a few hours there'll be a bus from Sari.' Rainclouds loomed overhead, with no shelter in sight. I hunkered down, perching on my bulging backpack, and stared hatefully at the reeking ball of wool that was the cause of my woes. 'In a few hours,' my driver had said. In Iran that could mean anything between now and never. Just as I began to contemplate the fastest and most effective route to self-destruction, I spotted movement on the road in the distance. It was a vehicle trundling along. Soon a dilapidated yellow bus pulled up.

'Mash'had?' I shouted speculatively. To my utter surprise, the doors groaned open.

★ ★ ★

Mash'had, tucked into the north-eastern corner of Iran that borders Afghanistan and the plains that sweep into central Asia, has firmly established itself as Iran's second city, overtaking Esfahan and Tabriz and making the province of Khorasan-e Razavi the most affluent in the country. This wealth is due almost entirely to two things: saffron and a shrine. Mash'had houses the mausoleum of Imam Reza, the eighth Shi'i Imam – in other words, the eighth descendant of the Prophet Mohammad from the line of Ali, whom the Shi'a revere as the Prophet's legitimate successor. The Imam Reza is the only one of the Prophet's successors to be buried on Iranian soil. Millions of pilgrims from across the globe flock to the city to become *mashtis* – the honorific title, like a *hajji*, bestowed upon one who has performed the pilgrimage to Imam Reza's tomb.

As the taxi from the bus terminal drove through the thronging streets of Mash'had to the house of a family friend who had agreed to put me up, the brightly lit shops and neon signs that drifted past the window spoke volumes about the city's fortunes. Every few metres were hotels and rental apartments to cater for the myriad pilgrims. Also striking in their number were gaudy furniture shops; mock Louis XIV furniture, garish chandeliers and over-embroidered curtains screamed newfound wealth from expansive showrooms all over town. The city was dripping with the proceeds of pilgrim-spending.

Mash'had started out as a village by the name of Sanabad. In 808 CE, the fifth Abbasid caliph, Harun al-Rashid, was on his way east from Baghdad to quash an uprising when he became ill and died. He was buried where he died, in the garden of the governor of Khorasan in Sanabad. Harun al-Rashid had declared that the empire of the caliphate should be split between his two sons. Amin, being born to an Arab mother, would get control of the Arab portion of the Abbasid Empire and Mamun, born to a Persian mother, the Persian portion. But Mamun's ambitions were greater than Persia alone; he wanted the whole empire for himself. As a means of legitimising his claims to the caliphate proper, Mamun decreed it should pass to Reza upon his own death, knowing that the aged Imam was more than likely to pass away first. But patience gave way to certainty and Mamun decided to hurry things along. Whilst accompanying him on a trip to Tus in 818, he is said to have killed Imam Reza with poisoned grapes. Reza's body was buried alongside that of Harun in Sanabad.

From that time, Shi'i adherents have been making the pilgrimage to visit the grave of their beloved Imam. The name of Sanabad was replaced by that of Mash'had, meaning 'the Place of Martyrdom'. Mamun built a mausoleum over the body of his father and that of the Shi'i Imam he is suspected of murdering. This was the first building of what was to become one of the largest religious complexes in existence, being expanded by a string of monarchs keen to display their devotion to both Reza and God.

The shrine was first expanded 200 years after its initial construction, this time upon the orders of Mahmud of Ghazni. The next stage in the evolution of the city was born out of the destruction wrought by the Mongols. The shrine of Imam Reza was looted but left intact. Survivors from the devastated region of Khorasan – the primary target of Genghis's ire, because of the then governor's slaughter of the Great Khan's envoys – poured into the city, swelling its population. As the only town in the area to be spared, Mash'had flourished whilst other great cities like Neyshapur disappeared, stagnated or slowly rebuilt themselves.

It was the influence of a later queen descended from the Mongols that was to transform the city into one of the most revered sites in the

Islamic world. Queen Gohar Shad and her husband Shah Rukh, the fifteenth-century Timurid ruler, were huge patrons of the arts and were fundamental to the recovery of Iran, especially in the re-emergence of the arts and architecture. Being a devout Shi'a, the Queen commissioned the building of the mosque that to this day bears her name and, according to Sir Percy Sykes, 'perhaps constitutes the crowning architectural achievement of the Mongols'. Shah Abbas also added to the complex, as did Nader Shah (1736–47), who made Mash'had the country's capital during his brief reign and whose tomb is also located in the city.

★   ★   ★

My hosts in Iran's holy city were Kami, a childhood friend of my uncle's and my mother's, and his family. A successful Dublin nightclub owner in bygone student days, an artist and ex-war correspondent, Kami now teaches English literature, paints and writes in the city he moved to in order to escape the overcrowded, oppressive streets of Tehran.

'Damn. We're going to have to move again. Where to this time?' came the response upon learning from our taxi driver that the population of Mash'had had climbed over the 2.5 million mark. 'In my father's day it was 200,000.'

The taxi dropped us off outside the vast, ever-expanding shrine complex of Imam Reza. 'It must be one of the greatest, if not the greatest, concentration of religious buildings in the world, Mecca not excluded,' wrote Sir Roger Stevens in the late 1950s. Security checks needed to be negotiated, searches having been in place since a bombing in 1994. Inside the complex giant carpets covered vast courtyards with their red and white patterns as countless pilgrims knelt on them, weeping, praying and picnicking. Incongruous images jumped out from all around: a *chadori* with a hard, rural face chatting on an expensive mobile phone between sobs of mourning; the ornate shimmering of the gold minarets of old and the dull grey cement of the new under construction; ageing rural types, unshaven and with tatty, ill-fitting jackets, next to young men wearing orange T-shirts with American slogans, their eyes hidden behind large, expensive-looking sunglasses. Military men in khaki slacks performed the necessary prostrations beside Arabs in white robes.

Through the glittering golden arch that led inside the shrine itself, I was dazzled by the twinkling of the mirrored mosaic walls, their refractions and the unravelling geometric and floral patterns disorienting the senses. Piercing wails from the female section of the shrine combined with the sobs of the men creating a kind of operatic chorus of grief, all lamenting the death of Reza twelve centuries ago. Dr Arthur Upham Pope writes of the shrine that 'One is enclosed in a world of glory that makes the world of common fact seem remote and curiously unreal.'[2]

I was pushed away from Kami and swept by a frantic scrum towards the grille that enshrined the tomb of the Imam. Hands flew forward from all around, anxiously groping, reaching out to touch the sacred silver bars. A solitary voice shouted an invocation, the *salavat*, to which an avalanche of voices replied in unison with the ritual response. Quickly realising that being passive about the process would leave me tossed about like a dry leaf in an autumn gale, I drew on my rugby-playing days, dropped a shoulder and shoved and squirmed my way as close to the front as I could manage before reaching out a long arm just far enough to be able to make contact with the cold metal worn with devotional caresses. As I turned to try and force my way out of the stampede I was suddenly pushed forward, pinning a weeping old man against the grille he had been kissing so devoutly. Unable to move even my arms, the pressure increased and for a moment panic began to creep in. The forward thrust soon subsided just long enough for me to stumble my way out and back into welcome daylight, where I found Kami waiting anxiously.

★　★　★

From Mash'had I returned to Tehran by overnight train. The taxi driver who drove me to the station spoke of the thirty years he had served his country and the twelve years he had spent at the front in Khuzestan, having been stationed there for the entirety of the war period and beyond. For his services he had been rewarded with an army pension of $250 a month. He told me how he had spent most of his savings on his son's education. Despite the young man's degree, the taxi driver still spent almost all of this pension supporting his son, who was a heroin addict. 'I am a veteran of thirty years, I was decorated for my service in the war. I'm in my sixties, I have a busted leg that hurts like hell when I drive and I have to spend over twelve hours a day in my cab just to make ends meet.' It was a depressingly common story and one that I had heard many times.

The express overnight train to Tehran was modern and comfortable, having recently been built to help transport some of the estimated

20 million pilgrims that visit Mash'had annually. In the morning I went to use the WC to find a queue of six people impatiently shifting their weight from one leg to the other. I was about to turn back to the compartment when I noticed one of the toilets was vacant. Pushing the door open, I discovered that it was being ignored because it was the unfamiliar and clearly mistrusted 'Western' sit-down toilet and not the squat toilet preferred by Iranians.

Chapter Eighteen

B orn in Qom in 1056 and brought up in Rey, just south of modern Tehran, Hassan Sabbah was raised a Shi'a at a time when the fledgling schismatic sect was being persecuted by the Seljuk dynasty, orthodox Sunnis of Turkic origin. A serendipitous meeting took place in an inn between three young men who would go on to become the era's key figures, so legend would have us believe. Sabbah, Omar Khayyam, the legendary astronomer and author of the *Rubaiyat*, and Nizam ul-Mulk, tireless vizier of the Seljuk sultan Malek Shah (1072–92), crossed paths, sharing conversation and swearing an oath that, were any of them to achieve a position whereby they could aid the others in the advancement of their own causes, they would do so. It was Nizam ul-Mulk who was first to succeed, acquiring an administrative role in the king's court and soon being appointed vizier. True to his word, Nizam ul-Mulk aided Khayyam in getting considerable patronage, allowing him to cultivate his fledgling talents in relative freedom and security. To Sabbah he offered the administration of a province, but the young man, brimming with ambition, rejected the appointment, demanding a place in the king's court, particularly coveting the ministerial role held by Nizam himself.

The young man's administrative skills were so exceptional that he took on a job the vizier had declared to the king would take two years to complete, claiming he could do it in just forty days. When Nizam saw that Sabbah was close to completing this onerous task within the specified timeframe he conspired to sabotage the young man's good work, fearing for his own position in the court. On the day of his big presentation to the Seljuk monarch, Sabbah discovered that his documents had been tampered with. Disappointing an expectant monarch can often prove a poor career move and even worse for one's well-being. Sabbah lost his position but was lucky to escape with his life, eventually fleeing to Egypt.

The fact that Nizam ul-Mulk was at least twenty years the senior of the other two protagonists casts some doubt over this legend. What we do know is that Sabbah did leave Iran for Egypt, where the Fatimid Caliphate had replaced the Sunni Abbasids. The Fatimids were Shi'a and, like Sabbah, of the Ismaili tradition. The Ismailis believe that the sixth Shi'i Imam, Ja'far Sadegh, should have been succeeded by his eldest son, Ismail, whom they regard as the seventh and last of the divinely guided Imams. For this reason Ismailis are known as Sevener Shi'a, rather than the Twelvers (twelve recognised Imams) of the Shi'i majority. The Ismailis continue to thrive, the line of succession having continued right up to the present day, with the Agha Khan recognised as the forty-ninth legitimate heir and spiritual leader of this influential sect.

The Ismaili heterodoxy thrived under the Fatimids in Egypt, but their rule was short-lived as they were overthrown by the iconic Saladin, who restored Sunni Islam to Egypt. The situation for the Ismailis back in Iran under Sultan Malek Shah, also a Sunni harbouring anti-Shi'i sentiment, was just as difficult. Hounded out of livelihoods and towns, the Ismailis were persecuted at every turn. With his band of dedicated followers, Sabbah, now back in Iran, retreated into Daylamite territory in the mountains north of Qazvin. The Daylamites are an ancient mountain people who have populated remote regions of the Alborz Mountains since before the Common Era. Being Shi'a themselves and staunch opponents of the crown, the Daylamites sheltered the Ismailis, helping them repel the soldiers sent by Nizam ul-Mulk to capture Sabbah.

★ ★ ★

Hassan Sabbah managed to elude capture and ensconced himself in Alamut, the legendary Castle of the Assassins, which later came to be known as the stronghold of the Old Man of the Mountain. According to legend the castle was given its name by a king of Daylam in the ninth century. He was out hunting in the mountains when he released his eagle. The bird took flight and soared into the air before coming to land on a rocky outcrop. The king recognised the strategic importance of the place and built a fortress on the site, which he named Alamut: 'the Eagle's Nest'.

Nearly 240 years later, in 1090, Sabbah also instantly recognised the value of the fortress and set about acquiring it. Various myths surround the acquisition of the castle. The most romantic of these is that Sabbah offered the owner 3,000 gold *dinars* for a piece of land as big as a cow's hide. This offer being so ludicrously in favour of the owner, he agreed instantly. With the deal struck, Sabbah took the hide and carefully cut it into minutely thin strips which he then laid out around the perimeter of the entire castle, thus claiming it as his own.

Behind the sturdy walls of his impenetrable stronghold Sabbah disappeared, never to be seen again before his death in 1124. Less than two years after taking Alamut, Hassan Sabbah had established more strongholds in the surrounding mountains, effectively creating an independent Ismaili state in the heart of Seljuk Persia. For thirty-four years Sabbah lived as the reclusive ruler of an ascetic sect of Shi'i Islam, dedicating his time and skills to studying religious texts and contributing to what was to become a legendary library. Even so, his name would reverberate through courts the length and breadth of the Islamic Empire, and even in the halls of European palaces, sending a shudder of fear down many a courtly spine.

Backed into a corner, Sabbah turned his fearless temperament and astonishing intellect to fighting for the survival of his faith. Recognising the impossibility of a successful direct confrontation with the might of the sultanate, he resorted to more covert subversion. Long is the history of guerrilla warfare, but Sabbah's ruthless tactics have earned him the ignoble reputation of the father of terrorism.

Sabbah was stoic in his faith, demanding an ascetic dedication from his followers, known as the *fidais*, or those willing to sacrifice. This sacrifice was to give up their lives to the faith. The recalcitrant Sabbah demanded more. Hand-picked *fidais* would be trained and sent on missions to infiltrate key households and courts where they might spend years gaining the trust of their employers and working their way into suitable positions. Here they would wait patiently, unquestioningly, until given the order to strike. The victims were usually people in positions of authority who had directly opposed or threatened the sect. The killers would not even attempt to flee, resigned to the gruesome fate of being torn to pieces once the deed was done. The fame of the victims, coupled with the tactic of striking in the most public of places (the mosque at Friday prayers was a particular favourite), soon garnered Sabbah and his band a chilly respect.

The old nemesis, Nizam ul-Mulk himself, was struck down in 1092, though conspiracy theorists posit that this order was given by the Sultan himself, wary of his vizier's increasing popularity. Sultan Malek Shah also died suspiciously soon after his vizier. Again, accusatory fingers were pointed at Alamut. Whether responsible for these deaths or not, Sabbah's ploy had worked. The impregnability of his castle and the fear cultivated by his actions slowly allowed him a certain amount of freedom. Much like modern-day terrorism, the threat thrives on attention. The public nature of the killings had caused rumours to sweep through the Middle East and Asia Minor and had even reached as far as Europe via returning Crusaders who told tales of the legend of the Old Man of the Mountain. Every death of an influential figure was surrounded by suspicion, with worried eyes looking up to Alamut. Many, no doubt, used this to their advantage, settling old scores or furthering growing ambitions only to deflect the blame onto the Ismailis. The maelstrom of rumours and whispers played straight into the wily Sabbah's hands.

The rumours continued on through the next century, only to be immortalised by Marco Polo in his *Travels*. To this day countless writers and artists across the globe, from Vladimir Bartol to William Burroughs and Amin Maalouf (in his superb historical novel *Samarkand*), have been inspired by the tales of decadent deception in which Sabbah would drug young men with 'a certain potion which cast them into a deep sleep. When therefore they awoke and found themselves in', according to Polo, 'a place so charming, they deemed that it was Paradise in very truth. And the ladies and damsels dallied with them to their hearts' content.' Sabbah had, according to rumour, recreated the Islamic ideal of Paradise. 'The Old Man had caused a certain valley between two mountains to be enclosed, and had turned it into a garden, the largest and most beautiful that ever was seen, filled with every variety of fruit. And there were runnels flowing with wine and milk and honey and water; and numbers of ladies and of the most beautiful damsels in the world. For the Old Man desired to make his people believe that this was actually Paradise.'[1] Other rumours claim that he kept his *fidai* faithful by feeding them hashish and opium, making them unthinking addicts willing to die at any moment for their leader – or for their next fix. One myth has Sabbah ordering a youth to jump to his death from the parapet of the castle onto the jagged rocks far below as a demonstration designed to impress a visiting dignitary.

Given that Hassan Sabbah was a deeply religious man and a fervent ascetic who had both of his sons executed (one on suspicion of murder and the other for drinking wine) and banished another man from Alamut for playing the flute, accusations of drug use to inspire faith and a sacrilegious garden to deceive his disciples seem wholly implausible. However unbelievable, these myths have stood the test of time and even found their way into European language, the word 'assassin' deriving from 'hashish'. Sabbah's followers were known as the *hashishian*, or 'ashishin', as Polo transliterated. Farhad Daftary explores the truth behind these rumours in his scholarly work, *The Assassin Legends*, coming to the conclusion that the majority of these legends were cultivated and propagated by the Crusaders and other Europeans as they do not appear in any contemporary Muslim sources.[2] Whatever the truth may be, the legacy of the fear with which Sabbah was regarded remains a testament to the effectiveness of his brutal methods.

★ ★ ★

The way to Alamut leads west from Tehran, past Karaj and on towards Qazvin, where a road winds up through tawny tentacles of rock reaching out from the base of the mountains and into the depths of the Alborz. My search for a lift had led me to Amirhossein, an exuberant artist who lived in central Tehran. His brazenness, sense of humour and chaotic energy made him a great travel companion and meant that he was always willing to drop everything and jump into his car at the merest hint of an adventure. We drove up and over a ridge to see the road plunge down into a picturesque valley with a series of hairpin bends. As we began our descent Amirhossein, behind the wheel of his Iranian-built Pazhan car, a thin Bahman cigarette clamped between his teeth, nudged me nervously.

'Cyrus,' he hissed as he tossed away the cigarette with paint-flecked fingers, 'the brakes aren't bloody working.' I looked down to see his right foot pumping the brake pedal to no effect. The gradient of the road was still relatively forgiving but we were gathering pace and the series of sharp turns that lay below us did not bode well. As we hurtled around a corner, Amirhossein spotted a straighter stretch of road and managed to stop our momentum by applying the handbrake and riding up the incline of the mountainside. Disaster averted, we very cautiously made our way down the mountain pass and soon came upon a man who claimed to be a mechanic in a small village.

Sitting on a nearby wall, we watched as he hopped into the driver's seat and started the engine. Giving us a big grin and a wave goodbye, he accelerated down the road. To our great relief, the car came to stop outside a little shack that turned out to be his house as he fell out of the car pointing at us and convulsing with laughter. 'You Tehranis really don't know how to take a joke,' he said, still chortling as he shuffled round the back of the shack to grab a grease-stained cloth bundle full of tools. From under the bonnet he told us that our brake line was leaking. He shouted to a little boy looking on fascinated by this interruption of his daily life. The boy scuttled off and came back with a length of hose. Our mechanic then cut this and attached it over the leak with duct tape.

'Will that hold?' I asked nervously. He shrugged his shoulders and then that deep, disconcerting laugh boomed out through the valley once more. I looked up at the treacherous mountain roads that lay on our path, then back at the red-faced mechanic, and was suddenly hit by the absurdity of our situation: entrusting our lives to an amateur mechanic from a remote mountain village in northern Iran who had claimed to fix our car with a piece of hosepipe and some duct tape. The man refused payment but instead insisted we stay and have a cup of tea with him. Our gratitude having been suitably conveyed, we set out again. 'In God's hands,' as the mechanic said with a wink, wiping the hydraulic fluid from his own.

In the fading light, we climbed over valley after valley as the road wound deeper into the mountains. We were in search of Lake Ovan, where we had planned to camp for the night. As the road twisted around a mass of rock, I spotted the unmistakable twinkle of electric lighting in the distance. Beyond a cluster of trees sat a lonely house and just beyond that was the lake, nestled in the folds of the mountain valley 1,800 metres above sea level. The sun soon disappeared behind the Alborz peaks and we were left to scout around the lake for a flat piece of terrain with our headlights. The few farmhouses dotted along the shoreline could offer no help in finding a campsite but instead invited us to join them for dinner. Declining politely, we pushed on and eventually found a spot. Within minutes we had erected our tent, lit a fire and set about the satisfying task of skewering meat with gusto.

Waking early, I decided to make the most of the glorious morning and set out for a wander along a path following a stream that ran off from the lake, around a hillock and down to the fields it irrigated below. The narrow valley spilt out into a wide plain tiered with the visible signs of cultivation. Bright grey rocks rose sharply from either side of the plain, their sheer surface given a blue-green tinge as the morning sun crept over them. On one side was a little village hemmed in by the now turquoise mountains to its left, a forest to its right and a sheer drop at its front. The other side rolled softly, with fold after fold of rock covered with the golden-brown shimmer of slowly desiccating grass. When I got back to the tent, I turned the embers of the previous night's fire, threw on some twigs and brewed a pot of tea with which to rouse my slumbering companion.

★ ★ ★

Back on the road, we drove past a few scattered mud-walled abodes and rusting painted depictions of martyrs from the recent war with Iraq, all the while speculating as to which jagged peak could house the Castle of the Assassins. Our conjecture was brought to an abrupt end, first by a sign, and then by the unmistakable sight of the fortress squatting on a peak, vaunting its impregnability.

As we pulled up at the site, the gravel of the car-park crunching under tyre, we were faced with an unexpected scene. A busload of *Basij* voluntary militia were posing for photographs in their drab green and grey militia outfits, their laughing and romping belying their fearsome reputation as upholders of morality. Another carload of tourists who had arrived at the same time as us were clearly made uncomfortable by their presence. 'Let's leave and come back later,' I heard one whisper to his companions. This reminded me of an observation of Freya Stark's in her account of travels through this very area: 'The way a Persian flattens out before a bully in authority is always the most depressing sight.'[3]

After a few minutes the *Basiji* photo session ended and they marched down the mountain path shouting the *salavat* prayers as they went. They were down amongst us in no time, in their olive and black mess of camouflage trousers, soulless grey shirts and heavy black boots. Each of them looked at us as they approached and greeted us as 'brothers' with warm, friendly smiles. Clearly they had identified Amirhossein and me as of their own. Given our scruffy, unshaven and unwashed appearance this was not surprising. But in those instances, as our eyes met, all I could see was a group of barely literate village boys on an outing – their reputation as ruthless enforcers of Islamic orthodoxy not in evidence on this sunny morning.

★ ★ ★

A towering mass of rock pierced the foothills, the grey sandstone looking unnatural in its surroundings; not least because the other peaks in view were all formed of sedimentary rock. Perhaps there was some truth to the legend recounted to Freya Stark by the villagers of Gazor Khan, a picturesque little village in the fertile plain at the foot of the mountain. She had been told that the mountain had been put there by Kayumars, the legendary first king of Iran's mythical Kayanian dynasty.

A pathway led from the car-park over a little stream and up the hillside to a set of large stone steps that climbed up to the castle on the only possible approach. Opposite, a scree slope rose into a dramatic jagged peak ripped away from the body of rock it stood beside.

The fortress itself was caught in a web of scaffolding; the site was still in the process of being excavated and preserved. Outlines of centuries-old stone walls traced out a floor plan whilst tacky but informative posters flapped in the light breeze. A leather-faced old man with a thick white moustache sat beside a large urn, shakily holding out a plastic cup of tea that Amirhossein exchanged for a cigarette. Sitting down on a lop-sided bench next to the urn, he tried to strike up a conversation as he first lit the old man's cigarette and then his own. The laconic man responded to his cheerful patter in grunts and monosyllables, only making Amirhossein even more determined to engage him in conversation. A few people came past, laughing as they photographed their way through the shapeless ruins.

To the south, beneath a sheer drop of a couple of hundred metres, lay the plain of Alamut, vibrant with its orchards and electric-green fields of fresh wheat. Neat rows of trees fanned out and surrounded the village below. Every cultivable surface of the plain had been used. Sabbah had improved the irrigation of these very fields all those centuries ago so that his fortress was self-sufficient. An intricate system of tunnels running through the mountain linked Alamut with the outside world, allowing food to be brought up even while the castle was under siege. But so hermetically sealed were the secrets of this network that archaeologists are only now beginning to excavate anything that resembles a passage in the hope of discovering the secret routes of access into the world of Hassan Sabbah.

There were over 300 forts dotted through this mountain range, spreading west to form a chain running all the way to Syria. Under the Syrian prince Ridwan (1095–1113), a supporter of the Ismailis, the sect found security and prosperity from which Sabbah and his followers greatly benefitted. And as for the epithet of *hashashin*, Sabbah and his followers were renowned for their knowledge of medicinal roots and plants so it is quite likely that rather than any sinister implications of drug-induced deception, the moniker related to their skill as herbalists.

The impregnable castle eventually fell to Hulagu, grandson of Genghis Khan, during the second Mongol invasion in 1256. Tired of the pervading threat of the Assassins, the Crusaders struck a deal with the Mongols to destroy the Ismaili stronghold, then under the leadership of Rokn al-Din Khurshah. The Ismailis' resolve had been weakened by the wholesale changes made by a successor and namesake of Sabbah's, Hassan II (1162–6), who replaced the founder's stoic principles with his own more flexible and pragmatic ideals. Hassan II's radical changes to the sect's principles proved so contentious that he was assassinated by followers faithful to the doctrines established by Sabbah. But Hassan II was succeeded by his son, who steadfastly implemented his father's changes despite their unpopularity. By this stage, links with the Syrian Ismailis, who were being governed independently by Rashid al-Din Sinan, had been almost completely severed.

With Alamut's influence already on the wane, Hassan III (1210–21) proclaimed himself a Sunni and moved to re-establish better relationships with the Sunni world. Meanwhile, outside the walls of the impregnable fortress, Persia was collapsing under the relentless onslaught of the Mongol armies, sending a wave of influential thinkers to take shelter at Alamut, which soon became practically the only surviving independent territory in the country. Hassan III's successor, Mohammad III, made a nominal effort at holding out against the Mongols, but he too was assassinated by Ismailis fearing his weak leadership. Mohammad's son, Rokn al-Din Khurshah, succeeded him and swiftly surrendered, hoping for clemency from Hulagu. Unmoved, the Mongol ordered the destruction of Alamut and everything in it. The castle was sacked and the legendary library set ablaze. As the ashes from the great tomes swirled in the mountain winds, the princes and viziers of the Levant and Persia breathed a sigh of relief. The Ismaili threat, which had seen many an opponent of Sabbah and his followers mercilessly assassinated by trusted members of their own courts, was finally at an end.

Chapter Nineteen

Our bleary eyes squinted in the ethereal dawn light as Amirhossein and I packed up his Pazhan jeep and left Alamut and its medieval legends behind us. We drove back towards Qazvin and then on to Zanjan under a breathtakingly blue sky. Rather than drive through the city, we looped around it on a sweeping ring road before turning onto a smaller road leading up and over a mountainous ridge into expansive volcanic valleys. Late autumn hues – the soft browns and gold of empty fields and harvested crops – stained the stunning view we had from the mountain road as it climbed higher and higher. Sparsely populated mud-walled villages lay somnolent in a sunshine that belied the fast-approaching chill of winter. Small roofs were stacked high with hay and mounds of dung as villagers prepared for the harsh months ahead. The few trees that had not lost their leaves were covered in canopies of delicate reds and golden browns, yet the sun was high in a cloudless sky and the air was crisp.

As the minutes turned into hours, the road wound over fold after fold of mountainous valleys, leading us further and further into an austere wilderness. Suddenly a formation of industrial titans appeared, casting their shadows over the foothills and fields of the sweeping valley. These pylons supported a cable carrying a constant stream of carts full of gold and bauxite mined in the area, rich as it is with the minerals that colour its landscape.

The endless road led over another high pass before descending into a wide plain. It was here, encircled by volcanic peaks reaching upwards of 3,000 metres, that we found the site we had come these 400 kilometres to visit. Fields and orchards surrounded a little village that lay in the shade of a volcanic plateau of limestone raised 60 metres above the rest of the plain. Inside this raised crater, surrounded by thick stone walls, was a temple complex built by the Sasanians in the fifth century CE. But the significance of this site to the Magi stretched back many centuries further.

★ ★ ★

The Magi are shrouded in mystery. Thought to be one of six Median tribes, they formed the priestly caste of the early elemental religion of this nomadic Aryan people. The earliest mention of the Magi currently documented dates to the sixth century BCE but it is not known when their role as ceremonial and sacrificial priests originated. By the Achaemenian era, they had become the official priests of the kings and the tutors to their sons. They were prominent under the rule of Darius I, but it was under Xerxes I (486–465 BCE) that their influence grew. Herodotus writes in his *Histories* that Xerxes consulted with the Magi before making any important decisions.

'The Magi accompanied the army to celebrate the sacrifices, they interpreted dreams and took part in the coronation of the new King – a ceremony performed in the temple of Pasargadae [Cyrus the Great's capital],' writes Professor Ghirshman on their role under the Achaemenians. 'Very little is known about their origins or their religion, which was not that of the Persians ... In contradiction to the Persians, who buried their dead, the Magi exposed all corpses to be torn by wild beasts or birds of prey.'[1]

There is great debate as to whether the Magi were followers of Zoroaster or whether they were opposed to his teachings, many of which went against pre-existing Median beliefs. Some historians suspect that the Magi only adopted the teachings of Zoroaster in the fourth century BCE, while others posit that, over a period of time, their own beliefs and those of Zoroaster were adapted and evolved into a system more in line with popular belief.

It was during the Sasanian era that a more universal set of beliefs was formed and adopted as the state religion, and it was only then that the oral traditions passed down from the time of Zoroaster – possibly as many as 2,000 years earlier – were finally committed to writing. As previously mentioned, the latest scholarly opinion is that the Magi adapted certain details of the history and beliefs of Zoroastrianism to be more in line with their traditional beliefs and with the message they were seeking to promulgate.[2] R.C. Zaehner writes that 'It is they ... who would be responsible for the cut-and-dried division of creation into two mutually antagonistic halves – the creatures of the Holy Spirit on the one hand and the creatures of the Destructive Spirit on the other. Thus they can be regarded as the true authors of that rigid dualism that was to characterize the Zoroastrianism of a later period, but which is only implicit in the *Gathas* of Zoroaster.'[3]

By the time of the Sasanians, this holy city – first known as Praaspa and later as Shiz – was the focal point of the Zoroastrian religion. So much so that a new Sasanian king would go on foot from the palace at Ctesiphon (south of modern Baghdad) to Praaspa, where the coronation ceremony would take place at the sacred-fire altar of Adhar Gushnasp, one of the three most sacred fires of the Zoroastrian faith. The 500-odd kilometres travelled on foot by an enormous royal retinue made my pilgrimage seem paltry in comparison. The ancient city of Praaspa in the province of West Azerbaijan is now known by the name of Takht-e Soleiman.

The name Takht-e Soleiman, meaning Solomon's Throne, was undoubtedly attributed to the site from the time of the Arab Muslim invasion in the seventh century. The name of Solomon was adopted by several Zoroastrian sites, the biblical link saving them from destruction. Once the misnomer had stuck, local legends blanketed the truth, leaving behind it, as with many pre-Islamic sites in Iran, a legacy inspired by myth that has usurped reality and woven itself into the very fabric of Iranian culture.

Like their ancient city-temple, so shrouded in mystery are the Magi that this priestly caste has, throughout history, been tarred with a nefarious reputation. This is thanks to their less than flattering depiction in the *Histories* of Herodotus – hardly an admirer of the Persians and their ways. This negative depiction by the Greek historian evolved and distorted as it caught the imagination of many later authors and poets who depicted the Magi as mysterious sorcerers, manipulators of evil spirits and keepers of such esoteric secrets as the Philosopher's Stone, the mythical key to the obscure metaphysical science of alchemy. It is from these ancient

Persian priests' unfounded reputation for sorcery that we get the word 'magic'. Nowadays the Magi are more readily associated with the Three Wise Men of the East who visited Jesus at his birth in Bethlehem – a stark contrast to their earlier portrayal by Herodotus.

★ ★ ★

Thirty-eight towers built into a high wall surround a volcanic crater at the centre of which sits a sacred lake fed by a warm spring. The reflective inky-blue surface of this near-perfect circle is disturbed only by an occasional ripple. Legend has it that this lake is bottomless and that the Magi drew spiritual energy from its sacred waters. The principal temple of the site, dedicated to Anahita, the ancient goddess of water and fertility, was built on its shore, surrounded today by a series of Sasanian-origin buildings. These were enhanced and expanded by Abaqa, the second of the Mongol Ilkhanid rulers in the mid-thirteenth century. The crumbling outer walls surrounding the plateau are now being restored to their former state. Inside, the ruins of the sanctuaries are humbled by the majesty of their surroundings. The site has seen such illustrious visitors as Alexander the Great who, so legend (or, more accurately, Magian historical propaganda) has it, destroyed the original copy of the sacred Zoroastrian book, the *Avesta*, said to have been written on thousands of skins in letters of gold. It was in the shade of these walls, on the very plain beyond them, that Mark Antony and his invading Roman army were so roundly defeated by the Parthians in 36 BCE.

In the distance, just the other side of the village of Nosrat Abad, rises another remarkable volcanic formation, a conical hill that plateaus at its top, similar in form to the Towers of Silence used by Zoroastrians to dispose of their dead. This teat-like mass of stone with its hollow interior is known as Solomon's Prison (the locals also referred to it as Alexander's Prison, only adding to the confusion), the mythical crater in which King Solomon was said to imprison the monsters he vanquished.

★ ★ ★

At the foot of an ochre hill, before a sparse but immaculate orchard and beside a little rivulet that had been channelled to irrigate the trees and surrounding fields, Amirhossein and I pitched tent as he excitedly told me where he was going to set up his easel in the morning. His explanation of how he was going to try and capture this pastoral scene soon turned into a detailed lecture on the genius of Titian's use of colour. As we scurried around erecting our tent, collecting kindling and preparing a fire, the sun swiftly disappeared behind the mountainous horizon, prompting a sudden and ferocious drop in temperature. We had come prepared for harsh conditions, but the speed of the drop to well below freezing had caught us by surprise and we could not stray more than a metre away from the warmth of the campfire. A few hundred metres on from our camp stood Takht-e Soleiman, the sacred monument to an ancient faith, possibly the earliest monotheistic religion and a great influence on all subsequent religions of the Book.

Shortly after sunset, as if by some kind of divine magic, the world around us was suddenly illuminated – powerful lights bathed the outside of the walled sanctuary, producing a ghostly effect. Amirhossein flattened out some coals to one side of our campfire and lit a cigarette off one before placing two skewers of marinated chicken over them. As the chicken sizzled and the bitter night pushed us ever closer to the fire, I found myself being drawn into the world of the Magi. I imagined the royal train arriving after its 800-kilometre pilgrimage from Ctesiphon in full pomp and procession, snaking around the abodes of the awe-struck local villagers, climbing up to the royal southern entrance of the site and on to the open-air throne. Here, before the altar of the sacred fire of Adhar Gushnasp, the Warrior King's Fire, the new Sasanian monarch would swear his allegiance to Ahura Mazda, the Wise Lord of his Zoroastrian faith, and acknowledge his role as the champion of *Asha*, divine Truth and Righteousness, and the mortal enemy of *Drauga*, the corrupting influence that permeates our daily lives. Kneeling before the altar, the Magi would approach in their flowing tunics and hand the king a chalice of *haoma*, a mysterious intoxicant prepared by the priests. This sacred drink was said to be fatal to those not imbued with the *farr*, or divine approval, so that if the monarch's claims to divine kingship were fraudulent, he would drop dead instantly, poisoned by the secret concoction made from a sacred plant.

* * *

The next morning we awoke to find a thick layer of ice frozen to the inside of our tent. Outside, the morning sun was making a valiant effort to dismiss the frost and slowly raise the temperature. Cirrus clouds streaked the blue sky as a small herd of cows was busy grazing beside us. Ambling over to the bovine assembly, I soon spotted their herder sprawled on a grassy knoll, a woollen hat pulled over his eyes, the crook resting on his chest rising and falling with the steady rhythm of sleep.

I started a fire and began to boil some water when I noticed the man, now awake, striding towards me. I got up and offered him some tea. He declined. I enquired whether the orchard was his. Yes, he answered, it belonged to the village. I motioned to a big pile of wood that lay beside us and asked if we could use some for firewood. '*Befarma*,' he said. 'It is yours.' Our terse exchange soon ran out of steam and the visitor, his curiosity satisfied, returned to his cows.

Our next visitor was dressed for the occasion in an ill-fitting coarse woollen jacket and approached us with an authoritative gait. After cocking an eye at Amirhossein standing before his easel, palette in hand and caked in paint, he informed us that the orchard was in fact his. More garrulous than the cowherd, this mustachioed man joined us for a pot of tea. Times were hard, he told us. A couple of bad harvests had caused much hardship to the 200-odd families of the village of Nosrat Abad. Surely they benefitted from a steady stream of tourists to the site, I enquired. The man gave me a look that spoke volumes. The only thing they got from the site was headaches, he huffed. The government had placed severe restrictions on the building of houses in an attempt to keep the traditional feel of the village. They had imposed traditional, out-dated dress on the local women, who found their enforced attire impractical and embarrassing. The man calmly yet passionately told of his woes trying to dig a much-needed well only to be buried under a blizzard of bureaucracy. Tourists were bussed in or drove straight to and from the site, ignoring the village entirely.

'We are getting old. Too old to work these fields like we used to and the youth … it is sad. All they seem to be interested in is drugs. Our village is awash with heroin, with opium and with hashish. They are ill. They become lazy, dishonest and disrespectful.' As rife as the drug problem in Iran may have been, I was still astonished that such a remote village could have problems with heroin. 'Do not camp here,' he went on, 'It is dangerous. Two days ago my brother was attacked by a bear just behind that hill there,' he pointed directly behind us, 'and there are plenty of wolves about, too. It's getting cold and the animals are getting bolder. You are safer down below, by the village.' The guards at the site had told us the same thing on our arrival the previous afternoon. 'It's cold; too cold to sleep outside. Usually at this time of year there is a metre of snow everywhere. It is late in coming this year. Winters are harsh. People barely leave their houses, let alone the village. The roads are buried and we are cut off from everything until *Nowrouz.*' Bearing this statement in mind, it was easy to understand the critical significance of the spring equinox, the key festival of Zoroastrian and Aryan belief, and its fundamental role in the lives of Iranians through the millennia.

After lunch a paint-covered Amirhossein and I decided to hike up the hill beside our camp. The short climb led through a cluster of eerily destitute abodes opposite a bizarre series of what looked like furnaces, presumably for extracting some kind of ore. Above this, a scree slope led to the top of a ridge, where we sat and took in the panorama with the holy site perched regally on its limestone plateau. Even from this distance the deep blue of the lake created a sense of tranquillity and the walls lost none of their grandeur. Beyond this, an attractive pattern of harvested fields gently rippled along the valley floor. Further still in the background, a strong volcanic ridge undulated across the plain. Directly beneath us, the trees of the orchard stood like soldiers on parade. Beside the ancient site, the beleaguered village of Nosrat Abad languished in the early afternoon sun. Soon the temperature began to drop and had us scuttling back to camp to prepare ourselves for the onset of night and the coming cold.

As we were readying some food, the rumble of motorcycles tore through the silence of the night. Out of the obscurity a single round light appeared, soon joined by another. The two lights wound their way down the dirt track towards us. A minute later five men hopped off the motorcycles, their faces concealed by scarves. As is customary, we offered then dinner. They declined. They asked how many we were. 'Only two?' they replied glancing at each other. After an awkward few moments, they mounted their bikes and drove off back to the end of the dirt track. They stopped there a few minutes before their lights swung back around to face us, hanging threateningly in the darkness. Both Amirhossein and I had felt uncomfortable with the exchange. Their aggressive manner was not reassuring and the fact that we were in the middle of nowhere did little to allay our concerns. The warnings of the old man and the guards about the perils of our campsite, the drug problems and the dissolute swagger of the young men did not bode well.

'They'll probably wait until we're asleep,' I said.

'Let them come. I've got an axe,' said Amirhossein rummaging around in the back of the car. 'There's only five of them.' This was a response I did not welcome. If I acquiesced to his bravado we could end up with our throats slit. If I insisted we leave, I would lose face – and in Iran to lose face can be a fate worse than a slit throat. We ate our dinner in uncomfortable silence, but as we did so I made a decision: life over pride. 'Amirhossein, we're leaving.'

We were soon packing up our tent and hurriedly tossing everything, including the easel and still-drying canvas, into the back of the car. The speed of Amirhossein's collaboration suggested he was relieved at the decision to move out. Since it was I who had taken it, his face was saved. We soon realised that it was simply too cold and too dark to find another campsite and pitch tent again so we decided to drive straight back to Tehran, or as far as we could before exhaustion set in.

Chapter Twenty

I boarded that Iran Air flight back in 2006 with a clear aim: to attempt to understand Iran as best I could. At some stage during the course of this quest I developed a deep affinity with the country and began to view myself as one if its own. This left me pondering what exactly it was that I identified with so much as to cause this radical reversal in my self-perception. I was fascinated by the country's history, enthralled by its poetry and enchanted by the majesty and diversity of its nature. But what makes Iran such a beguiling and intoxicating country, at once so fantastic and yet so flawed, is the Iranians themselves.

Sir Roger Stevens writes, 'Persia grows out from her past to as great an extent as any evolving nation; her geography, her history, her religion, and her art tell more perhaps about the Persian character and the nature of the country than any account of her modern economy or form of government.'[1] This statement is all the more poignant for having been made prior to the Revolution and is crucial to understanding the national psyche. Certainly no discussion of the form of governance of Iran can be complete without mention of the history of monarchy. Even after the events of 1979 and the accompanying anti-imperialist sentiment, many Iranians look upon their much-touted (yet inaccurate, as it was in fact much longer than) 2,500 years of uninterrupted monarchy with pride. In her book *The Iranians*, Sandra Mackey explores the inextricable bond between the ideal of the strong and charismatic just ruler, the prototype for which was Cyrus the Great, and the inherent nature of the Iranian people. Even when revolting against the institution of monarchy, Iranians still look for this archetype, clearly embodied in Ayatollah Khomeini, the figurehead of the Islamic Revolution. It is no accident that despite over a hundred years of agitating for a working constitution, Iranians settled upon an absolute theocracy headed by a strong and charismatic champion of the people. With Khomeini's brain-child, the *Velayat-e Faqih*, Iran essentially switched one form of absolute rule for another.

One of the more interesting theories one hears in the frequent conversations about the state of Iran is that a tried and failed theocracy is a necessary step towards a working democracy. Certainly for a country with a history of kingship so inextricably intertwined with that of the clergy – 'Church and State were born of the one womb, joined together and never to be sundered,' declared the Sasanian-era *Letter of Tansar* – the separation of the two is fated to be a long and tortuous process. Whether the consequences of this theocratic regime result in a successful dissolution of the ties between these two institutions or whether Iran's struggles to find a working democracy more suited to the modern era are destined to rumble on indefinitely, only time will tell.

With the amount of coverage it gets, many would be forgiven for assuming that the Islamic Revolution of 1979 and the resultant regime are the defining characteristics of the country as a whole. One cannot get away from it: from street names and murals to the endless grainy montages and the fiery rhetoric of the Friday Prayers beamed out over the airwaves; from the ubiquitous uniforms of authority to the legless limping of veterans; from the organised marches and celebrations to the religious months of mourning; from the stubble-flecked cheeks to the scurrying black chadors – all speak of the events of 1979. Just as the gaze of the two Grand Ayatollahs, Khomeini and his successor Khamenei, is unshakable, so too is the shadow cast by their revolution.

Yet one very quickly learns to see through the veneer. It is no coincidence that Iranians more readily quote their poets than their prophets; that they turn to the *Divan* of Hafez for guidance before the Qur'an. From the impertinent get-ups and suggestive glances of the youth to the bawdy banter and innuendos of the old, there is a playful, pleasure-seeking side to the national character that has diffused itself throughout Iran's culture. It is brought to life in the piquant verses of its great poets just as it is on display in the soft curves and stunning mosaic-work of its celebrated buildings. Only by understanding this contradictory synthesis between innate hedonism and austere piety can one begin to truly understand Iran.

The American writer Terence O'Donnell observes in *Garden of the Brave in War*, his memoir of the fifteen years he spent in Iran during the 1960s and 1970s, that 'the word romantic, as applied to a person, does not exist in Iranian, nor does its opposite, realist. No Iranian would so limit his sense of the world by being one or the other.'[2] In the same way that an Iranian sways his political beliefs with the force of each new gust to blow through his land, so too does he adapt his personal beliefs to serve his own purpose: 'he exposes his virtues on the palm of his hand, and hides his vices under his armpits,' as James Morier wrote in *Hajji Baba of Ispahan*, paraphrasing a verse of Sa'di's.[3] To view religion in Iran with the same self-serving cynicism as Morier's legendary character Hajji Baba did, though – as a means to an end, as image over substance – is to wholly misread the situation.

Undeniably, many an Iranian with his 'passion for metaphysical speculation' would refer to the Sufi philosophy of *erfan* to justify his incongruous actions by stating that one's own sincere love of God triumphs over any conventional religious orthodoxy: 'men who, in true Persian fashion,' in the words of E.G. Browne, 'disguise atheism in the garb of religion, and bedeck it with the trinkets of a mystical terminology'.[4] To imply that this is the basis of Sufism is wholly inaccurate and downright insulting to those that have genuinely dedicated their lives to the spiritual path. Equally, to imply that the majority of Iranians look upon their religion either as 'irksome ceremony', as Morier puts it, or as a means to an end is to grossly misjudge the piety and blind faith of the majority of the population.[5]

In the same way that Sufism embodies the Iranian propensity towards metaphysical speculation and a more spiritual bent, so too does the adoption of Shi'ism speak volumes of another character trait. The need to dissociate from the Arabs and their caliphate stems from the Iranian tendency towards self-aggrandisement and a pride in Iran's heritage that occasionally borders on arrogance. Many a myopic Iranian is all too ready to denigrate the Arabs and their culture one minute and to extol all that Islam has brought the country the next, as though it is only Iran that has made Islam great.

The study of history has, until very recently, not been a part of the Iranian experience. Iranians revel in the sense of entitlement that a vague conception of past glories grants them, yet they often have little real interest in the country's history. Whether a palace was Solomon's or Cyrus's is irrelevant. What is important is that it is old and was once great. Perhaps this is why Iranians will treat an event that occurred millennia ago with as much relevance as something that happened last week and why they mourn the martyrdom of centuries-old imams as though it happened just recently. Freya Stark writes: 'The Persian's mind, like his illuminated manuscripts, does not deal in perspective: 2,000 years, if he happens to know about them, are as exciting as the day before yesterday.'[6] Thus time does not fade the glories of Iran's past, irrespective of its present state.

This arrogance is combined with a 'general assumption of self-deprecation' observed by Robert Byron and a flaccid fatalism;[7] 'that comfortable feeling', writes Morier, 'of predestination which has been so wisely dispersed by the holy Prophet for the peace and quiet of all true believers'.[8] Pride commingles with servile sycophancy: 'a string of cold assents, such as constantly hang on every Persian's lips, whatever may be his real feelings'; 'truth [is] a matter of mood and wish and dream, not a matter of objective fact,' writes O'Donnell,[9] and Sandra Mackey notes 'the Iranian propensity to make the grand gesture at the expense of reality'.[10]

So Iranians are deceitful and derisive, Machiavellian and melodramatic, arrogant and xenophobic, yet they possess an 'easy courtesy and unaffected hospitality wherein [they] excel all other nations', according to Browne, who was impressed by 'the quick, versatile, subtle mind of the Persian, stored as it usually is with anecdotes, historical, literary, and incidental … flashes forth … in coruscations of wit and humour, interspersed with pungent criticisms and philosophical reflections which display a wonderful insight'. 'We are apt', he goes on, 'to think of the Persians as an entirely sedative, grave, and almost melancholy people, philosophers, often pessimist, seldom mirthful. Such a type does indeed exist, and exists in plenty. Yet among all Orientals the Persians are perhaps those whose idea of humour most nearly approaches our own, those in whom the sense of the ludicrous is most highly developed.'[11]

This confusing cocktail of contradictions is nowhere better expressed than by Lord Curzon, who in 1892 wrote:

> The finest domestic virtues coexist with barbarity and supreme indifference to suffering. Elegance of deportment is compatible with a coarseness amounting to bestiality … A creditable acquaintance

with the standards of civilisation does not prevent gross fanaticism ... Accomplished manners and a more than Parisian polish cover a truly superb faculty for lying and an almost scientific imposture. The most scandalous corruption is combined with a scrupulous regard for specified precepts of the moral law. Religion is alternately stringent and lax, inspiring at one moment the bigot's rage, at the next, the agnostic's indifference. Government is both patriarchal ... and Machiavellian ... the people at once despicable and noble; the panorama at the same time an enchantment and fraud.[12]

It is this paradoxical nature of the Iranian character that has contributed to the many ebbs and flows of the country's fortunes over the millennia, and it is this Jekyll and Hyde tendency that is the root of the country's current woes, embodied in the nation's struggle to come to terms with its own modernity. Whether one can view this struggle as that of 'two warring identities – one evolving from the values, social organisation, and arts of ancient Persia, the other from Islam', as Sandra Mackey posits – or whether the dichotomy is deeper-rooted than this, is a matter of opinion; what the antidote may be is a matter for speculation.[13]

Iran's is a youthful population in an ancient country. In many respects this youth is dragging the country towards modernity – powered by the influence of the internet – faster even than at any time under the Pahlavi dynasty and despite the reactionary theocratic regime determinedly digging its heels in to prevent this progressive movement. The youth is looking to embrace a more global, technologically inspired future, whilst the government is still looking back to the musty traditions and ideals of the past for a sense of identity. As long as these two antagonistic forces continue to pull in opposite directions, the tension and uncertainty that are destabilising the country will continue to escalate and hamper the forging of a coherent contemporary identity. The move towards modernity that was started by the Constitutional Revolution just over a hundred years ago will only be allowed to reach its completion, whatever that may be, when the past and present stand side by side and look together towards the future.

The pendulum of global fortunes has swung from East to West and West to East almost metronomically throughout the centuries. With the recent emergence of strong Asian economies, it seems that once again the balance of power is shifting towards the East; a shift that may prove

significant for Iran, shunned and distrusted by the West for its reactionary ideology and isolationist policies but much coveted by the emerging
powers for its plethora of resources.

I set out to look for a national essence; those characteristics taken by
a people and moulded to its own style that go on to separate it from the
races and cultures around it. Iranian society, as with any other, evolves
with the passing centuries, adapting to the changing moods of the various eras. Certainly contemporary Iran is very different from any other
time in its history, but the essence of being Iranian has not changed, nor,
ensha'llah, shall it. Thus Curzon's and Browne's astute observations on
the Iranian character are just as valid and valuable now, nearly 130 years,
two dynasties and an Islamic Revolution on, as they were when they
were written, despite Iranian society being turned on its head.

Browne transports us to a world of razor-tongued, hypocritically
principled, obstinately illogical yet loveable companions and servants: the
languid lifestyle of loafing in gardens by a *ghalyan* or *manghal*; the extraordinary passion for poetry and philosophy; the necessary deceitfulness
of people in a country in which they are so free with their tongues yet
keep their cards so close to their chests, and the accompanying tensions
created by these opposing forces of freedom and constraint; the larger-
than-life characters riddled with fantastic eccentricities embodied perfectly by Sheykh Ibrahim the wandering loafer, the ascetic hedonist.
A drunkard and a dreamer, he was by turns despicable yet delightful,
obstinate yet intelligent, irksome yet insightful, loathsome yet somehow
lovable. This dervish 'presented a combination of qualities impossible in
any but a Persian. Antichrist, antinomian, heretic and libertine to the
very core, he gloried in drunkenness, and expressed the profoundest
contempt for every ordinance of Islam'. And what could be more Iranian
than 'quoting in excuse for his orgies of hashish and spirits this couplet
from the *Masnavi* – "Thou disgracest thyself with bang [hashish] and
wine in order that for a moment thou mayest escape thyself."'[14]

This was the Iran that a twenty-five-year-old E.G. Browne had
found all those years ago and it was the same Iran that I found when I
explored it at a similar age. Iran is a country with a pervasive sense of
adventure, with unpredictability and uncertainty waiting around every
corner. Iranians are a people who combine touching hospitality and faux
sincerity with loathsome intolerance and an intrusiveness that, though
occasionally irksome, eventually endears. In short, it is a place so different in its wiles and ways that any free-thinker or romantic is guaranteed

to form an inextricable bond with the place. This is Iran and thus are its inhabitants, the heart and soul of the country that remain constant despite whatever latest clamour may break out on its surface; a country whose many imperfections only serve to highlight its alluring qualities.

Many times have I heard concerns expressed for a generation of Iranians growing up scattered all over the world, often oblivious to their rich heritage. Extraordinary familial situations have arisen in which three generations – grandmother, mother and daughter – live under one roof but in which grandmother and granddaughter cannot communicate; the elderly generation fluent only in Persian and the youth all too often only in the language of their adoptive homelands. As I was to find out, there is no greater tonic for this curious condition than to go to Iran and discover it for oneself. Not only are Iranians living and growing up abroad worse off for any denial or ignorance of their heritage, Iran itself is ailing from this disconnect. As Rumi put it, the reed is crying out to be reunited with the reed bed.

★ ★ ★

I was invited to a friend's house one evening shortly before my departure from the country. Most of the friends I had made over the course of my three years in the country were there, congregated in an old-style house in one of the few remaining garden compounds in Tehran. It was a warm, convivial gathering with the dinner table groaning with the traditional rices, sauces and *khoresht* stews that made up the canon of Persian cuisine.

As the evening wore on, someone appeared with a *tambour* and began to drum it softly as people milled about talking. He was soon joined by another friend brandishing a couple of small hand-drums. Within five minutes, the twenty people in the house were sitting in a circle on the floor. Various percussion instruments had been passed around and were keeping time with the rhythm set by the *tambour* and the singing of one of the group. Many eyes were closed and smiles had crept across nearly every face as bodies swayed gently to the sound of the drums. The next thirty minutes were lost in a communal jam of traditional Iranian folk music. Every so often, led by the breathless gasps of the singer, the tempo would quicken and then tail off again. At the end of the impromptu musical interlude faces beamed with beatific serenity as the performers applauded one another and embraced.

As I wandered into another room of the house, I saw a young carpet trader and aspiring artist whom I knew sitting at a round wooden table. A few others huddled around him as he closed his eyes and began to breathe deeply in and out. As the light from a candle danced across his features he began to sway slowly, all the while cradling a leather-bound copy of Hafez's *Divan* – a book of poetry often used for *faal*, or bibliomancy, in Iran – lovingly in his arms. His lips began to move, his brow was furrowed with concentration, his face radiated an eerie intensity in the flickering light of the flame. After a few minutes of this meditative swaying he seemed to have been transported to another realm, oblivious to the intense curiosity of the growing crowd gathered to observe his trance-like state. Suddenly he splayed the book open with a deep sigh and collapsed onto its pages. He then shot back bolt upright, opened his eyes and looked down at the words his index finger was tracing over. The finger came to an abrupt halt and he began to read the passage aloud, perfectly capturing the cadence of the mystical quatrains. As he read over the lines one by one, he interpreted the meaning of the words within the verses for the young woman whose *faal* he was reading. From this message, one line stood out: 'The future is yours to shape.'

Notes

Chapter One

1 The first and third of the Shi'i Imams, both of whom were martyred in the struggle to claim the succession of the Prophet Mohammad that led to Islam splitting into its two great branches, Sunni and Shi'a.

Chapter Two

1 Browne, *Year amongst the Persians*, p. 552.
2 Sykes, *History of Persia*, vol. II, p. 540.

Chapter Three

1 The term *Il-Khan* literally means 'leader of a nomadic tribe'. So this was a Mongolian-origin dynasty, its rulers, the leaders of the Mongol conquerors of Iran who never actually settled in the country's cities.
2 Sykes, *History of Persia*, vol. II, p. 192.
3 Browne, *Year amongst the Persians*, pp. 74–5.
4 Sykes, *History of Persia*, vol. II, p. 214.

Chapter Four

1 Jafari, 'Noruz (New Day); the New Year of the Iranian Peoples'; http://www.cais-soas.com/CAIS/Celebrations/noruz.htm (accessed 7 August 2014).

2 The prophet Zoroaster's actual dates are much debated by scholars and range from 600 BCE to 1800 BCE. The dates given are those put forward by the late Professor Mary Boyce.

3 Frye, *Heritage of Persia*, p. 39.

4 Boyce, *Zoroastrians: Their Religious Beliefs and Practices*, p. 26

5 Jafari, 'Noruz (New Day); the New Year of the Iranian Peoples'; http://www. cais-soas.com/CAIS/Celebrations/noruz.htm (accessed 7 August 2014).

Chapter Seven

1 The design of the Tower of Babel was supposedly based upon that of the Mesopotamian ziggurat.

2 The name Pahlavi was adopted by Reza Shah for his dynastic title, drawing on the ancient culture as a way of aggrandising his otherwise lowly origins.

3 *Chambers Dictionary of Etymology*, p. 754.

4 This detail of the ground pomegranate skin was found in Terence Ward's account of his family's return to Iran in *Searching for Hassan*.

5 Pope, *Introducing Persian Architecture*, p. 73.

Chapter Nine

1 Zaehner, *Dawn and Twilight of Zoroastrianism*, p. 128.

2 Nayer Nouri, *Iran's Contribution to the World Civilization*, vol. I, p. 9.

Chapter Ten

1 Stevens, *Land of the Great Sophy*, p. 149.

Chapter Eleven

1 Rumi, *Selected Poems*, p. 125.

2 Stark, *Valleys of the Assassins*, p. 126.

Chapter Twelve

1 Daryaee, *Sasanian Persia*, pp. 17–19.

2 Frye, *Heritage of Persia*, p. 97.

3 Stevens, *Land of the Great Sophy*, p. 166.

4 Stark, *Valley of the Assassins*, pp. 143–4.

Chapter Thirteen

1 Pope, *Introducing Persian Architecture*, pp. 1–2.

2 *Ibid.*, pp. 1–3.

3 *Ibid.*, pp. 14–15.
4 Nehemiah 1:1; Esther 1:2; 2:3; 3:15; 9:11; and Daniel 8:2.

Chapter Fourteen

1 Browne, *Year amongst the Persians*, p. 260.
2 Sykes, *History of Persia*, vol. II, p. 135.
3 'The children of Adam are limbs of each other, having been created of one essence. When the calamity of time afflicts one limb, the other limbs cannot remain at rest. If thou hast no sympathy for the troubles of others, thou art unworthy to be called by the name of man.' Sa'di, *The Golestan*.
4 Yarshater, *Encyclopaedia Iranica*, pp. 461–5; http://www.iranicaonline.org/articles/hafez-i (accessed 6 August 2014).
5 Figures taken from Axworthy, *Iran: Empire of the Mind*, pp. 168–9.
6 See Chapter Seventeen for my visit to Mash'had.
7 Battutah, *Travels*, p. 70.
8 Frye, *Heritage of Persia*, p. 92.
9 Stevens, *Land of the Great Sophy*, p. 229.
10 Pope, *Introducing Persian Architecture*, p. 18.
11 *Ibid.*
12 Feiler, *Where God Was Born*, p. 303.
13 Stevens, *Land of the Great Sophy*, pp. 223–4.
14 Pope, *Introducing Persian Architecture*, p. 24.
15 Quoted from an interview with BBC Persia, 4 October 2005.
16 Pope, *Introducing Persian Architecture*, p. 22.
17 For more details see Dandamaev and Lukonin, *Culture and Social Institutions of Ancient Iran*, pp. 160–2.
18 Pope, *Introducing Persian Architecture*, p. 18.
19 Browne, *Year amongst the Persians*, p. 87.
20 Stevens, *Land of the Great Sophy*, p. 214.

Chapter Fifteen

1 Sykes, *History of Persia*, vol. I, p. 495.

Chapter Sixteen

1 Stevens, *Land of the Great Sophy*, p. 122.
2 This mythical figure is also known as Kaveh of Esfahan, although this is because he is believed to be buried on a hill outside the city.
3 Pope, *Introducing Persian Architecture*, p. 44.
4 Gonbad-e Kabus literally means 'Domed Mausoleum of Kabus'. Mil-e Gonbad means 'Pole of Gonbad'.

Chapter Seventeen

1 Sykes, *History of Persia*, vol. II, p. 184.
2 Pope, *Introducing Persian Architecture*, p. 98.

Chapter Eighteen

1 Quoted from Sykes, *History of Persia*, vol. II, p. 110.
2 See Daftary, *Assassin Legends*, pp. 88–127.
3 Stark, *Valley of the Assassins*, p. 256.

Chapter Nineteen

1 Ghirshman, *Iran: From the Earliest Times to the Islamic Conquest*, p. 156.
2 Although the works of Ghirshman and Zaehner predate this latest scholarly research, the opinions expressed here are still considered valid.
3 Zaehner, *Dawn and Twilight of Zoroastrianism*, p. 162.

Chapter Twenty

1 Stevens, *Land of the Great Sophy*, p. xvi.
2 O'Donnell, *Garden of the Brave in War*, p. 51.
3 Morier, *The Adventures of Hajji Baba of Ispahan*, p. 249.
4 Browne, *Year amongst the Persians*, p. 493.
5 Morier, *The Adventures of Hajji Baba of Ispahan*, p. 253.
6 Stark, *Valleys of the Assassins*, p. 164.
7 Byron, *The Road to Oxiana*, p. 300.
8 Morier, *The Adventures of Hajji Baba of Ispahan*, p. 283.
9 O'Donnell, *Garden of the Brave in War*, pp. 51, 138.
10 Mackey, *The Iranians*, p. 200.
11 Browne, *Year amongst the Persians*, p. 121.
12 Curzon, *Persia and the Persian Question*, vol. I, p. 15.
13 See the back cover of Mackey's *The Iranians*.
14 Browne, *Year amongst the Persians*, pp. 475–6.

Bibliography

Al-Ghazali. *Al-Ghazali's Path to Sufism: His Deliverance from Error*, trans. R.J. McCarthy (Louisville, KY: Fons Vitae, 2000).

Armstrong, Karen. *Muhammad: A Biography of the Prophet* (London: Phoenix Press, 2001).

———— *Islam: A Short History* (London: Phoenix Press, 2004).

Aslan, Reza. *No God but God: The Origins, Evolution, and Future of Islam* (New York: Random House, 2006).

Axworthy, Michael. *Iran: Empire of the Mind* (London: Penguin Books, 2008).

Boyce, Mary. *Zoroastrians: Their Religious Beliefs and Practices* (London: Routledge, 2001).

Browne, Edward. *A Year amongst the Persians* (Port Chester, NY: Elibron Library, 2005).

———— *The Persian Revolution 1905–1909* (Washington, DC: Mage Publishers, 2006).

Byron, Robert. *The Road to Oxiana* (London: Penguin Books, 1992).

Chambers Dictionary of Etymology (New York: Larousse Kingfisher Chambers Inc., 2006).

Curzon, George N. *Persia and the Persian Question*, vol. I (London: Frank Cass & Co. Ltd, 1966).

Daftary, Farhad. *The Assassin Legends* (London: I.B.Tauris, 1994).

Dandamaev, Muhammad and Lukonin, Vladimir. *The Culture and Social Institutions of Ancient Iran* (Cambridge: Cambridge University Press, 1989).

Danziger, Nick. *Danziger's Travels: Beyond Forbidden Frontiers* (London: Flamingo, 1993).

Daryaee, Touraj. *Sasanian Persia: The Rise and Fall of an Empire* (London: I.B.Tauris, 2013).

de Bellaigue, Christopher. *In the Rose Garden of the Martyrs* (London: Harper Perennial, 2005).

———— *The Struggle for Iran* (New York: New York Review Books, 2007).

———— *Patriot of Persia: Muhammad Mossadegh and a Very British Coup* (London: Vintage, 2012).

Della Valle, Pietro. *The Journeys of Pietro Della Valle: The Pilgrim*, trans. George Bull (London: Folio Society, 1989).

Elliot, Jason. *Mirrors of the Unseen* (London: Picador, 2006).

Farman Farmaian, Sattareh. *Daughter of Persia* (London: Bantam Press, 1992).

Feiler, Bruce. *Where God was Born: A Journey by Land to the Roots of Religion* (New York: Harper Collins, 2005).

Ferdowsi, Abolqasem. *Shahnameh: The Persian Book of Kings*, trans. Dick Davis (New York: Mage, 2006).

Frye, Richard. *The Golden Age of Persia* (London: Weidenfeld and Nicolson, 1975).

———— *The Heritage of Persia* (London: Cardinal, 1976).

Ghirshman, Roman. *Iran: From the Earliest Times to the Islamic Conquest* (Harmondsworth: Penguin Books, 1954).

Hamilton, A.M. *Road through Kurdistan: Travels in Northern Iraq* (London: I.B.Tauris, 2004).

Herodotus. *The Histories*, trans. Robin Waterfield (New York: Oxford University Press, 1998).

Holland, Tom. *Persian Fire* (London: Abacus, 2009).

———— *In the Shadow of the Sword: The Battle for Global Empire and the End of the Ancient World* (London: Little, Brown, 2012).

Ibn Battutah. *The Travels of Ibn Battutah*, trans. Tim Mackintosh-Smith (London: Picador, 2003).

Irving, Clive. *Crossroads of Civilisation: 3000 Years of Persian History* (London: Book Club Associates, 1979).

Jafari, Ali A. 'Noruz (New Day); the New Year of the Iranian Peoples'; http:// www.cais-soas.com/CAIS/Celebrations/noruz.htm (accessed 7 August 2014).

Kaplan, Robert. *The Ends of the Earth: A Journey to the Frontiers of Anarchy* (New York: Vintage Departures, 1997).

Kapuscinski, Ryszard. *Shah of Shahs* (London: Penguin Classics, 2006).

Keddie, Nikki. *Modern Iran* (New Haven and London: Yale University Press, 2003).

Kriwaczek, Paul. *In Search of Zarathustra* (London: Phoenix Books, 2003).

Lewis, Franklin. *Rumi: Past and Present, East and West* (Oxford and Boston: Oneworld Publications, 2000).

Maalouf, Amin. *The Crusades through Arab Eyes* (London: Saqi Books, 2004).

———— *Samarkand* (London: Abacus, 2004).

Mackey, Sandra. *The Iranians: Persia, Islam and the Soul of a Nation* (New York: Plume Printing, 1998).

Mas'udi. *From 'The Meadows of Gold'*, trans. Paul Lunde (London: Penguin Books, 2007).

McDowall, David. *A Modern History of the Kurds* (London: I.B.Tauris, 2004).

Molavi, Afshin. *The Soul of Iran* (New York and London: Norton Paperbacks, 2005).

Morier, James. *The Adventures of Hajji Baba of Ispahan* (New York: Cosimo, 2005).

Naipaul, V.S. *Among the Believers: An Islamic Journey* (London: Picador, 2003).

Nayer Nouri, A.H. *Iran's Contribution to the World Civilization*, 2 vols (Tehran: General Department of Publications, Ministry of Culture and Arts, 1970).

O'Donnell, Terence. *Garden of the Brave in War: Recollections of Iran* (Washington, DC: Mage, 2013).

Perrot, Jean. *The Palace of Darius at Susa: The Great Royal Residence of Achaemenid Persia* (London: I.B.Tauris, 2013).

Pezeshkzad, Iraj. *My Uncle Napoleon*, trans. Dick Davis (New York: Random House, 2006).

Pope, Arthur Upham. *Introducing Persian Architecture* (Tehran: Soroush Press, 1976).

Rohl, David. *Legend: The Genesis of Civilisation* (London: Century, 1998).

Rumi, Jalaluddin. *Selected Poems from the Divan-e Shams-e Tabrizi*, trans. R.A. Nicholson (Washington, DC: Ibex Publishers, 2001).

Said, Edward. *Orientalism* (London: Penguin Books, 2003).

Shah, Idries. *The Sufis* (London: Octagon Press, 1999).

Smith, Anthony. *Blind White Fish in Persia* (London: Readers Union Ltd, 1954).

Stark, Freya. *The Valleys of the Assassins and Other Persian Travels* (New York: Modern Library, 2001).

Stevens, Roger. *The Land of the Great Sophy* (London: Methuen & Co., 1965).

Sykes, Percy. *A History of Persia*, vol. II (London: Macmillan and Co., 1915).

———— *A History of Persia*, vol. I (London: Macmillan and Co., 1963).

Theroux, Paul. *The Great Railway Bazaar* (London: Penguin Books, 1996).

Ward, Philip. *Touring Iran* (London: Faber & Faber, 1971).

Ward, Terence. *Searching for Hassan: A Journey to the Heart of Iran* (New York: Anchor Books, 2003).

Watson, Robert. *A History of Persia from the Beginning of the Nineteenth Century to the Year 1858* (London: Smith, Elder & Co., 1866).

Wiesehofer, Josef. *Ancient Persia* (London: I.B.Tauris, 2004).

Xenophon. *The Persian Expedition*, trans. Rex Warner (London: Penguin Books, 1972).

Yarshater, Esan. 'Hafez', *Encyclopaedia Iranica*, vol. XI, fasc. 5, online edition (New York: Bibliotheca Persica Press, 1996).

Zaehner, R.C. *The Dawn and Twilight of Zoroastrianism* (New York: Phoenix Press, 2002).